Chains of Babylon

Critical American Studies Series

George Lipsitz, University of California–Santa Barbara, Series Editor

Chains of Babylon
The Rise of Asian America

Daryl J. Maeda

Critical American Studies Series

 University of Minnesota Press
Minneapolis
London

Excerpts from the poem "To My Asian American Brothers," by Pat Sumi, appear courtesy of Tetsuji Gotanda and Kiyoko Gotanda.

Lyrics from "Yellow Pearl," "We Are the Children," "Something about Me Today," "Jonathan Jackson," "Warrior of the Rainbow," "Somos Asiáticos," "Divide and Conquer," and "War of the Flea," by Nobuko JoAnne Miyamoto and Chris Iijima, appear courtesy of Nobuko JoAnne Miyamoto and Jane Dickson.

Lyrics from "Wandering Chinaman" appear courtesy of Charlie Chin.

Quotations from "Firepot" and "Jungle Rot and Open Arms," by Janice Mirikitani, were originally published in *Time to Greez! Incantations from the Third World* (Third World Communications and Glide Publications); reprinted courtesy of Janice Mirikitani.

Lyrics from "Song for a Child," by Chris Iijima, appear courtesy of Jane Dickson.

Chapter 3 was previously published as "Black Panthers, Red Guards, and Chinamen: Constructing Asian American Identity through Performing Blackness, 1969–1972," *American Quarterly* 57, no. 4 (December 2005); reprinted with permission of The Johns Hopkins University Press.

Published by the University of Minnesota Press
111 Third Avenue South, Suite 290
Minneapolis, MN 55401-2520
http://www.upress.umn.edu

Library of Congress Cataloging-in-Publication Data

Maeda, Daryl J.
    Chains of Babylon : the rise of Asian America / Daryl J. Maeda.
    p. cm. — (Critical American studies series)
    Includes bibliographical references and index.
    ISBN 978-0-8166-4890-0 (hc : acid-free paper) — ISBN 978-0-8166-4891-7 (pb : acid-free paper)
    1. Asian Americans—Politics and government—20th century. 2. Asian Americans—Social conditions—20th century. 3. Asian Americans—Ethnic identity. 4. Political activists—United States—History—20th century. 5. Social movements—United States—History—20th century. 6. Third World Liberation Front—History. 7. Vietnam War, 1961–1975—Protest movements— United States. 8. African Americans—Relations with Asian Americans. 9. United States—Race relations—History—20th century. 10. United States—Social conditions—20th century. I. Title.
    E184.A75M34 2009
    305.895'073—dc22
                                                                2009017762

Printed in the United States of America on acid-free paper

The University of Minnesota is an equal-opportunity educator and employer.

15 14 13 12 11   10 9 8 7 6 5 4 3

In the spirit of Pat Sumi and Chris Iijima

In memory of George Maeda

In hopes for the future of Alex and Kenji

Chains of Babylon
　　bind us together
　　but we do not touch
With this sword
　　I would free you
But where are your chains?
　　They are not like mine
In your eyes
　　I see your spirit
　　bound by chains
　　　by burdens
　　　by weight
　　　by hearts
　　　　so heavy
　　the sword cannot free you
　　　　　yet

—Pat Sumi, "To My Asian American Brothers"

Contents

Preface   ix

Acknowledgments   xiii

Abbreviations   xvii

Introduction: From Heart Mountain to Hanoi   1

1. Before Asian America   19

2. "Down with Hayakawa!" Assimilation vs. Third World Solidarity at San Francisco State College   40

3. Black Panthers, Red Guards, and Chinamen: Constructing Asian American Identity through Performing Blackness   73

4. "Are We Not Also Asians?" Building Solidarity through Opposition to the Viet Nam War   97

5. Performing Radical Culture: A Grain of Sand and the Language of Liberty   127

Conclusion: Fighting for the Heart of Asian America   154

Notes   161

Bibliography   183

Index   199

Preface

This book is a cultural history of Asian American activism and identity in the late 1960s and early 1970s. By tracing ideas about race, ethnicity, nation, and empire expressed in social movement cultures and formal cultural productions, it recuperates a set of political actions that brought into being the category of "Asian American." Throughout, it argues that cultural critiques of racism and imperialism, the twin "Chains of Babylon" of the title, informed the construction of Asian American identity as a multiethnic formation committed to interracial and transnational solidarity. This focus on cultural manifestations follows Lisa Lowe's dictum, "Where the political terrain can neither resolve nor suppress inequality, it erupts in culture."[1] Indeed, this book proceeds from a conviction that the cultural sphere—defined broadly, from everyday performances and ways of being to drama, music, and poetry—cannot be reduced to an aftereffect of the political but rather must be understood as in constant dialectical relation with the political.

The topic of Asian American activism during the 1960s has garnered much scholarly attention but not nearly enough. It is a politically charged subject that demands that its critics take stands and stake positions, for interpretations of the past are inevitably informed by present-day concerns. Because I want to be clear about the partiality and limitations of this project, I must begin with three caveats. First, throughout the book

I have chosen to refer to the "Asian American movement" rather than the "Asian American Movement." Capitalizing "Movement" suggests, to me, a solidity or uniformity that overly schematizes this tumultuous period. All narratives seek to organize chaos into order, and in constructing this narrative I have chosen the noncapitalized form as a gesture to suggest that messiness and contradiction were inherent in an ad hoc movement comprised of loosely associated groups and organizations that adopted a variety of ideological approaches; differed by ethnicity, immigrant status, class, and region; addressed a multiplicity of issues; arose spontaneously; and lasted for varying lengths of time.

The second caveat flows directly from the first. Given the breadth of its subject, this narrative is necessarily selective and does not aspire to, let alone achieve, comprehensiveness. Many highly important and noteworthy examples of Asian American activism of this period receive scant attention, if any. One example deserves particular mention. In arguing for the primacy of anti-imperialism among Asian American radicals, I focus on the anti–Vietnam War movement but do not substantively engage with the anti-Marcos movement. Filipino and Filipino American opposition to the Marcos regime provides a primary example of Asian American anti-imperialism, for, as Estella Habal argues, Filipino American radicals of the 1960s were deeply influenced by radicals in the Philippines and saw opposition to the Marcos dictatorship as integral to their struggles in the United States. For instance, the KDP (Katipunan Ng Ma Demokratikong, Union of Democratic Pilipinos) simultaneously engaged in a domestic campaign to save the International Hotel, an important community institution in San Francisco that was under attack by redevelopers, and vigorously opposed Marcos's imposition of martial law in the Philippines.[2]

Third and finally, choices about periodization are never neutral. For a book on Asian American activism during the movement era, 1968 presents an eminently plausible beginning point. Many consider the Third World Liberation Front strike at San Francisco State University an inaugural event for Asian American radicalism, and the black power and anti–Vietnam War movements (both of which heavily influenced the Asian American movement) were becoming ever more powerful. The year 1968, which saw the assassination of Robert F. Kennedy, the chaos of the Chicago Democratic Convention, and the militancy of the Free Huey Movement, has been apotheosized as a near-perfect distillation of late 1960s fractiousness. But this point of supposed divisiveness provides an ideal moment around which to counterargue, as this book does, that resisting racism and imperialism enabled many types of interconnections.

If choosing a beginning point for this narrative is fairly straightforward, choosing an ending point is more complicated. Two developments suggest that Asian American activism reached a turning point in the mid-1970s. First, the antiwar movement's fervor waned after 1973, when the United States withdrew its troops from Viet Nam. Subsequently, after the fall of Saigon in 1975, a wave of Vietnamese refugees entered the United States. Many of these newest Asian Americans had fought in the South Vietnamese army, served in its government, or otherwise supported the South Vietnamese and American forces. The perhaps overly romantic view of Asian American radicals, who insisted that all Vietnamese wanted independence from the United States, had to be tempered by the real presence of Vietnamese people of anticommunist persuasions. Second, a wave of consolidation and party building transformed the relationship of radicals to communities, as all of the primary Asian American radical organizations, along with many other race-specific groups, merged into multiracial parties. Max Elbaum notes that party building was prioritized over mass and community organizing, and defining leftist orthodoxy led to excessive dogmatism and divisiveness, to the detriment of what he calls the New Communist Movement.[3] Together, the qualitative changes in the makeup of Asian America coupled with ideological and organizational shifts in the Asian American left marked, if not an ending point, at least a pivot point in the mid-1970s. By ending this narrative in 1975, however, I do not mean to consign the Asian American movement to the past or to impugn its legacies, which have endured into the present and will, I hope, inform the future.

Acknowledgments

Throughout the research and writing of this book, I have accrued a great many debts, which I acknowledge here with deep appreciation. My immersion in Asian American studies and ethnic studies began at San Francisco State University, where I was fortunate to learn from Jeffrey Paul Chan, Ben Kobashigawa, and Roberto Rivera. At State I met Mel Escueta, first learned of his play *Honey Bucket,* and heard his concerns about the first Gulf War. At the University of Michigan, George Sanchez molded many of the ways that I think about race and identity, as did Terry McDonald with regard to ethnicity and politics. Steve Sumida and especially Gail Nomura mentored me every step of the way. I was also fortunate to be part of an extraordinary cohort of co-conspirators in graduate school, in particular Anna Pegler Gordon, Tom Guglielmo, Peter Kalliney, Richard Kim, Larry Hashima, Nhi Lieu, Anthony Macias, Kate Masur, Andrew Needham, and Tom Romero. Tom Ikeda and the crew at the Densho Project enlarged my sense of what history could and should be. At Oberlin College, I was surrounded by a tight-knit community of scholars and friends, including Pawan Dhingra, David Kamitsuka, Wendy Kozol, Pablo Mitchell, Gina Perez, and Meredith Raimondo. At the University of Colorado at Boulder, my *comadres* and compadres in and around the Department of Ethnic Studies (especially Elisa Facio, Emma Perez, and Reiland Rabaka), the Pan-Asian Faculty/Staff Association, and the Center for Multicultural Affairs provided inspiration through their constant examples of engaged scholarship, teaching, and service to the community. I am especially grateful to Arturo Aldama, who provided helpful comments on the manuscript, and to Seema Sohi, who has become my sister-in-arms.

My ideas about race, identity, culture, and power have been greatly enriched by many scholars who have engaged in conversation with me and critiqued portions of this work. Among others, May Fu, Diane Fujino, Ed Hashima, Moon-Ho Jung, Paul Kramer, Lon Kurashige, Josephine Lee, Ken Mochizuki, Gary Okihiro, Laura Pulido, Mary Renda, Greg Robinson, Jere Takahashi, and Henry Yu all pushed my work in useful ways. Friends around the country alternately lifted my spirits and kept me grounded. The boys I grew up with—Clark Davis, Rudy Hilado, Dan Lantry, Dan Lau, and Brian Mohr—formed my original multiethnic, multiracial crew; Clark, who convinced me to become a historian, left far too soon, but we're grateful that he brought Cheryl Koos into our circle. Elham Kazemi and Mark Purcell kept me sane in a time of insanity, and my sparring with Mark over the salience of race within a radical framework lasted many rounds.

This project could not have gone forward without the generosity of individuals who shared their memories, perspectives, and documents. My deepest gratitude goes to Frank Abe, Charlie Chin, Bob Fuchigami, Kim Geron, Marc Hayashi, Jim Hirabayashi, Pam Tau Lee, Steve Louie, Greg Mark, Nobuko Miyamoto, Nelson Nagai, Glenn Omatsu, and other sources who wish to remain anonymous. Although not all of their words may have reached the pages of this book, they were all instrumental in shaping it.

The staffs of many institutions facilitated archival research, and I am thankful to Marjorie Lee of the Asian American Studies Reading Room at UCLA, the staffs of the Special Collections Library of the Harlan Hatcher Graduate Library at the University of Michigan, the Department of Special Collections of the Charles E. Young Library at UCLA, the California Ethnic and Multicultural Archives at the University of California–Santa Barbara, the Special Collections Division of the University of Washington Libraries, the unparalleled Helene Whitson of the Department of Special Collections and Archives of the J. Paul Leonard Library at San Francisco State University, the San Francisco History Center of the San Francisco Public Library, the Bancroft Library at the University of California–Berkeley, and the Hoover Institution.

A portion of the writing and research was accomplished on a leave funded by the University of Colorado at Boulder and through research support from Oberlin College. I am grateful for the insights and challenges of my students at the University of Washington, Oberlin, and Colorado.

Many thanks to Richard Morrison, my wonderful editor at the University of Minnesota Press, to Adam Brunner for his patience and diligence, and to series editor George Lipsitz, who has been a role model of intellectual and political commitment.

My parents, George and Amelia Maeda, inspired my interest in race, ethnicity, and justice in ways they may not truly fathom; they never questioned my decision to abandon a useful career in favor of academia, and they supported me in every way. My fondest wish is that my father had lived to see the publication of this book. Ken, Fran, Katie, and Keith Dutro have proven time and time again that they are not in-laws but my true second family. The lights of my life, Alex and Kenji, cannot remember a time when their dad was not immersed in this project; in turn, I cannot imagine a life without the welcome distractions and daily inspirations they provide, which made completing this book not only possible but indeed necessary. Elizabeth Dutro has been my constant companion along this journey of a thousand steps, my most trusted critic and confidante, staunchest ally, and best friend.

Abbreviations

AAA	Asian Americans for Action
AAPA	Asian American Political Alliance
AATW	Asian American Theater Workshop
AC	Asian Coalition
AFL	American Federation of Labor
AFT	American Federation of Teachers
BAACAW	Bay Area Asian Coalition Against the War
BSU	Black Student Union
CCBA	Chinese Consolidated Benevolent Association
CEA	Chinese Exclusion Act
CHLA	Chinese Hand Laundry Alliance
CICN	Community Interest Committee of Nihonmachi
CINO	California Intercollegiate Nisei Organization
CIO	Congress of International Organizations
CMWAA	Chinese Workers' Mutual Aid Association
CPUSA	U.S. Communist Party
FAIR	Federation for American Immigration Reform

ICSA	Intercollegiate Chinese for Social Action
ILD	International Labor Defense
IWK	I Wor Kuen (Righteous Harmonious Fists)
JACL	Japanese American Citizens League
JMLA	Japanese-Mexican Labor Association
KDP	Katipunan Ng Ma Demokratikong (Union of Democratic Pilipinos)
KMT	Kuomintang (Chinese Nationalist Party)
LASO	Latin American Student Organization
MASC	Mexican American Student Coalition
MDM	Movement for a Democratic Military
NMU	National Maritime Union
NPAC	National Peace Action Coalition
PACE	Pilipino American Collegiate Endeavor
RNA	Republic of New Africa
SDS	Students for a Democratic Society
SIU	Seamen's International Union
TWLF	Third World Liberation Front
WMS	Wei Min She

Introduction

From Heart Mountain to Hanoi

By the time Pat Sumi arrived in Hanoi in the summer of 1970, she had traveled a great geographical distance and had progressed far in her journey to understand the politics of race. Yet she still had far to go. A third-generation Japanese American (Sansei) born to parents newly released from the Heart Mountain concentration camp in Wyoming, Sumi is rightly regarded as a luminary of the Asian American movement of the late 1960s and early 1970s. She first participated in the southern civil rights movement, later joined the anti–Viet Nam War movement, and traveled with Eldridge Cleaver as part of a delegation that visited North Korea, North Viet Nam, and the People's Republic of China. After returning from Asia, she became involved in the Asian American movement and played an important role in organizing the 1971 Indochinese Women's Conference in Vancouver, Canada, which brought together 150 North American women and six women from Viet Nam. Studying Sumi's journeys reveals much about the trajectory of Asian American identity in the mid- to late twentieth century, and introduces the major themes of this book, by showing how Asian American people encountered whiteness and blackness, constructed a multiethnic Asian American racial identity, and adopted anti-imperialism as a way to build solidarity with people of color in the United States and abroad.[1]

Asian Americans have long occupied an uneasy position within the

American racial order. Throughout the twentieth century, they have struggled with and against both blackness and whiteness. Decisions by Asian Americans—including the politics they practiced and the groups with which they chose to build sympathies and alliances—responded to existing relations of power and bespoke dreams of new identities. This book is concerned with the racial making of Asian Americans. It reveals historical shifts in how they have been positioned by the dominant society in relation to blacks, whites, and each other. More important, it explores how they have defined themselves in terms of ethnicity, race, and nation while grappling with the constraints of preexisting political, social, and cultural systems.

Chains of Babylon examines how Asian American radicals of the late 1960s and early 1970s challenged prior ideas about their race and national belonging and articulated a new form of Asian American identity as a multiethnic racial formation. Chapter 1 briefly surveys the racialization of Asian Americans during the nineteenth and twentieth centuries, then examines major trends in pre-1960s Asian American politics. It shows how Asians began the twentieth century imagined by the dominant society to be an inassimilable Yellow Peril composed of perpetual foreigners who could never become good Americans, then during the cold war were transformed into an eminently assimilable "model minority," providing proof that a minority group could overcome prejudice through hard work, education, and eschewal of vocal protest.

In the early part of her life, Pat Sumi dealt directly with the specter of whiteness. She was raised in a "mostly white, upper middle class neighborhood" and wondered, "[Am] I white?"[2] She went on to attend Occidental College, which was also "very white."[3] Assimilation has been a critical presence in Asian American experiences in the twentieth century, as I argue in chapter 2. Denied the privileges of whiteness, some Asian Americans actively sought assimilation as a palliative to the racism they faced. Typifying this position, Samuel Ichiyé (S. I.) Hayakawa professed faith in the American system's ability to eradicate racial disparities through assimilation. Hayakawa proved to be a pivotal figure in Asian American history; he was acting president of San Francisco State College during the Third World Liberation Front strike of 1968–69, when his assimilationism was contradicted by Asian American radicals (as well as black, Latino, white, and Indian radicals) who argued for the durability and exploitive nature of race and contended that nonwhites should take pride in their racial identities. By the 1960s, many Asian Americans were experiencing the Cold War contradictions of simultaneously suffering discrimination and yet being praised as a "model minority." Hence, Asian American identity emerged during this period in part through struggles *against* whiteness.

Sumi took two international journeys during college that broadened the horizons of her racial consciousness. In 1963, she traveled to Japan, where she met her Japanese relatives for the first time and witnessed their culture and lives as rural farmers. She credited this trip with connecting her for the first time to a sense of being Japanese: "Going to Japan was one of the things which kept me from falling all off into a white, middle class bag, marrying a white man, living in a white neighborhood, and telling everyone how assimilated I was." Although she did marry a white man, she felt a voice telling her, "You're really Japanese, and you're separate from white people."[4] Connecting to her Japanese heritage did not automatically make Sumi sympathetic to African Americans, however, for she still believed that blacks' poverty in the United States was due to their cultural deficits. This belief was destroyed when she made her second trip, to Africa, in 1965. There she observed peasant farmers and noted the deep similarities they shared with her relatives in Japan. Seeing the rich culture of Africa made her realize that segregation and discrimination in the United States could not be justified by the claim of black cultural inferiority.[5] Sumi's journeys to Japan and Africa were pivotal moments that together brought her closer to identifying herself as an Asian American and awakened her to similarities in the travails of Asians and blacks.

After graduating from college, the idealistic Sumi went south to Mississippi, where she worked during 1966 and 1967 in an Office of Economic Opportunity program. This experience exposed her to the harsh realities of crushing poverty among African Americans and rabidly violent racism among whites. She had entered the civil rights movement confident of the ability of the democratic system to ameliorate injustice but became thoroughly disillusioned by the indifference displayed by state and federal elected officials. She left the south and wound up in a hippie commune in Palo Alto, California, where she kept house, cooked, and did laundry for about eight men and eventually came to see the commune as "male chauvinist, elitist, [and] racist."[6] Just as was the case in Sumi's experience, for many radical Asian Americans, a dawning racial consciousness sometimes coincided with new appreciation for the importance of gender equality.

When she left the commune, Sumi turned to the antiwar movement. Along with other activists, she opened a coffeehouse called Green Machine outside of the Camp Pendleton Marine Corps base near San Diego. Green Machine, like other coffeehouses operated by antiwar activists near military bases nationwide, offered "free coffee, live music, and political conversation," along with antiwar literature and programs, in a laid-back atmosphere. Thousands of GIs visited these venues, and political activities at bases often increased after they opened.[7] Green Machine merged with an underground antiwar newspaper based in San Diego to form the first chapter of Movement for a Democratic Military (MDM), which by 1970 was affiliated with seven coffeehouses nationwide.[8] MDM was one of the six major organizations of the GI movement[9] and had a membership estimated at somewhere between five thousand and ten thousand.[10] MDM sought to extend civil liberties and constitutional rights to members of the military, abolish racism, stop the draft, and end the Viet Nam War. But although much of its twelve-point program concentrated on improving conditions for U.S. servicepersons, it also struck an anti-imperialist note by concluding, "We refuse to repress the Vietnamese who are struggling for liberation. END THE WAR NOW!"[11]

In Oceanside, Green Machine and MDM held picnics; distributed pamphlets and their newspaper, *Attitude Check;* screened movies such as *Battle of Algiers;* and hosted speakers, including prominent antiwar activists and members of the Black Panther Party. Jane Fonda attended an open house at Green Machine on 22 March 1970 and met with about thirty marines. And of course Green Machine and MDM sponsored protest marches. Their first major march was held on 19 December 1969. Several thousand participants, including between four hundred and a thousand marines, waved North Vietnamese flags, chanted North Vietnamese slogans, and carried the U.S. flag upside down. They heard speeches from antiwar veterans, Black Panthers, and Angela Davis. A subsequent march in May 1970 attracted a similar number of protesters and marines and featured speakers from *Ramparts* magazine, Students for a Democratic Society, the Chicano organization Los Siete de la Raza, and Tom Hayden.[12]

The activities of Green Machine and MDM attracted significant surveillance from authorities, and violent repression, too. The House Committee on Internal Security went so far as to compile a dossier on Pat Sumi and others involved in MDM.[13] The Oceanside Police Department also spent considerable time and resources (an estimated $100,000) on its MDM operations and concluded that Sumi was one of the three "principals" behind Green Machine and MDM in Oceanside.[14] The police regularly observed happenings at the coffeehouse, collected flyers, and carefully surveyed the defensive setup of MDM facilities. They raided a Green Machine house and confiscated eight or nine rifles and shotguns, which had to be returned when it was determined that they were legally possessed. Police deemed two different MDM facilities to be "fortified," with perimeter trenches and concertina wire at one house and a "warning system" and sandbags arranged with "gun ports" at the other.[15] The level of surveillance and depth of attention directed to Green Machine and MDM indicate the degree to which local and federal authorities viewed them as serious threats. Indeed, nationally MDM had a reputation for stealing weapons from military bases.[16] The fortifications and arsenal at the MDM house outside Camp Pendleton might seem to have been the products of excessive paranoia, but in fact, on 28 April 1970 the MDM staff house was struck by gunfire. Unidentified assailants fired approximately twelve rounds of .45-caliber ammunition at the house, wounding one marine.[17]

MDM drew heavily upon black power rhetoric and prominently featured Black Panthers in its operations. Like Pat Sumi, many Asian Americans radicals were inspired by the black power movement. As I discuss in chapter 3, during the late 1960s and early 1970s, adaptations and performances of blackness proved integral to building an understanding of Asian Americans as a racial bloc. The Red Guard Party of San Francisco, which had mobilized Asian American youth into an organization explicitly modeled on the Black Panther Party, performed blackness as a way to signal their militancy, to suggest that Asians were racialized in ways similar to those experienced by blacks, and to declare solidarity with blacks. In contrast, Frank Chin, in his 1971 play *The Chickencoop Chinaman*, linked Asian Americans to blacks through masculinity, which he defined in sometimes troubling ways. The Red Guards and Chin sparred vigorously over the nature and politics of Asian America, but both drew upon and performed blackness in order to reject assimilation, argue that Asian Americans constituted a racialized bloc, and emphasize linkages between Asian Americans and African Americans.

While MDM strove for multiracial unity, calling itself a "black-brown-white coalition" in solidarity with "Vietnamese freedom fighters,"[18] Asian Americans remained conspicuously absent from its consciousness. Though MDM envisioned black, brown, and white soldiers in alliance with the Vietnamese, it did not consider the racial commonality between Asian American soldiers and the Vietnamese people. Despite the critical role

Pat Sumi played in Green Machine, the local chapter of MDM showed no greater awareness of Asian Americans than did the national organization. This suggests that Sumi's racial vision was still colored in black and white and that her awareness of the racial positioning of Asian Americans in the United States was, as yet, incipient. However, the fact that she was Asian was not lost on other members of the new left and antiwar movements.

In 1970, Sumi was selected on the basis of her MDM work as a member of the U.S. People's Anti-Imperialist Delegation. Under the leadership of Eldridge Cleaver, the delegation was intended to build solidarity between American new leftists and the communist nations of Asia. Sumi, who was remembered by co-traveler and Black Panther leader Elaine Brown as "a young diminutive Japanese woman," believed that her ancestry was an important factor in her selection.[19] Significantly, Alex Hing of the Red Guard Party was invited on the journey. Sumi and Hing's inclusion points to the delegation's theatrical staging and casting: as a performance of interracial solidarity traveling to Asia, it required the inclusion of Asian faces.

The delegates arrived in Pyongyang, North Korea, on 14 July 1970.[20] They toured the country, attending athletic and cultural events; visiting museums, schools, clinics, farms, and factories; and meeting local activists.[21] From North Korea they issued a message that read in part, "Since the peoples of the world have a common enemy, we must begin to think of revolution as an international struggle against U.S. imperialism."[22] This statement reflected the growing internationalist perspective that would inform the Asian American antiwar movement, for it located U.S. imperialism as the common enemy of leftists both within and outside of American borders. While in North Korea, the group was invited to visit Hanoi by the North Vietnamese ambassador. They spent twenty days in North Viet Nam, where the Vietnamese government honored them by celebrating an International Day of Solidarity with Black People of the United States on 18 August.[23] Sumi came to admire the intense resolve that enabled the Vietnamese people to endure almost unspeakable difficulties in their quest for national liberation.[24]

Asian American radicals opposed the war in Viet Nam because they, like Sumi, understood the connection between an anti-Asian war in Viet Nam and the oppression and exploitation of Asians in America. Chapter 4 shows how Asian Americans who hoisted signs reading "Stop Killing Our Asian Brothers and Sisters" came to identify with the Vietnamese as fellow Asians and how doing so strengthened multiethnic Asian American solidarity. "Asian continents" and organizations such as the Bay Area Asian Coalition Against War (BAACAW) comprising Filipinos, Chinese, and Japanese Americans marched at demonstrations across the nation under the flags of left Asia—China, North Korea, and North Viet Nam. Viet Nam veteran Melvyn Escueta also struck the theme of Asian unity in his play *Honey Bucket,* which chronicles the coming-to-consciousness of a Filipino American soldier in Viet Nam, his increasing identification with the Vietnamese people, and the psychic trauma he suffers for being an "Asian killing Asians."

Upon returning from Asia, Sumi was eagerly embraced by the Asian American left, even though to that point she had not been centrally involved in Asian American organizations or causes. She made herself available to Asian American groups and spent the next year speaking across the United States.[25] By late 1970, Sumi was a regular contributor to *Gidra,* a monthly newspaper that was the most widely read periodical of the Asian American movement in the nation. She wrote articles warning against Japanese militarism, tracing the history of Asian American radical activism, decrying historical discrimination against Asian Americans, commemorating the atomic bombing of Hiroshima and Nagasaki, and, most prominently, covering the Asian American antiwar movement.[26] Sumi's rapid integration into Asian American radical circles was due in part to her eagerness to join the movement, perhaps as a result of what must be understood as her dawning racial consciousness. However, the movement's acceptance may also be attributed to the particular way that Sumi performed a racial critique of racism and imperialism, for she had, after all, traveled to Viet Nam as a member of a Black Panther–led delegation. By comparison, another similar traveler did not receive such adulation from the Asian American movement. A Japanese American woman, Marii Hasegawa, visited Hanoi in 1973 as a representative of the Women's International League for Peace and Freedom, an old pacifist organization dominated by middle-class white women, yet remained unknown and unlauded by Asian American radicals.[27]

Sumi soon developed a critical discourse linking Asians in the United States to those in Indochina, which she expressed in her poem "To My Asian American Brothers," published in *Gidra* in November 1970 (p. 3). The poem juxtaposes Asian American oppression with the suffering of Vietnamese people in parallel constructions:

Do you see
grandfather back bent
worked to the ground?

Do you see
father barb bound
concentration sent?

Do you see
brother Asian death
Vietnam sent?

The first two stanzas allude to the exploitation of Asian American laborers in the agricultural industry and the imprisonment of Japanese Americans in concentration camps during World War II. The word "brother" in the third stanza has a double function. As a generational marker contrasting with "grandfather" and "father," it refers to a Sansei, perhaps a Japanese American soldier sent to his death in Viet Nam. But it also suggests that if Asian Americans are brothers to the Vietnamese, their familial ties are built through racial exploitation in the United States and genocide in Viet Nam. Sumi looked for inspiration to the left Asia that she had just visited, writing, "The world has turned/a revolution/a great victory in the East." And she envisioned the politics of this radical Asia infusing Asian America, for she stated, "A home of revolution/of love/for us is possible/ in Los Angeles."[28]

"To My Asian American Brothers" marks Sumi's full immersion in an Asian American perspective on the war, for it expressed a conviction that the war in Viet Nam and the oppression of Asian Americans were but two facets of U.S. imperialism. In this, Sumi echoed the critique of the war leveled by the Asian American antiwar movement that forms the subject of chapter 4. Asian American antiwar activists believed, as did Sumi, that Asian Americans shared "a blood relationship to those peoples of Indochina who are fighting for their freedom against the United States," a relationship that was "a kinship of oppression" between peoples subject to capitalist exploitation and neocolonialism on both sides of the Pacific.[29] Building a sense of racial commonality with the peoples of left Asia helped to consolidate the conglomeration of ethnic groups that formed Asian America. Furthermore, advocating a distinctive Asian American line against the war which differed from the discourses of the mainstream antiwar movement furthered the construction of Asian American identity.

Gidra devoted considerable space to cultural expressions of Asian

American perspectives, regularly featuring graphic art, photography, fiction, and poetry. The newspaper's emphasis on visual art and literature provides compelling evidence that Asian American radicals viewed culture as integral to politics. Chapter 5 focuses on the music and performances of the folk trio A Grain of Sand, which many thought provided the soundtrack to the Asian American movement. Performing across the United States at demonstrations, on campuses, and in community centers, the trio enacted a version of racial politics that encapsulated the cultural formation of Asian America. Their self-titled 1973 album expressed solidarity with blacks, Latinos, and Native Americans; supported the Vietnamese people's quest for self-determination; and argued that the efforts to construct Asian American identity were part of the larger struggle against U.S. imperialism at home and abroad.

Pat Sumi's journeys illustrate the four major themes of this book—Asian American struggles with and against whiteness, the emergence of Asian American identity in relation to blackness, transnational sympathies with Asians in Asia constructed through opposition to the war in Viet Nam, and the cultural formation of Asian American identity. The title of this book, *Chains of Babylon,* is drawn from the aforementioned poem, in which Sumi wrote: "Chains of Babylon/bind us together."[30] In the parlance of the 1960s, Sumi's usage of "Babylon" points to the United States as a racially oppressive empire; the twin chains of Babylon to which she refers are American racism and imperialism. Asians in the United States have been historically divided by ethnicity, culture, language, and nationality and have been estranged from Asia by geographical distance and cultural and linguistic differences. But in this poem Sumi argues that the dual chains of American racism and imperialism "bind" all of "us"—Asians of all ethnicities in the United States, along with Asians struggling against American hegemony in Asia—"together" by forcing us to recognize our common struggles and interests. Despite the strength of these chains, Sumi suggests that powerful oppositional alliances and solidarities can emerge from recognizing the common oppression they impose and struggling together to break them.

Significance

Studying how multiethnic Asian American racial identity emerged in the 1960s and 1970s helps build a more general understanding of race in the United States in three main ways. First, it shows the importance of conceptualizing racial formations as processes that unfold in relation to each other. Second, it revises the historiography of the 1960s by redressing Asian American invisibility and also by extending the periodization of the 1960s to include the early 1970s. Third, it provides a fuller, more ideologically diverse account of the political organizing and cultural work that led to the creation of Asian America.

Neither Black nor White: The Racial Triangulation of Asian Americans

It is widely accepted by now that race is a historically contingent social construct that is always in the process of becoming, and that racial identities are defined in relation to each other. This book explores how Asian Americans have confronted a system of race that positions them differentially in relation to whites, African Americans, Latinos, and Native Americans. In her book *Asian American Dreams,* the Chinese American journalist Helen Zia recounts a conversation from her childhood during the 1960s in which she was discussing the civil rights movement with two friends, one black and the other white. In the midst of the conversation, her black friend declared, "Helen, you've got to decide if you're black or white!"[31] The insistence that Asian Americans must choose between being black or white typifies the binary model of race, which features only two possible racial categories. But a black-white binary cannot adequately address the enduring existence of racial categories such as Asian American, Latino, and Native American. Indeed, as geographer Laura Pulido perceptively notes in her examination of the multiracial left in Los Angeles, various groups are positioned in relation to each other in a process that she terms "differential racialization."[32] Differences of class, culture, and historical inclusion in the nation all impact the particular ways that racial categories are partitioned. Thus, the fact that Asian Americans are racialized as inferior to whites does not make their racial categorization equivalent to that of African Americans.

Instead, sociologist Claire Jean Kim proposes the enormously useful concept of "racial triangulation" to assess how Asian Americans are racialized in the United States.[33] Racial triangulation asserts that the formation of the category "Asian American" always occurs in dialogue and dispute with both blackness and whiteness, and it examines the multidimensionality of racial comparisons. Blacks, whites, and Asian Americans are positioned differently on multiple scales of fitness as Americans: suitability for citizenship, fitness for civic and corporate participation, worthiness of government assistance, and so on. For example, Asian Americans are often seen as perpetual foreigners yet industrious; blacks are perceived as unquestionably American but indolent; and, in contrast, whites are most often portrayed as both suitable citizens and hardworking. According to this typology, Asian Americans and African Americans are both inferior to whites but in different ways. Racial triangulation enables us to understand how Asian Americans exist not simply as intermediaries between black and white but instead as a racial group formed through constant comparisons to both blacks and whites. Adopting the racial triangulation framework demands that we pay attention to cross-racial interactions, interventions, and imaginations and forces us to consider how Asian Americans encountered both blackness and whiteness as they built their own racial identity.

A growing body of scholarly literature examines encounters between Asian Americans and African Americans. Although a significant amount of attention has been paid to conflicts, particularly urban, class-based clashes including the 1992 Los Angeles riots, scholars have increasingly examined commonalities and alliances.[34] Special issues of the *Journal of Asian American Studies* and *positions: east asia cultures critique* have examined transracial crossings and exchanges.[35] The literature on black and Asian American encounters can be categorized into three main strands. First, some studies examine how the dominant society has conceptualized and positioned African Americans and Asian Americans in relation to each other. In this vein, Henry Yu demonstrates how social scientists conceived of American "Orientals" in frameworks first rehearsed in discussions of the "Negro Problem," and Moon-Ho Jung examines the intertwined images of blacks and Chinese "coolies" in debates about slavery and emancipation.[36] Second, some scholars explore African American admiration of Asian cultures and politics, particularly in the realm of anticolonialism. George Lipsitz, Ernest Allen, and Marc Gallicchio have examined black hopes for Japan as the "champion of the darker races" before and during World War II, and Robin Kelley and Betsy Esch have remarked on black radical affinity for Red China in the 1960s.[37] The third strand of writing—including works by Laura Pulido, Daniel Widener, Scott Kurashige, and Vijay Prashad—examines black and Asian American social organizing on the ground and reminds us that Asian Americans and African Americans have not only coexisted under systems of racial domination but also have seen similarities in their experiences and at times built tenuous alliances.[38]

Although scholars have begun to explore the linkages between Asian

Americans and black people, to date there has been little discussion of Asian American contemplations of the category of *blackness,* per se. It is crucial to distinguish between blackness and black people. Blackness is an abstraction, a racial category constructed by a vast array of social actors who imbue it with a variety of meanings. In contrast, black people are the human beings who are sorted into this category, are ascribed the qualities of blackness, and as a result are often oppressed and exploited. In addition to the alliances between Asian Americans and black people, I argue that thinking about blackness per se provided Asian Americans with important ways to consider their own racial positioning in the United States.

Throughout their histories, Asian Americans have contended with whiteness by struggling for its privileges in the face of denial and also, in some cases, by vying for inclusion within its ranks. From the mid-1800s through World War II, the dominant portrayal of Asians in the United States relied on Orientalist notions of difference and incompatibility. Asians were imagined to be a threatening Yellow Peril incapable of assimilating into the nation, which was raced as white. The cold war and its imperatives opened up new ways of thinking about Asians that were part of a more general pattern of an American reassessment of race in the 1950s and 1960s.[39] This revision attempted to portray the United States as an egalitarian nation in order to counter Soviet allegations of American racism and to persuade newly liberated nonaligned Third World nations to join the western alliance against communism. Rather than posing an inassimilable threat to the nation, Asians came to be represented as an eminently assimilable "model minority," proof that the United States had overcome its racist past.[40] Asian American scholars and activists have labored mightily to dispel the model minority myth not only by proving its empirical falsity but also by pointing to the ideological work it performs in blaming people of color for their own economic exploitation and in driving wedges between Asian Americans and other people of color.[41] However, to simply dismiss the model minority myth as false or politically suspect is to miss a crucial point: that during the cold war Asian Americans for the first time faced the possibility (whether fulfilled or not) of being accepted into whiteness.

The field of Asian American studies is beginning to actively debate and theorize the relationship between Asian Americans and whiteness. The scholarship that emerged in the 1960s argued that Asian American experiences could best be comprehended within a framework that emphasized racial discrimination, including immigration exclusions, labor exploitation, denial of citizenship, cultural representations, and incarceration. But focusing exclusively on anti-Asian racism occludes the fact that some Asian Americans have aspired to whiteness as a palliative to the discrimination they faced, as Susan Koshy has shown.[42] At present, the relationship of Asian Americans to whiteness is in dispute. Aihwa Ong points to the "whitening" of ethnic Chinese and Vietnamese immigrants, in contrast to the "blackening" of Cambodians and Laotians.[43] James Kyung-Jin Lee contends that after World War II, Asian Americans attained a "structural alignment whiteness," and Viet Nguyen speculates that Asian Americans may become assimilated ethnic rather than racial subjects.[44] In contrast, Min Zhou believes that classifying Asian Americans as "white" is "premature and based on false premises."[45]

That some Asian Americans would aspire to whiteness tells us something about the hegemonic hold that existing systems of race have exercised on the imaginations of their subjugated subjects. More important, it is critical to appreciate the significance of the fact that other Asian Americans chose to *reject* the disingenuous proffer of whiteness in the postwar era and opted instead to cast their lots with other people of color.

Asian Americans and the Historiography of the 1960s

When I made my way to San Francisco in 1990, the International Hotel was no more than a gaping pit in a weed-strewn lot at the corner of Kearny and Jackson streets. Once the home of many elderly Filipino and Chinese men, in 1968 the hotel became the target of urban redevelopers seeking to demolish it. For nine years, a broad-based coalition waged a protracted battle to save the hotel, but on 4 August 1977, riot-equipped law enforcement officers forced their way through thousands of protesters to evict the last of the seniors from their homes.[46] Thus, when I made my pilgrimage to the site, only an empty hole in the ground enclosed by a chain-link fence bore mute testimony to the struggles of Asian American elders and radicals.

The I-Hotel speaks to Asian American radicalism of the 1960s and 1970s and its legacies in three ways. First, its physical obliteration represents the near-total absence of Asian Americans from the existing historiography on social activism during the civil rights and black power period. The otherwise excellent and definitive *Columbia Guide to America in the 1960s* omits Asian Americans entirely; Todd Gitlin's influential account, *The Sixties: Years of Hope, Days of Rage,* is utterly blind to

Asian Americans; Terry Anderson's authoritative *The Movement and the Sixties* mentions Asian Americans once in passing; and the widely assigned documentary collection *Takin' It to the Streets* includes only two documents produced by Asian Americans.[47]

Second, unity and separatism among Asian American radicals can be mapped onto the physical layout of the I-Hotel, as scholar May Fu has pointed out.[48] The I-Hotel was a "hotbed" of activity encompassing nearly every aspect of Asian American activism in the San Francisco Bay area. Its labyrinthine basements comprised multiple spaces, both divided and shared, occupied by many organizations, including the I-Hotel Tenants Association, the cultural organization Kearny Street Workshop, the Chinatown Draft Help Center, Kalayaan (the Filipino group that evolved into KDP or Katipunan Ng Ma Demokratikong, the Union of Democratic Pilipinos), Wei Min She (WMS) and its affiliates, Everybody's Bookstore and Asian Community Center, and I Wor Kuen (IWK) and its affiliate, the Chinese Progressive Association.[49] The hotel was a place where young radicals could rub elbows with elderly manongs who had migrated to the United States in the 1920s and in the 1960s and 1970s gathered at the Lucky M Pool Hall and Tino's Barbershop to reminisce, swap stories, and share laughter. Asian American activists of the time were famously fractious, often differing fiercely about the correct line on nationalism, the vanguard, and culture. Situating these internecine disputes within the spatial context of the I-Hotel emphasizes that despite deep disagreements, participants in the Asian American movement also shared much common ground. Though separated by walls within the massive edifice, they chose these shared spaces because they were united by an urge toward social justice.

Third, although I first encountered the I-Hotel as an absence, during the time in which I have been working on this book the I-Hotel has risen like a phoenix from its ashes. When the tenants were evicted in 1977, it seemed to close the book on Asian American radicalism. However, in 2003, community activists cheered the groundbreaking for a new building that would include 104 units of affordable senior housing.[50] Just as the site of the hotel lay dormant for a quarter century, the Asian American movement lapsed into quiescence by the end of the 1970s. President Richard Nixon's trip to Beijing in 1972 dispirited much of the left, the influx of anticommunist South Vietnamese refugees after 1975 dispelled the notion among Asian American radicals that all Asians were inherently anti-imperialists, and both IWK and WMS had turned away from community organizing and toward building multiracial communist parties.[51] However, the reconstruction of the I-Hotel suggests that the ideals and dedication of the Asian American radicals of the 1960s and 1970s were not razed to the ground but rather persevered through the ascendance of conservatism in the late twentieth century to find new expression in the twenty-first.

In addition to broadening our understanding of Asian American participation in "The Sixties," this book is also centrally concerned with correcting a popular misunderstanding of that period. White-centric historiography often charges that the political movements of the late 1960s betrayed the new left's promise of the early 1960s. This "good sixties/bad sixties" model portrays the post-1968 movement as hopelessly fractured by the rise of narrowly divisive identity politics. Historian David Burner excoriates the black power movement for engendering a "narcissistic absorption in the group content of self-identity" and a "solipsistic examination" of the self. Similarly, the former 1960s activist Gitlin mourns the left's supposed abandonment of universalism in favor parochialism, which he laments as the "twilight of common dreams."[52] However, the case of Asian American mobilization serves as a powerful rejoinder to naysayers of the late 1960s.[53] Asian American adaptations of black power's emphasis on race and racial identity not only contributed to the construction of Asian American identity but also provided points of conjunction around which African Americans and Asian Americans could connect political and cultural movements. To a lesser extent, Asian Americans supported Chicano, Puerto Rican, and American Indian causes. Furthermore, Asian American adoptions of anti-imperialism led them to declare their solidarity with the Vietnamese as fellow Asians. Only by envisioning white people as the center of the 1960s movements can we see the late 1960s as a time of racial separatism.

Understanding Asian American Identity

Historians, sociologists, and cultural studies scholars have produced differing accounts of the construction of Asian American identity, none of them entirely satisfying. William Wei's 1993 pioneering monograph *The Asian American Movement* remains the most extensive historiographical account of Asian American radicalism of the 1960s. However, it mistakenly places Asian American activism within a civil rights rather than a Third World liberationist framework. The Asian American movement bloomed from the late 1960s to the mid-1970s and, like contemporaneous social movements of blacks, Chicanos, Puerto Ricans, and American Indians, demanded self-determination rather than integration. Furthermore,

Wei consistently lauds "reformers" over "revolutionaries." While I agree with Wei that by the mid-1970s sectarianism and party building were impediments to the effectiveness of some Asian American organizations, I argue for the primacy of radicalism (especially antiracism and anti-imperialism) to the ideological underpinnings of Asian American identity and recognize the crucial roles that leftists played in nearly every facet of Asian American organizing. Finally, whereas Wei treats culture as a realm in which Asian Americans could find self-affirmation, I emphasize the richly generative role that culture, defined broadly, played in mustering Asian American identity and politics.

Sociologists have examined Asian American identity as a category that includes multiple ethnicities largely through the lens of "panethnicity," an idea first advanced by Yen Le Espiritu.[54] Scholars adopting the panethnic approach concentrate primarily, though not exclusively, on Asian American interactions with the state, arguing that Asian Americans gain traction with local, state, and federal agencies and institutions such as colleges and universities by building plausible claims to representing larger, multiethnic communities.[55] In addition to increasing the numerical basis of Asian America, making racially based appeals to the state allows Asian Americans to more easily conform to categories that the state already recognizes, for claims made on the basis of race are much more likely to be accepted than are those based on ethnicity.[56] This strategy of conforming to state-recognized categories builds what I would call a "state-sponsored identity." Although a state-sponsored panethnic Asian American identity may be common today, analyzing the emergence of Asian American identity exclusively through a panethnic, state-centric lens tends to obscure the grassroots politics that first infused the building of multiethnic coalitions during the 1960s and 1970s. The state-sponsored identity approach cannot account for radical ideologies and organizations that rejected the state as repressive and complicit in the maintenance of capitalism and instead sought transnational racial solidarity.

Finally, the field of Asian American cultural studies has yet to properly account for the birth of Asian America. Works by literary scholars that examine Asian American identity tend to rely on untenable mythologies of 1960s activism, chiefly the belief that Asian American identity emerged primarily out of American nationalism.[57] This approach oversimplifies the complexity of a diverse ideological field that included sophisticated analyses of imperialism and transnational racial identifications. Whereas literary scholars tend to restrict their attention to published plays, poems, fiction, and so on, my study is the first to consider the rich and eminently readable political theater of protests, rallies, and proclamations as cultural productions. Indeed, culture in this larger sense played an essential role in the creation of Asian American identity by providing a vital stage upon which Asian Americans forged multiethnic solidarity and argued for racial solidarity between Asian Americans and other people of color in the United States and abroad.

Like many other Asian American radicals, Pat Sumi ultimately connected the racialization of Asian Americans to more extensive systems of race, exploitation, and imperialism, arguing that Asian Americans should stand "shoulder to shoulder" with other "third world people." On 21 February 1974, she spoke at the Third World People's Solidarity Conference at the University of Michigan. Her co-speakers in Ann Arbor included Angela Davis, Clyde Bellecourt of the American Indian Movement, and Ramsey Muñiz of La Raza Unida Party in Texas. In her speech she brilliantly interwove the histories of oppression and resistance of Asian Americans, Chicanos, blacks, Native Americans, and Third World people, stating:

> Our lives, along with the lives of all Third World peoples of the world have been conditioned by imperialism. Therefore, our struggles to liberate the Asian, African and Latin American peoples from imperialism. Our lives have been conditioned by racism. Therefore, our struggles as Asian Americans must be part of the struggle to end racism and win genuine equality for all people.[58]

Sumi had traversed continents and ideologies to arrive at this understanding of Asian American identity. Renouncing the assimilationism of her childhood, Sumi came to see Asian Americans as racial subjects of the United States and embraced an Asian American identity that sought solidarity with other people of color in the United States and across the globe.

Tracing Asian American racial politics of the late 1960s and early 1970s enables us to see the allure that whiteness exercised on racialized peoples, the complexity of the racial field in which Asian Americans were triangulated, and the political commitments that emerged from their contemplations of blackness and interactions with other nonwhite people. If in the period after World War II Asian Americans faced new racial possibilities, the choice of some to reject whiteness and instead practice a politics of multiethnic unity, interracial solidarity, and transnational anti-imperialism seems all the more remarkable.

One

Before Asian America

Tensions over sameness and difference have unsettled Asian America from the late 1800s to the present. While the dominant society tends to lump Asians together regardless of ethnicity or national origin, Asians view themselves as distinct from one another. Migrants from Asia never set foot on American soil already thinking of themselves as Asians, let alone "Asian Americans." Instead, they arrive with identities tied to nations, regions, ethnicities, or even tribes. Some immigrants gravitate toward enclaves that feature ethnic communities, employment opportunities, and the familiar sounds, aromas, and foods of home. Others settle into areas with dense Asian American populations but find few who share their particular languages or cultures. Still others disperse into the wider terrain of the United States, where they encounter majority populations that are white, black, or Latino. Longstanding national and ethnic antagonisms in Asia often continue to fester in the United States and at times inhibit political organizing across ethnic lines. But although new immigrants may not consider themselves Asian Americans upon arrival, they enter into a racial landscape not of their own making, which positions them according to its own logic.

From the mid-nineteenth century onward, the category "Oriental" has been a critical organizing principle under which diverse peoples of various Asian nations, cultures, and ethnicities in the United States were collapsed into a monolithic bloc. Orientalism, as Edward Said has famously argued, constructs the East and West as dichotomous opposites, with the Orient embodying weakness, immorality, and irrationality, in contrast to the Occident's strength, virtue, and reason. Nineteenth- and early twentieth-century American versions of Orientalism imagined Asians within the United States as unwanted perpetual foreigners who could never be assimilated or become good Americans, a Yellow Peril that threatened white racial dominance.[1] Many different Asian groups entered the United States separately, only to exploited, legislated, and discriminated into uniformity in the eyes of the dominant society.

Before the 1960s, in response to this American system of race that agglomerated them together as "Orientals," Asian ethnics employed political strategies that emphasized their differences or rejected distinctions between Asians and whites. Supporting Asian homeland nationalism highlighted differences among Asians and exacerbated ethnic tensions in the United States. Promoting assimilation rejected the idea that Asians were racially distinct from whites and instead argued that they could be seamlessly incorporated into the nation. Organizing by labor unionists and radicals tended to emphasize class solidarity over racial identity.

Racializing Asians

Asians in the United States were racialized in three main ways. First, as subjects of capitalism and imperialism, waves of Asians from various nations were impelled to migrate across the Pacific. Each group, in turn, was exploited for their labor and then, subsequently, had immigration restrictions imposed upon them. Second, each ethnic group petitioned for naturalized citizenship but was denied by court rulings and legislation, leaving Asians uniquely and uniformly considered "aliens ineligible to citizenship" under the law. Third, social discrimination against each group constructed them as inassimilable and undesirable. Chinese, Japanese, Koreans, Indians, and Filipinos—the five Asian immigrant groups before World War II—all found themselves caught in cycles of migration, exploitation, and exclusion that left them similarly positioned vis-à-vis the state and dominant society.

Immigration and Exclusion

From the beginning of large-scale Asian immigration to the United States and its territories in the mid-1800s, Asians provided cheap labor to the rapidly expanding capitalist economies of Hawaii and the West Coast.[2]

Chinese began immigrating in large numbers in the 1850s, some 46,000 to Hawaii by 1900 and about 380,000 to the mainland by 1930.[3] Initially drawn to California by dreams of the riches to be found on Gold Mountain, they worked in agriculture, mining, and small manufacturing and on the railroad. While employers welcomed the Chinese, white workers viewed them as labor competition and formed a vigorous anti-Chinese movement. Historian Alexander Saxton argues that in California, the Chinese functioned as an "indispensable enemy" that allowed Europeans of various ethnicities and immigrant statuses to unite under the banner of whiteness.[4] Chinese exclusion began in 1875 with the enactment of the Page Law, which was intended to bar the importation of Asian women for prostitution. However, according to George Anthony Peffer, "Government officials recklessly applied popular anti-Chinese stereotypes to exclude women whom the Page Law technically regarded as eligible," in effect erecting a "formidable barrier" to the immigration of all Chinese women.[5] Exclusionists triumphed in 1882 with the passage of the Chinese Exclusion Act (CEA), which prohibited the entry of laborers into the United States, effectively ending large-scale Chinese immigration. The CEA gave the Chinese the dubious distinction of being the first people whose immigration was restricted based on "race and nationality."[6] Chinese exclusion was renewed in 1892 and made permanent in 1904.[7]

While the flow of Chinese workers was largely staunched, the need for cheap labor continued unabated, and Japanese began migrating in large numbers in 1885. By 1924, some 200,000 Japanese had migrated to Hawaii and another 180,000 to the mainland. While Japanese Americans managed to build urban enclaves, agriculture proved to be the mainstay of their community as they rapidly became major growers of fruits and vegetables.[8] The nativist movement that had previously targeted the Chinese remobilized to oppose Japanese immigration. In 1907–8, the federal government engineered the so-called Gentlemen's Agreement, in which the Japanese government agreed to end the emigration of workers from Japan.[9] This allowed Japan, a rising power in the Pacific, to evade the humiliation of outright unilateral exclusion that had befallen China while still impeding the flow of male laborers.[10] However, Japanese women continued to immigrate; many were "picture brides" who had been married in absentia in Japan and would meet their new spouses for the first time at the dock in America. Exclusionists, distressed that Japanese women were evading the Gentlemen's Agreement and functioning as de facto laborers (which was in some sense true, because they worked in the fields alongside the men, in addition to performing household work and caring for children), again pressured the federal government. In 1920, the two governments reached a second agreement that ended the immigration of picture brides.[11]

While Chinese and Japanese composed the largest Asian immigrant streams, Koreans and Asian Indians also entered the United States and Hawaii, albeit in smaller numbers. Some seven thousand Koreans (40 percent of whom were Christian converts) immigrated to the mainland and Hawaii, where they worked primarily in agriculture.[12] After Japan colonized Korea in 1905, it severely restricted Korean emigration, and after the Gentlemen's Agreement, Koreans became subject to the bans against Japanese emigration.[13] Indian emigrants tended to follow the contours of the British Empire, but a small number ended up in the United States, some by crossing the border from Canada.[14] By 1910, the Indian population of the United States topped five thousand.[15] Some Indians worked in the lumber industry in the Pacific Northwest, while others were agricultural laborers.[16] Despite their small population, Indians attracted ample attention from exclusionists: in 1907 the Japanese and Korean Exclusion League renamed itself the Asian Exclusion League in order to target Indians as well.[17] Indian immigration was ended by the passage of the 1917 Immigration Act, which created an "Asiatic Barred Zone" including the Indian subcontinent.[18]

The 1924 Immigration Act was one of the most important pieces of American legislation of the twentieth century. It substantially diminished mass immigration from southern and eastern Europe by allotting those nations minuscule quotas. But while it drastically reduced European immigration, it virtually ended Asian immigration. Most important, the 1924 legislation, sometimes known as the Asian Exclusion Act, conglomerated the peoples of multiple Asian nations into a monolithic, distinctly nonwhite racial bloc of undesirables. Despite the near-wholesale ban on Asian labor migration, however, the agricultural industry continued to require cheap labor.

Immigrants from the Philippines constituted the sole exception to the Asian Exclusion Act. Filipinos could not be easily excluded, because they were American subjects due to the U.S. colonization of the Philippines. Filipinos thus made up the third large wave of Asian migrants to Hawaii and the U.S. mainland. Takaki states, "By 1930, some 110,000 Filipinos had gone to Hawaii and another 40,000 to the mainland."[19] In Hawaii, they worked the sugar plantations. On the mainland, they labored in the salmon canning industry, as domestic workers, and, most frequently, in agriculture. The overwhelmingly male workforce composed an itinerant army that followed the crops across the west. Though initially valued by growers as docile, Filipinos proved highly organized and militant.[20] When the Great Depression greatly reduced the need for Filipino labor, calls for their exclusion began to reverberate more loudly. The 1934 Tydings-McDuffie Act disposed of the problem of Filipino immigration by promising independence for the Philippines in the future while immediately making Filipinos aliens and giving them an immigration quota of fifty per year.[21]

By 1934, U.S. immigration policy had aggregated "Orientals" into a bloc of racial undesirables. Chinese, Japanese, Koreans, Indians, and Filipinos were all excluded, either unilaterally by the United States or by means of coerced agreements with foreign governments. Although they confronted the United States in separate ways and at different times, Asian immigrants were exploited and excluded in remarkably similar fashion and were legally and socially discriminated against in ways that differed significantly from the treatment of white European immigrants.

Naturalization Bars

While immigration restrictions impaired the ability of Asians to enter the United States, they did not generally address those who had already landed on American shores. As legal scholar Leti Volpp points out, "The terms Asian American and American citizenship stand in curious juxtaposition," for Asian immigrants were banned from naturalization for over a century and a half.[22] Asian immigrants of many different ethnicities sought to gain the benefits of U.S. citizenship through naturalization, but, as historian Mae Ngai contends, the state's responses once again constructed Asians as a monolithic racial bloc.[23] From its inception in 1790 until 1952, U.S. naturalization policy was based on an explicit racial criterion. The 1790 Naturalization Act restricted the ability to obtain naturalized citizenship to "free white persons." After the Civil War, Congress debated how to extend naturalization to blacks. While Senator Charles Sumner advocated removing the racial qualification altogether, others sought to limit the extension to blacks, specifically in order to exclude Asians. In the end, the Naturalization Act of 1870 extended the right to naturalization to people of "African nativity" and "descent," thus leaving claims to whiteness or Africanness as the only routes by which immigrants could pursue citizenship.[24]

Between 1878 and 1923, Chinese, Japanese, Asian Indian, Korean, and Filipino immigrants made numerous unsuccessful bids for naturalization, almost universally by claiming that the Asian petitioners were white.[25] As legal historian Ian Haney Lopez demonstrates, in the "prerequisite cases" (so named because they tested whether petitioners possessed the racial prerequisite for naturalization), federal courts repeatedly denied Asian claims to whiteness.[26] In 1878, a federal circuit court ruled that the first Asian litigant, a Chinese man by the name of Ah Yup, was Mongolian, not white, and hence ineligible for naturalization.[27] Subsequently, the Chinese Exclusion Act specifically barred Chinese from naturalized citizenship.[28] After the Chinese petitions came petitions from Japanese (In re Saito, 1894), Asian Indians (In re Balsara, 1909), and Filipinos (In re Alverto, 1912), all of whom federal courts ruled were nonwhite and therefore ineligible for naturalization. The final authority on race and citizenship, however, lay with the U.S. Supreme Court, which heard three definitive cases between 1922 and 1925.

The Japanese immigrant Takao Ozawa should have been the perfect candidate to become an American citizen. After arriving in 1894, he graduated from high school in Berkeley and attended the University of California for three years. He settled in Hawaii and raised a family. In his petition for naturalization, he stated that he did not drink, smoke, or gamble; he spoke English at home and sent his children to Sunday school; and he had not registered his children for dual Japanese citizenship upon their births.[29] Despite his qualifications, the U.S. Supreme Court ruled in 1922 that Ozawa was not eligible for naturalization because he was "clearly of a race which is not Caucasian."[30] In other words, he and all other Japanese were disbarred from naturalization not because of their appearance or skin color but because of their race.[31]

Just three months after disposing of Ozawa's claim, the Supreme Court took up the case of Bhagat Singh Thind. An Indian immigrant who had served in the U.S. military during World War I, Singh had been naturalized in 1920 by the U.S. District Court in Oregon. Federal officials sought to deport Thind because of his advocacy of Indian independence from Great Britain, but in order to do so, they first had to strip him of his citizenship. Thind's defense of his citizenship claimed that Indians are Aryan and therefore white. The Supreme Court conceded that although Thind, unlike Ozawa, might be racially Caucasian, he was nevertheless not white according to "the understanding of the common man." Furthermore, it referred to the 1917 Immigration Act's exclusion of Indians, concluding that it was "not likely that Congress would be willing to accept as citizens a class of persons whom it rejects as immigrants."[32] The high court thus stripped Thind of his citizenship and decreed that Indians were ineligible for naturalization.[33] In so doing, it reversed its logic in *Ozawa,* for it ruled that Indians were ineligible because of their appearance, not their "scientifically" determined race.

Filipinos occupied an ambiguous position with regard to citizenship. On the one hand, they were American nationals by virtue of being colonial subjects of the United States, but on the other hand, as nonaliens, they were not specifically eligible for naturalization. The question as to their eligibility was answered by the Supreme Court in a rather circuitous fashion. In 1925, in *Toyota v. United States,* the Court ruled that Japanese were ineligible to apply for naturalization under legislation aimed at facilitating citizenship for veterans of World War I. In finding that the law was specifically applicable to Filipinos, the Court further ruled that Filipinos were eligible for naturalization only under this law, not more generally.[34] Earlier, in 1921, a Korean American veteran named Easurk Emsen Charr had petitioned for naturalization under this same law, but a district court had ruled that as a member of the "Mongol family" he was ineligible for naturalization.[35]

By 1925, Chinese, Japanese, Koreans, Asian Indians, and Filipinos formed a bloc of "aliens ineligible to naturalization." In contrast, European immigrants, even those like Irish and Italians deemed racially inferior to Anglo-Saxons, enjoyed unfettered rights to naturalization, making them what historian Thomas Guglielmo terms "white on arrival."[36] After 1870, blacks enjoyed the right to naturalization, and even American Indians could attain citizenship through the 1890 Indian Naturalization Act. Asians thus stood as the sole group to be barred from naturalization on racial grounds. Ah Yup, Alverto, Charr, Ozawa, and Thind approached the courts separately and advanced divergent claims, yet all were denied with equal certainty. The category "aliens ineligible to citizenship" thus consolidated various Asian immigrants into a uniform bloc in the eyes of the law.

Social Discrimination

Asians of various ethnicities encountered numerous forms of social discrimination, including violence, bans on union membership, employment and housing discrimination, unequal pay, bars from certain public facilities, and antimiscegenation laws. But beyond simply noticing that Asians faced racism, it is perhaps more important to trace out how people of different ethnicities and nationalities came to be discriminated against in similar fashions. Interracial marriage provides one key way to measure the social status of sundry Asian groups, for as scholars such as Peggy Pascoe and Susan Koshy have argued, the regulation of intimacy has been an important technique for enforcing racial hierarchies.[37] Furthermore, Asians were seen as a threat to white racial purity, and indeed, much anti-Asian animus was expressed as anxiety about sexuality between "Orientals" and "whites," as Henry Yu has shown.[38] Hence, the degree to which diverse Asians were targeted by antimiscegenation laws provides evidence that they were not only viewed as distinct from whites but also understood by the dominant society to be alike in their inferiority.

Although immigration and naturalization fall within the domain of the federal government, the regulation of marriage has been left to states, and no nationwide consensus emerged with regard to the question of whether Asians could marry people of other races. However, the case of California's antimiscegenation legislation is instructive. California's antimiscegenation law, first enacted in 1850, forbade whites from marrying blacks; it was amended in 1880 to include Chinese, to whom it referred as "Mongolians."[39] The state's antimiscegenation statutes were again amended in 1905, with the critical intention of including Japanese in the forbidden category of "Mongolian."[40] Filipinos who were barred from intermarriage argued that they were not Mongolians in *Roldan v. Los Angeles County*. Although the California Appellate Court agreed, the antimiscegenation statutes were again amended in 1933 to forbid whites from marrying anyone of "the Malay race," as Filipinos were then classified.[41]

California's stringent antimiscegenation law thus made clear that people of various Asian ethnicities were equivalently undesirable. The state's ban on interracial marriage remained in force until after World War II, when the California Supreme Court struck it down in *Perez v. Sharp* (1948). California was far from exceptional, for antimiscegenation laws were enacted in forty-one states and colonies, with most remaining on the books through the mid-1960s. In all, fourteen states forbade intermarriage between whites and Asian Americans (Chinese, Japanese, and Koreans), and nine included Filipinos. The national demise of antimiscegenation laws did not occur until 1967, when the U.S. Supreme Court decreed them unconstitutional in *Loving v. Virginia*.[42]

From the mid-1800s to World War II, the state had consolidated the category "Oriental" through a series of legislative and juridical maneuvers that sharpened racial definitions and made Orientals of a diverse stream of immigrants from various nations. These immigrants and their descendants hailed from an assortment of nations, spoke different languages, worshiped in sundry ways, and practiced a variety of cultures. Nevertheless, the state formed them into a monolithic bloc with regard to their rights to immigrate, naturalize, and assimilate through intermarriage with whites.

Political Mobilizations before the 1960s

Asians who encountered racism and exploitation in the United States did not passively accept their subordination but instead actively resisted, using a variety of ideologies throughout the late nineteenth and early twentieth centuries. Asian nationalism, assimilationism, and radicalism all provided means by which Asians in the United States sought to better their lives and diminish the racism they faced. However, none of these avenues built multiethnic solidarity among Asians; instead, they exacerbated ethnic tensions at times.

Asian Nationalism

Although the state and popular discourses conflated Asian nationalities and ethnicities, Asians themselves resisted this presumption of their uniformity and instead emphasized their distinctions, often through embracing a variety of Asian nationalisms.[43] Immigrants in the United States often supported the liberation, establishment, or strengthening of their home nation-states. These diasporic nationalist movements were shaped in part by the American conditions that immigrants faced. For one thing, in an instrumental sense, supporting their homelands could improve their life in the United States, for, in the words of Robert G. Lee, a "strong diplomatic presence on the part of Asian countries would be one of the few sources of protection for immigrants who had been declared ineligible for citizenship."[44] But beyond instrumentality, diasporic nationalists also drew upon quintessentially American discourses of democracy and puzzled over the contradictions between America's promises and its realities in terms of racism and colonialism. For example, historian Augusto Espiritu comments that the critiques of colonialism deployed by expatriate Filipino intellectuals in the United States were deeply rooted in the "American realities" of discrimination that they encountered.[45] Finally, diasporic nationalisms were sustained by complicated and ongoing relationships between migrants and their countries of origin, for, as historians increasingly recognize, transnational ties endured for decades and generations.[46]

The United States proved to be a useful base from which immigrants could mobilize to liberate their homelands from colonial rule. Among Asian Indians, the Ghadar ("Revolution") Party was organized in 1913 to fight for Indian independence from Britain. It unified Indians across ethnic and class lines, bringing together Bengali intellectuals and Punjabi Sikh agricultural workers, and its newspaper, *Ghadar,* was distributed throughout the Indian diaspora. Led by the exiled intellectual Har Dayal, who studied Marx, Bakunin, and Kropotkin and served as secretary of the Radical Socialist Club in San Francisco, the party's opposition to British imperialism drew support from the Social Labor Party and the Industrial Workers of the World (the Wobblies). The Ghadar movement was broken during World War I, when over a thousand Ghadarites returned to India to instigate a rebellion, only to be promptly arrested and imprisoned; some were hung. When the United States entered the war, party leaders were arrested, tried and convicted, and threatened with deportation for their anti-British activities.[47]

Koreans in the United States also fought for independence for their homeland, which Japan had formally annexed in 1910. Prominent nationalist leaders, including Ahn Chang-ho, Park Yong-man, Syngman Rhee (who became the first president of the Republic of Korea in 1945), and Philip Jaisohn, lived at various times in Hawaii or the United States and drew faithful support for their organizations from Korean immigrants.[48] As Richard S. Kim argues, the diasporic nationalism practiced by Koreans in the United States drew heavily upon "American political ideals and values" and sought to mobilize Wilsonian internationalism to liberate their homeland.[49]

Chinese nationalism also flourished on American soil. In 1905, immigrant workers joined their compatriots in China in a boycott of American goods organized to protest the United States' lack of respect for Chinese national sovereignty.[50] Chinese leaders, both revolutionaries and reformers, traveled to the United States and sought support and financial aid for their causes. Sun Yat-sen, who sought to overthrow the Qing Dynasty and establish a Chinese republic, founded the Xingzhonghui (Revive China Society) in Hawaii in 1894. Meanwhile, the reformist Baohuanghui (Chinese Empire Reform Association) drew thirty thousand members in Hawaii and North America. Later, during a period of struggle following the overthrow of the Manchu emperor in 1911, Sun's Kuomintang party

(KMT, the Chinese Nationalist Party), was dissolved in China but continued to operate in North America, where it claimed a membership of more than fifteen thousand. By World War II, the KMT had established itself as the dominant political force in Chinese America.[51]

Competing Asian nationalisms often caused conflicts or exacerbated existing rifts between Asians in the United States. At the beginning of the twentieth century, Japanese protesting against proposals to exclude them argued vigorously against being grouped with Chinese. The Japanese insisted that they were the equals of whites and therefore should not be subject to exclusion, even while agreeing that exclusion of the inferior Chinese was justified.[52] Conversely, Chinese Americans were largely unperturbed by the anti-Japanese movement in California.[53] Korean loathing of Japan continued to resonate in the United States, where Korean immigrants seethed with resentment when they were mistaken for Japanese, to the point of refusing Japanese consular intervention and assistance.[54] After Japan invaded Manchuria in 1931, Chinese Americans quickly mobilized to defend China, raising millions of dollars for relief, boycotting Japanese goods, and attempting to curb shipment of scrap metal to Japan.[55] Meanwhile, Issei (Japanese American immigrants) in communities across the west mobilized to support the Japanese war effort, and the Japanese American press, including the English-language papers such as Jimmie Sakamoto's *Japanese-American Courier,* parroted the Japanese government's official line of blaming China for the conflict.[56] During World War II, when Japanese Americans were incarcerated in concentration camps and Japan was occupying much of Asia, various Asian Americans vigorously sought to dissociate themselves from the Japanese by posting signs saying, "This is a Chinese shop," wearing buttons proclaiming "I am Chinese" or "I am a Filipino," carrying identification cards that announced "I am Korean," or wearing Korean dresses.[57]

Competing Asian nationalisms were thus clearly not suited to fostering multiethnic solidarity in the United States. Diasporic nationalisms, in particular, tended to be embraced most ardently by immigrants and often attenuated over subsequent generations. As exclusion restricted the entrance of new migrants, the proportion of native-born Asian Americans grew dramatically, from 10 percent to 52 percent between 1900 and 1940.[58] Some of these second-generation Asian Americans, who enjoyed citizenship by birth yet continued to face racial discrimination, fiercely proclaimed their American identity.

Assimilation through Americanism

In 1938, James Y. Sakamoto, President of the Japanese American Citizens League (JACL), declared that the JACL was "definitely aligned" with "patriotic organizations [such] as the American Legion, the Veterans of Foreign Wars, the Daughters of the American Revolution, and all that uphold American institutions."[59] This was an astonishing statement given the notoriously anti-Asian histories of the organizations he named, yet Sakamoto and the JACL sought to prove to nativists that Japanese could become good Americans through assimilation. In particular, Sakamoto performed Americanism by collaborating with nativists, highlighting the patriotic citizenship of Japanese Americans, and portraying Japanese culture as compatible with American values. Throughout the 1930s, he and the JACL advocated an ideology that I call "liberal assimilationism," which argued that Japanese could prove their worthiness as Americans through civic participation in the public sphere while retaining their cultural particularities in the private sphere. Liberal assimilationism rejected Anglo conformity, that is, the idea that immigrant groups had to forsake their unique cultural identities. Contrary to the ideal of the melting pot, it envisioned unmelted cultural groups continuing to coexist alongside each other. Although it resembled cultural pluralism most closely, liberal assimilationism reflected a more sophisticated analysis of power. Whereas cultural pluralism imagined that everyone, regardless of ethnicity or race, could participate equally in the political sphere, liberal assimilationism understood that whiteness represented the ultimate position of power and thus sought to gain racial equality by collaborating with whites and arguing implicitly for the extension of the privileges of whiteness to Japanese Americans.

Sakamoto was a key figure in the establishment of the JACL, which, as its name implies, was composed of Nisei (second-generation Japanese Americans), the only Japanese Americans who possessed American citizenship. Initially formed in 1929, the JACL had chapters in urban centers and farming communities across the west. Sakamoto, a Nisei born in Seattle in 1903, had earned renown within the community as a professional boxer who fought in Madison Square Garden. But when detached retinas in both eyes cost him his eyesight and career, he returned to Seattle, where he applied the dogged determination he had displayed in the boxing ring to the task of organizing his fellow Nisei. He began publishing a weekly newspaper, the *Japanese-American Courier*, the first all-English-language Japanese American periodical, and used its pages to proclaim his message of Americanism.[60] The first edition of the *Courier* rolled off the press at 4:15 p.m. on January 1, 1928. As Sakamoto recalled later, "The trials and hardships of the paper were to be many."[61] Indeed, the publisher and his wife, Misao, struggled through financial privation to publish the *Courier* (which had a circulation of only thirteen hundred in 1940), but persevered until the paper was shut down on April 24, 1942, by the mass incarceration of Japanese Americans.[62]

The eminent JACL member Bill Hosokawa, who cut his journalistic teeth at the *Courier*, recalls Sakamoto as "preaching militant, unquestioning loyalty to the United States" and embracing an American identity so zealously that he even banned the Japanese word "Nisei" from the headlines of his newspaper, insisting instead on the more cumbersome term "Second Generation."[63] Sakamoto was far from a lone crusader, for he and the *Courier* not only proved instrumental in building the fledgling JACL but indeed typified the JACL ideology of liberal assimilationism. JACL practices were remarkably consistent across the organization, in chapters and regions near and far from Seattle. Mike Masaoka, perhaps the central figure of the JACL during World War II, agreed on the organization's prewar uniformity, asserting that "most of the local chapters carried on almost identical programs, varied, of course, to meet local situations and conditions."[64]

The young Jimmie Sakamoto had received his first lesson in identity from his father, who had asked him what he would do if war broke out between the United States and Japan. When the boy tried to playfully evade the question, his father admonished him, "If war comes you'll fight for America even to the extent of pointing your gun at me. That son is the spirit of Bushido, the code of ethics and chivalry of the Samurai, who knows no two masters." Sakamoto recalled, "That, might I say, was my first lesson in Americanism."[65] His father's declaration had neatly encapsulated the version of Americanism that Sakamoto would advocate throughout his life, for it posited that Japanese Americans' political fealty to the United States was demonstrated through performing their civic duties but derived from Japanese cultural traits. Sakamoto's father had drawn upon a dominant strain in Issei thinking that identified Nisei Americanism as a product of Japanese values such as bushido.[66]

Sakamoto and Pacific Northwest JACL members collaborated with nativist organizations, including the American Legion, Veterans of Foreign Wars (VFW), and the Daughters of the American Revolution (DAR).

Sakamoto himself spoke before the women's auxiliaries of both the American Legion and the VFW. He claimed that the JACL program of Americanism would help the Nisei to "become contributing factors to the community, . . . strengthen the foundation of society, . . . [and] perform their function at the polls at election times in accordance with their conscience and convictions."[67] Sakamoto thus constructed Japanese Americans as independent and fit for self-government, both traits that scholars such as David Roediger and Matthew Frye Jacobson agree were key to claims of whiteness.[68]

Nativists embraced Sakamoto's work eagerly. Clark Frasier, the state commander of the American Legion in Washington state visited Sakamoto in the fall of 1937, and Sakamoto provided him with a report on the JACL's Yakima convention. Frasier warmly praised "the very excellent work" that Sakamoto and the JACL were doing with Japanese American citizens, especially the resolutions regarding Americanism adopted at the conference.[69] Similarly, when National JACL planned to meet in Seattle, Harry Weingarten, adjutant of Seattle Post No. 1, wrote, "The Seattle Post Number One of the American Legion wishes to extend to both the Northern and Southern California League a welcome to hold their Fourth Biennial Convention in the city of Seattle." Weingarten effused, "We are very proud of the Washington League, with whom we have cooperated 100%."[70] The warm relations between Sakamoto and local American Legionnaires can be seen in the informal language used in their correspondence. Department adjutant Fred Fueker opened one letter, "My dear Jimmie," and enthused in another, "I am darn glad to be able to do this as you don't know how much we appreciate the fine work you are doing in your American born Japanese Americanism work."[71]

The interests of the JACL, the American Legion, and the VFW converged on one issue in particular. All three groups backed the Nye-Lea Act, which would confer citizenship upon Asian veterans of World War I. Tokutaro "Tokie" Slocum, an immigrant from Japan who had fought in the U.S. Army during the war, was a leading actor in this episode. In 1921, Slocum had applied for naturalization under the Act of May 19, 1918, which promised citizenship to aliens who had served in the armed forces during the war. The Bureau of Naturalization informed Slocum that as an Asian he was racially ineligible for naturalization, to which he replied despondently, "I know what you mean; you mean that I am yellow. I may be yellow in face, but I am not yellow at heart."[72] As a veteran who had himself been denied citizenship, Slocum managed the JACL efforts in Washington and liaised with veterans' organizations. Although the JACL's desire to extend citizenship rights to certain Asian immigrants was in keeping with its general mission, it is somewhat surprising that the American Legion and the VFW would concur. This episode demonstrates that all three organizations saw the performance of the civic duty of military service as trumping the racial exclusion from naturalization. In other words, they agreed that through good behavior Japanese Americans could surmount their racial restrictions. After the passage of Nye-Lea, Charles McCarthy of the American Legion praised Slocum's work and presented the pen with which President Franklin D. Roosevelt had signed the bill to the national president of the JACL.[73] Conversely, the JACL presented Japanese swords to two influential Legionnaires and two VFW leaders in gratitude for their support.[74] The act of thanking white veterans by presenting them with Japanese swords makes clear that in 1937, the JACL was not afraid to be associated culturally with Japan. Thus, in keeping with the ideal of liberal assimilationism, the JACL was eager to emphasize that Japanese Americans performed the duties of citizenship and yet also happily underscored their ethnic particularity.

Flag presentations constituted a recurring motif in the JACL play. In 1933, the Yakima chapter of the DAR presented the Yakima Citizens League with an American flag as a token of its approval of the JACL chapter's Americanization program.[75] The DAR did so with remarkable self-importance: in a letter of commendation, the chapter regent enthusiastically called the banner, the "American Flag–The Emblem of our Country."[76] Similarly, Seattle Post No. 1 of the American Legion presented a flag to the Seattle JACL chapter in 1935 in recognition of its efforts in Americanizing the Nisei.[77] Ralph Horr, a member of the American Legion and Republican chair of King County, repeatedly addressed Seattle Progressive Citizens League and JACL meetings, urging members to "actively participate in the political activities of the nation."[78] Horr's seemingly open position—that Japanese Americans deserved citizenship rights—masked a less tolerant position that revealed itself when he ominously intoned, "By going to the polls you will be doing something for your community and country and you will be a part of them; but if you do not and disenfranchise yourself, you cannot be one of the community nor of your country."[79] Horr's thinly veiled threat begins to explain why Legionnaires and members of the VFW and DAR might have cooperated with a Japanese American group like the JACL.

The JACL's stated goal, like the American Legion's and the DAR's, was Americanization, and both American Legion and DAR flags were presented to the JACL in recognition of its Americanization efforts. Nativist organizations sought to impose uniformity upon the American population in two ways: by preventing further immigration (thus, the Legion's prior stand on Japanese exclusion) and, especially after 1924, by forcing assimilation in the guise of Anglo conformity upon those already in the United States (thus, the Legion's Americanization program). Horr's admonition contained elements of both strands of Legion strategy: on the one hand, it offered membership in the nation if the Nisei acquiesced to the Legion's brand of Americanism, but on the other hand it threatened exclusion or removal if they did not. As historian Matthew Frye Jacobson shows, discussions of the fitness for citizenship of various not-quite-white groups frequently hinged on the question of whether their members possessed the ability to make independent political decisions.[80] By emphasizing that Nisei were ready to make informed choices, the JACL argued that Japanese Americans were fully prepared to assume the duties and privileges of citizenship. Generally, in making their bid for full citizenship through their assimilability and readiness for self-government, Japanese Americans implicitly argued for their aptness for inclusion in whiteness.

Radicalism

Before World War II, Asian American communities contained few but vibrant lefts consisting of labor unionists, socialists, and communists. Asian American workers showed a remarkable willingness to organize from their earliest years in the United States.[81] As early as 1867, some two thousand Chinese workers building the transcontinental railroad high in the Sierras struck for better wages and working conditions. The railroad company responded by cutting off their provisions; consequently, the strike lasted for only a week before the workers capitulated.[82] Filipino laborers worked and organized up and down the West Coast, as chronicled by the great Filipino writer Carlos Bulosan in his fictionalized bildungsroman *America Is in the Heart*.[83]

Like Asian diasporic nationalism, ethnic nationalism—which sought to build cohesion among co-ethnics in the United States—also proved more divisive than unifying. In Hawaii, Japanese laborers struck against sugar plantations in 1909 to demand wages equal to those earned by Portuguese. Ronald Takaki characterizes the strike as an example of ethnic solidarity, for Japanese workers, merchants, and professionals supported the strike with money, food, and services. The limitations of ethnic nationalism became clear when planters broke the strike by bringing in "massive numbers of Filipinos to counterbalance the Japanese laborers."[84] Similarly, Eiichiro Azuma argues that ethnic nationalism inhibited labor from organizing and obscured class consciousness among Japanese and Filipino workers in the San Joaquin delta from 1936 to 1941.[85]

Although much early Asian American labor organizing followed ethnic or national lines, the 1920 sugar plantation strike in Hawaii stands out as an important exception. After the 1909 strike, planters consciously sought to balance the plantation workforce so that no single ethnic group would predominate. Consequently, comprehensive organizing required cross-ethnic cooperation. In 1920, more than eight thousand Japanese and Filipino plantation workers struck together. Plantation owners responded by evicting thousands of workers and their families from plantation housing in the midst of an influenza epidemic, and 150 died. Though workers stayed off the job for six months, the strike was largely unsuccessful.[86] Yen Le Espiritu astutely attributes the 1920 strike's cohesiveness to class solidarity rather than any sense of shared racial identity, a conclusion bolstered by the fact that Koreans organized themselves as strikebreakers, saying, "We are opposed to the Japanese in everything."[87]

The emergence of organized Asian American labor in the salmon canning industry on the Pacific Coast further illustrates ethnic tensions within the working class. Chinese, Japanese, and Filipino American workers in the Alaska Cannery Workers Union and the Cannery Workers and Farm Laborers Union vied for power not only with employers but among themselves. During the 1930s, these unions briefly succeeded in building a fragile multiethnic alliance based on shared class position, but the outbreak of World War II bolstered Filipino nationalism and removed Japanese Americans from the picture altogether.[88]

Asian American workers sometimes crossed not only ethnic but racial lines in organizing unions. They did so in spite of longstanding opposition to Asian workers from the American Federation of Labor (AFL), which was a staunchly nativist and exclusionary organization during the early twentieth century. In the first instance, the Japanese-Mexican Labor Association (JMLA) was formed in 1903 by Japanese and Mexican sugar beet workers in Oxnard, California. When the JMLA petitioned the AFL for membership, AFL president Samuel Gompers replied that a charter would be granted only if the JMLA agreed to ban Japanese and Chinese workers. The Mexican members of the JMLA bravely demurred.[89] Asians and

Latinos once again cooperated in California agriculture when the AFL granted a charter to a joint Mexican and Filipino union, the Field Workers Union, Local 30326, in 1936.[90] In addition to forming interracial alliances in agriculture, Asian American sailors and porters found acceptance in unions dominated by other racial groups. In 1933, the National Maritime Union (NMU) broke from an AFL affiliate, the Seamen's International Union (SIU), over the SIU's racism. In contrast, the NMU adopted a policy of racial inclusion, and some three thousand Chinese sailors joined in the NMU strike of 1936.[91] The primarily black Brotherhood of Sleeping Car Porters countered the Pullman Company's recruitment of Filipinos to dilute the union's power by incorporating Filipinos.[92] And in Hawaii, as Moon-Kie Jung demonstrates, the International Longshoremen's and Warehousemen's Union brought together Filipino, Japanese, and Portuguese workers in a movement that did not seek to obliterate racial distinctions as unavoidably divisive but rather rearticulated race as a category of exploitation.[93]

In addition to unionists, Asian American communities contained vital segments of political radicals. The eminent Asian American historian Yuji Ichioka has argued that socialism and communism, in addition to unionism, were central to Japanese American politics up to 1924. Sen Katayama, the founder of Japan's socialist movement, spent several years in exile in the United States, promoting socialism among Japanese immigrants, lecturing widely, publishing a newspaper, and participating as a founding member of the American Communist Party (CPUSA). Upon his death in Moscow in 1933, Katayama was lauded as a workers' hero and buried in the Kremlin. Japanese immigrant radicals included not only intellectuals like Katayama but workers as well. Ichioka demonstrates that Japanese American workers regularly organized in the agricultural and mining industries, despite being generally barred from the AFL and targeted for exclusion by the white labor movement.[94] Karl Yoneda's memoir, *Ganbatte*, takes up where Ichioka leaves off, chronicling worker activism and organizing from the 1920s through the 1970s. Yoneda, who adopted the first name Karl in honor of Marx when he joined the CP in 1927, edited *Rodo Shimbun*, the official organ of the Japanese section of the CPUSA, stirred up support for the 1934 Pacific Coast Maritime Strike, and organized Alaskan cannery workers into Congress of International Organizations (CIO) unions.[95] Yoneda met his wife, Elaine Black, through his political activism. She played a crucial role in International Labor Defense (ILD), a communist-affiliated organization devoted to the legal defense of arrested and jailed labor and political activists. Vivian Raineri's biography of Black, *The Red Angel*, shows that in the prewar period Japanese American communists were tightly interwoven into the fabric of the CPUSA, participating in demonstrations and actions, being bailed out by ILD, and so on.[96]

Despite the commitment of Japanese American progressives, the left never formed a primarily political tendency within the Japanese American community. Yoneda estimates that there were perhaps only two hundred Japanese American communists in the 1930s, and they, along with other progressives, were subject to red baiting and ostracism from the community.[97] Yet the historical significance of the Japanese American left cannot be evaluated simply in terms of numbers, for leftists were the most persistent critics of racism and imperialism. Unlike more conservative unionists, Katayama never shied away from impugning the AFL's anti-Japanese policies as racist.[98] At a time when Sakamoto's *Japanese-American Courier* defended Japan's annexation of Manchuria, Yoneda and other communists condemned it as imperialist.[99] In early 1942, a progressive organization called the Young Democrats wrote a letter protesting the expulsion of Japanese Americans from their homes on the West Coast. Although all of the community newspapers to which they submitted the letter refused to publish it, this act marks the Young Democrats as perhaps the only Japanese American organization to openly oppose the expulsion.[100]

Chinese Americans also organized extensively, and some joined socialist or communist parties, as historian Him Mark Lai has discussed widely.[101] The Unionist Guild, formed in 1919, won concessions on working conditions from shirt manufacturers in San Francisco and Oakland. Nearly two decades later, the Chinese Workers' Mutual Aid Association (CMWAA), established in 1937, became the first organization to develop links to the CIO and the AFL. In New York City, as Renqiu Yu has shown in *To Save China, To Save Ourselves,* the Chinese Hand Laundry Alliance (CHLA) organized in 1933 to oppose a proposed city ordinance aimed at eliminating small laundries. The CHLA membership was composed of small entrepreneurs, not the business elite of Chinatown, and their progressive politics led them to march in the National Recovery Act parade, support the Chinese revolution of 1949, and establish the leading left newspaper, the *Chinese Daily News.*[102] Following the communist revolution, American Chinatowns factionalized into pro–People's Republic of China contingents, which included the left-leaning CWMAA and readers of the *Chinese Daily News,* and pro-KMT camps, which were composed primarily of the business elite and represented by the Chinese Consolidated Benevolent Association.[103]

The linkage between the prewar Asian American left and the Asian American movement of the 1960s and 1970s is complicated. An argument for tenuous continuity between the Asian American old and new lefts could possibly be made in three ways. First, in some instances individual old leftists personally influenced and organized new leftists. The eminent Chinese American leftist Grace Lee Boggs, whose activism predated the Second World War and included a close association with the black Marxist C. L. R. James, started the Asian Political Alliance in Detroit in 1970.[104] Similarly, Kazu Iijima was one of two Japanese American women who were communists before the war, and then in 1968 she organized Asian Americans for Action, an early and important radical group in New York City.[105] Iijima functioned as an Asian American analogue to Ella Baker, who personally bridged the institutions of the pre–World War II black civil rights movements and the 1960s movement.[106] Second, a few activists in the Asian American movement grew up as "red diaper" babies. For example, Steve Yip, a prominent member of Wei Min She, was the son of a Marxist, and Chris Iijima, a radical musician who is one of the subjects of chapter 5, was the son of Kazu Iijima.[107] However, unlike Yip and Iijima, the vast majority of Asian American 1960s radicals did not inherit their parents' politics but rather rejected what they saw as their parents' assimilationism. The Asian American movement's third and by far most important linkage to the prewar left was its recovery of the history of Asian American radicalism. Movement participants recuperated the legacies of Asian American radical individuals and organizations, including Karl Yoneda, the JMLA, Carlos Bulosan, the CHLA, Sen Katayama, and Ben Fee. While living figures like Yoneda and Fee did not provide day-to-day leadership or point-by-point ideological guidance to the nascent Asian American movement, their very existence bespoke a legacy of Asian American resistance through radicalism, and their personal support buoyed the younger movement.

Despite these tenuous linkages, however, it is difficult to draw a solid, continuous line from the Asian American old left to the Asian American new left. Individual old leftists, scattered red diaper babies, and recuperation do not constitute continuity per se. Most important, there is no evidence of institutional continuity between the old and new lefts. For example, there was no Asian American analogue to the League for

Industrial Democracy, the old anticommunist socialist group that served as the parent organization for Students for a Democratic Society during its earliest days.[108] The lack of institutional continuity may be attributed to the fact that the Asian American left fell quiescent during the 1950s, the victim not only of McCarthyist red baiting from the mainstream society but also of repression from within Asian American communities. Furthermore, as Him Mark Lai contends, the Chinese American new left diverged in important ways from the Chinese American old left: the new left was dominated by native-born Chinese Americans rather than immigrants; it was composed of students, professionals, and intellectuals rather than workers; and it was more interested in local conditions than in Chinese nationalism.[109] While these generalizations may be disputable, Lai's observations about the Chinese American left apply more or less to the Asian American left in general.

The category "Asian American" is a social construction that groups together people of diverse ethnicities, religions, languages, nationalities, and cultures. Despite the fact that Asians have been present in the United States for over a century and a half, the term *Asian American* is a relatively recent invention. As the following chapters demonstrate, in the late 1960s and early 1970s, a variety of people of Asian ancestry in the United States recognized the similar ways Asians had suffered from exploitation and discrimination. They noticed the pattern in which groups of people from a series of Asian nations had been recruited to the United States to serve as cheap labor, encountered prejudice and discrimination, and were subsequently excluded from immigration, naturalization, and equal inclusion in the nation. Asian American radicals built the conceptual bridges that linked together peoples of divergent ethnicities and cultures into a political alliance devoted to ending racism and imperialism. That alliance and the political stance that it espoused marked the beginning of Asian America. Although Asian American identity emerged for the first time in the 1960s, it did not simply supersede its historical predecessors but instead opened up new avenues for political mobilization. Asian American identity contested with Asian nationalism, liberal assimilationism, and narrow ethnic and class-based radicalism by embracing multiethnic, interracial, and transnational solidarity. This contestation was illustrated in the 1968–69 Third World Liberation Front strike at San Francisco State College, a pivotal moment in Asian American politics that is discussed in the next chapter.

Two

"Down with Hayakawa!" Assimilation vs. Third World Solidarity at San Francisco State College

On 21 February 1969, S. I. Hayakawa, the acting president of San Francisco State College, addressed some three hundred Japanese Americans attending a dinner at the Athletic Club in San Francisco. Inside the building, Hayakawa bathed in the warm welcome of a standing ovation by two-thirds of the attendees on his entry and received sustained applause at intervals throughout his speech. Outside, a less friendly group of approximately one hundred Japanese Americans gathered. Picketing with signs reading "Support your local puppet" and "Hayakawa—Ronnie Rat's Houseboy," the protesters booed and shouted, "Down with Hayakawa!"[1] Hayakawa stood before both his supporters and his detractors as arguably the most famous and admired Asian American in history, having rocketed to national prominence for his bare-knuckled, get-tough stance against campus radicals.

Across town at the urban commuter campus of San Francisco State, the Third World Liberation Front (TWLF), a multiracial alliance of African American, Asian American, Latino, and American Indian students, was in the third month of a tumultuous strike. The TWLF demanded the establishment of a school of ethnic studies with a faculty and curriculum to be chosen by people of color, along with open admissions for all nonwhite applicants. The strike mobilized thousands of students and at times succeeded in shutting down the college. Appointed acting president during the strike, Hayakawa was the public face of opposition to the strike. He banned many student political activities, invited a substantial police force to campus, and cracked down harshly on strikers. (During the TWLF strike, the faculty of San Francisco State struck under the aegis of the American Federation of Teachers [AFT]. However, because the relationship between the TWLF and AFT actions was complicated, this chapter focuses on the students and Hayakawa.)

The confrontation between Asian American radicals and Hayakawa at San Francisco State represents a pivotal moment in Asian American politics, for radicals advocated multiethnic and interracial solidarity, while Hayakawa argued that Asian Americans should strive to assimilate into the mainstream. Japanese Americans in San Francisco—and, more widely, Asian Americans across the nation—were deeply divided over Hayakawa and his actions at San Francisco State. Indeed, the movement newspaper *Gidra* deemed the controversy surrounding Hayakawa a "struggle for the hearts and minds of the Asian community."[2] The struggle centered on the proper way to understand the racial position of Asian Americans and how to go about seeking justice and equality. Hayakawa believed that assimilation would eventually solve the problem of racism; invoked the model minority thesis, which asserted that Japanese Americans had gained acceptance and middle-class status by working hard and avoiding vocal protests; and consistently allied himself with conservative whites. In contrast, his radical critics believed that racism and exploitation were permanent and fundamental features of a capitalist and imperialist society, saw parallels between the racism faced by Asian Americans and that endured by other "Third World" people, and allied themselves with blacks, Chicanos, and American Indians. Asian American strikers and their supporters were intensely vexed by Hayakawa's racial politics, for he often represented himself, and, by extension, all Asian Americans, as proof that assimilation could overcome racism. Hence, they sought to distance Asian Americans from Hayakawa's actions. But with his flair for theatrics and penchant for self-promotion, no one could have performed the role of Asian American gadfly more brilliantly than S. I. Hayakawa.

Professor of Assimilation

Samuel Ichiyé Hayakawa had been born on July 18, 1906, in Vancouver, British Columbia, Canada. The son of Japanese immigrants, he was raised and attended public schools in Calgary, Alberta, and Winnipeg, Manitoba. He earned a bachelor's degree in English from the University of Manitoba and a master's degree from McGill University. In 1929, he migrated to the United States, where he earned a Ph.D. at the University of Wisconsin and went on to teach English at the Illinois Institute of Technology and the University of Chicago. Hayakawa first achieved modest fame in 1941 when he published *Language in Action,* which became a popular semantics textbook and a selection of the Book of the Month Club. In 1955, he moved west to San Francisco State College, where he taught part time until his appointment as acting president in 1968. Cashing in on the fame and popularity he had garnered in his conspicuous role as a campus hardliner, Hayakawa went on to win a seat in the United States Senate in 1976.[3]

From the 1930s through the 1980s, Hayakawa displayed a remarkably consistent commitment to assimilation, integration, and a shared public sphere as the solutions to the problem of racism. His academic work as a semanticist, his popular writing as a columnist for a black newspaper, his actions against the strike at San Francisco State, and his subsequent political career were all of a single piece: they sought sameness and sought to confine difference to the private sphere. Hayakawa argued that liberal assimilation would bring together people of different backgrounds for rational conversations in a single, shared language; this coming together, in turn, would diminish the irrational misunderstandings that he believed were at the root of racism.

General Semantics and Race Relations

Hayakawa's racial politics thoroughly suffused his academic work as a semanticist. General semantics, the theory of language that Hayakawa popularized, emphasized the distinction between signs and their referents, arguing that much human misunderstanding stemmed from mistaking words themselves for reality. In his most comprehensive explanation of general semantics, *Language in Action* (1941), he argued that linguistic solutions could be found for the problem of prejudice.[4] Hayakawa wrote the book with one eye focused on Nazi aggression in Europe during a period in which he saw "the world . . . becoming daily a worse madhouse of murder, hatred, and destruction." He attributed these animosities to people's mistaking "meaningless noises" for "actualities" and proposed as a solution—quite astonishingly—that people should study "how language works."[5]

Hayakawa argued that the misuse of language can lead to faulty thinking and that the study of general semantics could eliminate such irrationality. One of his fundamental premises was that the opacity of language could mislead people into unfounded prejudices.[6] Using anti-Semitism as an example, he explained the linguistic basis of prejudice thus: because the word *Jew* has historically carried negative connotations, anyone labeled a Jew is assumed to carry certain undesirable traits. Therefore, although there is no such thing as a Jew (there are only humans who are labeled as such), the category itself, as a linguistic construction, imposes its meaning upon unthinking minds.[7] Similarly, Hayakawa saw racism as arising from mistaking representation for reality—when, for example, "the comic strip stereotype for Negroes inside your head is identified with the actual Negro 'out there.'" He called these confusions "identifications" and defined general semantics as "the study of identifications, and how to reduce their number. . . . In other words, it is the science of how not to be a damn fool."[8]

Hayakawa viewed general semantics as a modernizing and moral project that would eliminate the atavistic hatreds and prejudices that fueled great wars and social inequalities. Using the scientific principles of semantics would enable people to put aside their preconceptions and see the world afresh. Applying this understanding to the race problem, Hayakawa wrote:

> We shut Negroes out of our most attractive places of entertainment, and we are told that "they really prefer to be by themselves." We deprive Negroes of the opportunity for advancement, and then wonder why some of them don't show the same degree of energy and ambition that are shown by people who are given the opportunities for advancement. Nowhere as in our social and racial thinking do we rely more upon shibboleths and formulas, and less upon the testing of our statements against the criterion of predictability.[9]

Hayakawa thus attributed racism to uncritical reliance on mistaken notions about other people, which he believed would be falsified when subjected to scientific "testing," a clear testament to his belief that racism could be ended through rationality. His faith in the transformative power of general semantics led Hayakawa to optimistically predict in 1946 that within two decades humans would overcome the outdated moral system that allowed such irrational social systems. (However, just over two decades later, Hayakawa would be confronted by a very different type of "racial thinking" at San Francisco State.)

The popularity of *Language in Action* made Hayakawa a highly visible public intellectual. Letters poured into his mailbox, many from fellow academics but others from ordinary citizens. Charles Hughes, a young

Dr. S. I. Hayakawa was appointed acting president of San Francisco State College in November 1968. Previously, he had been best known as a semanticist and author of a textbook on language. Photograph copyright Bettman/Corbis.

man who lamented that he could not afford to attend college, wrote from Lakewood, Ohio: "I have just finished reading your book, 'Language in Action,' and it has stimulated my mind to such active ferment that I have not been able to resist the impulse to write to you."[10] Hayakawa also began to receive speaking invitations. For example, the YWCA of Northwestern University asked him to give a talk on religious terminology.[11] Perhaps most outlandishly, he received a congratulatory case of KIX cereal from General Mills, whose director of public relations wrote, "The attention you have won as one who 'does things' leads us to feel that you will appreciate the nutritional advantages of a cereal which, in its way, promotes physical fitness."[12] It is not clear from the archival record the degree to which the professor enjoyed the cereal, but there is no doubt that the publication of his book made Hayakawa a highly public intellectual.

Before World War II, Hayakawa preached the virtues of assimilation. On his first trip to California, he was invited to address a gathering of his "fellow Americans of Japanese ancestry." A crowd of about three hundred mostly student-aged people attended his lecture at City College in Los Angeles on 11 September 1941. Amid the darkening clouds of war, speaking to an audience fearing the outbreak of hostilities between their native land and the land of their ancestors, Dr. Hayakawa chose semantics as the topic of his speech. He began, predictably, by explaining how people could rid themselves of preconceptions by carefully examining their use of language. But he went on to argue that free exchange between different cultures was the basis for the expansion of human knowledge. America was great, he told his audience, to the degree that it guaranteed "freedom of speech and the other liberties," because unfettered speech led to "free pooling of knowledge." This was why "we should be wholly dedicated to democracy as a system of government and as a way of life." Hayakawa explained that the science of general semantics pointed to the benefits of social integration. He implored his audience, "We ought to ally ourselves with organizations that tend to bring people together instead of separate them into labeled groups." Ironically, on the eve of World War II, Hayakawa was preaching the virtues of integration to a group that would within a year be segregated into concentration camps and deprived of their "liberties" en masse.[13]

Even during the war, Hayakawa continued to fervently believe in the power of semantics to overcome irrational prejudice. Around 1943, he wrote the following in an unpublished paper entitled, "Why I Want America to Win":

> We are not fighting the yellowness of the Japanese any more than we are fighting the whiteness of the Germans. If, through careless talk and misdirected anger, we make a "race" war out of this fight, we shall be doing the very thing which outrages us most about Hitlerism. This is not . . . a war of peoples, but a war of ideals: the open, free, equalitarian ideals of the democracies against the closed, barbaric tribalisms of the totalitarian mob-states. Let's not forget what the shooting is about.[14]

In this passage Hayakawa urged Americans to view the conflict in the Pacific not as a racial war but instead as a conflict of ideologies. But, critically, he viewed the cause of racism as linguistic, for it results from "careless talk." Furthermore, his labeling of "Hitlerism" as "barbaric tribalism" positioned it as outdated and irrational, and hence inferior to the modern rationality of democracy. In January 1945, Hayakawa connected this idea of racism as intellectual carelessness to his own racial positioning when he delivered a lecture in Chicago in which he cautioned audience members against succumbing to "habitual reaction patterns" that might wrongly convince them that he was "a Japanese spy."[15] According to this formulation, logical thought would root out linguistic laziness, which was the ultimate cause of irrational racial prejudice.

As the founding editor of *ETC.: A Review of General Semantics*, Hayakawa used the occasion of its first issue to link his concerns regarding race relations with his scholarly interests. Scoffing at those who might think that wartime was the wrong time to be laboring over a "dull old quarterly journal which nobody but college professors [were] going to be able to read," he offered general semantics as a solution to the very problem of prejudice that was fueling the war. He portrayed general semantics as "an attempt to blast from their very roots the old habits of mind, the old stupidities, the old prejudices, the old nonsense, that make otherwise civilized human beings behave like savages." Dividing the human mind into two compartments—one modern, scientific, and factual and the other superstitious and prejudiced—he proposed semantics as a way to bring the scientific portion of the mind to bear on its outdated superstitions. Rather than being "harmless idiosyncrasies," prejudices were "case[s] of serious mental deficiency. A 'prejudice' is a point at which your brains stop working."[16] Hayakawa's explication of semantics clarified his other pronouncements on race. According to his diagnosis, rational thought is a necessary and sufficient antidote to racism. For him, showing whites the errors of their ways—that is, the irrationality of their biases—constituted the best and in fact the only strategy to combat racism. Once attention was directed to their fallacious patterns of thought, whites would logically and inevitably begin to eradicate racism.

Hayakawa's theory of general semantics ignored questions of power, such as who defines terms, to whom they are applied, and who may be excluded from conversations and exchanges. Perhaps more important, it was bereft of any analysis of interests, ignoring the extent to which economic exploitation and social oppression convey benefits to some at the expense of others. This theoretical blind spot, which Hayakawa shared with most American liberals at midcentury and retained throughout the remainder of his life, would inevitably lead him into conflict with 1960s radicals who based their analyses precisely upon considerations of power and interests.

The *Chicago Defender* and Race Relations

Shortly after the publication of *Language in Action*, Hayakawa began writing a column titled "Second Thoughts" for the *Chicago Defender*, a prominent "Negro" weekly. The *Defender* carried news of interest to blacks, publicized accounts of racial discrimination, crowed about black achievements, and covered happenings in black society, sports, education, and entertainment. During World War II, its pages were filled with stories about black soldiers and home-front support for the war effort. The "Defender Platform for America"—which emphatically demanded that "American Race Prejudice Must Be Destroyed!"—insisted on economic, political, legal, social, and educational equality for all "American citizens." From 1942 to 1947, Hayakawa's column appeared each week on page 15 of the *Defender,* below Walter White's "People and Places" column and on the page following Langston Hughes's "Here to Yonder" column. Hayakawa's writings ranged over a variety of topics, including poetry, music, art, race relations, the war, economics, and local happenings. Throughout his tenure as a *Defender* columnist, Hayakawa expressed his faith in the democratic system, insisted on the value of interracial cooperation and cool-headed communication, and emphasized the intrinsic irrationality of racism.

Hayakawa's position on race mirrored that of Gunnar Myrdal, whose 1944 opus *An American Dilemma* represents the quintessential expression of midcentury American racial liberalism.[17] Myrdal posited racism in the United States as an aberration from democratic ideals rather than a structural feature of the capitalist socioeconomic system. In his model, racism could best be ameliorated by a rational appeal to whites, who, once confronted with the contradiction between their commitment to equality and the social reality of discrimination, would logically act to abolish racism. Widely recognized as a highly consequential work upon its publication, *An American Dilemma* exerted tremendous influence on American racial thinking—it was even cited in the Supreme Court's *Brown v. Board of Education* ruling—but subsequently came under attack from radicals in the late 1960s, much as Hayakawa himself did.[18]

Exhibiting his faith in what Myrdal termed the "American Creed," Hayakawa made a clear distinction between "biological" and "spiritual" ancestors, arguing that Americans of all colors could claim the Pilgrims, Jefferson, and Lincoln as their spiritual forebears. Noting that many biological Daughters of the American Revolution had turned out to be racist, he opined, "Let no one smile, therefore, when a little Chinese, or Mexican, or Hungarian, or Jewish, or Negro kid recites solemnly in school, 'Fourscore and seven years ago our fathers brought forth upon this continent a new nation.'"[19] He thus asserted that people of all races could claim the right of American citizenship, despite the fact that individual whites might be prejudiced. However, Hayakawa's use of a "Chinese" child to include Asians in the set of potential Americans masks a telling silence. What if he had instead claimed that "a little Japanese kid" could rightly claim to be an American? In December 1943, when this particular column appeared in the *Defender,* more than a hundred thousand Japanese Americans had been forcibly removed from their homes on the West Coast and were imprisoned in "relocation camps," charged with no crime other than being of Japanese descent. Hayakawa was perfectly aware of the incarceration, having that very year visited a family friend incarcerated at the Amache Relocation Center in Colorado.[20] The contradiction between Hayakawa's claim that everyone could claim the rights of citizenship and the reality of Japanese American imprisonment apparently proved too blatant, forcing him to use a Chinese child as an alternative example of America's inclusiveness.

Hayakawa devoted several of his *Defender* columns to lauding consumer cooperatives, insisting that "white, black, yellow, brown" people could find "genuine democracy at work" in co-ops because "they not only preach the principle of religious and racial equality—they practice it."[21] He explained that the economic incentives inherent in co-ops promoted nondiscrimination, for what rational person would reject potential members because of race when increasing co-op membership would lead to increased economies of scale? "If you reject a couple of prospective members because you don't like the color of their skins or the religion of the ancestors, you simply gyp yourself out of your savings," he argued. Cooperation based purely on economic motivations would eventually lead to "co-operative recreation and social life."[22] Thus, in Hayakawa's scheme, bringing people together for rational discourse and demonstrating to them their shared interests provided the key to interracial harmony, the ultimate goal of which was assimilation. At his talk to Japanese Americans in Los Angeles just before the start of the war, he urged them to join consumer cooperatives, arguing, "You will make white friends there and they will be your friends for life."[23]

In a similar vein, Hayakawa praised liberal whites, including the widely read newspaper columnist Westbrook Pegler, for writing essays from the perspective of "If I Were a Negro." Hayakawa believed that getting whites to explore the racial problem through their imaginations would help to alleviate the basic problem of prejudice, because bigots "don't often see the other fellow's point of view." He wrote, "The trouble with most whites is not cruelty or viciousness, but simply thoughtlessness."

Whites permitted discrimination to continue simply "out of ignorance" of its pervasiveness and consequences. Hayakawa claimed that if "only a few thousand" whites in Chicago would thoughtfully write essays such as Pegler's, "an enormous step forward [would be] taken in this whole matter of race relations."[24] Whites would quickly renounce racism, once made aware of it, because the problem was not that they benefited from systematic oppression of nonwhites but that they simply had never thought about it! In this sense, Hayakawa's position mirrored that of Myrdal, for he believed that merely exposing the "dilemma" of racism in a professedly egalitarian society would alleviate it.

Hayakawa wrote his last column for the *Defender* in 1947, and in 1955 he left Chicago for the Bay area, where he took a part-time teaching position at San Francisco State College. From his new position on the West Coast, the home of the vast majority of Japanese Americans, Hayakawa continued to advocate integrationism. In 1955, the California Intercollegiate Nisei Organization (CINO) held its northern California regional meeting at San Jose State College. One hundred twenty delegates attended the conference, where nineteen-year-old Yo Matsuda, an education major at Reedley College, was selected queen and reigned over the coronation dance. But S. I. Hayakawa, the best-known Japanese American educator in the nation, was notably absent. Or perhaps it would be more accurate to say that his conspicuous absence dominated the gathering.

Northern California CINO head Bob Fuchigami, who admired the book *Language in Action,* had invited Hayakawa to address the conference.[25] Hayakawa not only declined but also sent a letter advising CINO to disband. He claimed that discrimination against Japanese Americans had disappeared, "for all practical purposes," and that because the greatest barriers to integration existed "inside the Nisei's own mind . . . Nisei organizations only serve to perpetuate those internal barriers." Consequently, he contended that "Nisei social groups should cease to exist" because they were nothing more than "social crutches." He concluded, "We shall learn to walk as free men and women among equals in a democratic society when, and only when, we throw away the crutches."[26] In contrast to Hayakawa's sunny outlook, Nisei clubs were formed at many colleges and universities out of necessity, because Japanese Americans were excluded from most social organizations. CINO, which was intended to allow the members of these clubs to network across campuses, thus served a real purpose.[27] Hence, in 1955, a scant decade after the closing of America's concentration camps and before an ethnic organization was formed in response to segregation, Hayakawa denied the existence of anti-Japanese prejudice and saw ethnic-specific organizations for Japanese Americans as archaic detriments to social progress because they inhibited assimilation.[28]

In the early 1960s, Hayakawa turned his attention to the black civil rights movement, paying special attention to the role played by television. In a series of speeches, the renowned expert on communication argued that television advertising created a uniform desire for mass-marketed products across racial boundaries. He noted approvingly that many of the civil rights protesters were teenagers who had been exposed to TV commercials their entire lives and that they were merely attempting to force the nation to live up to its advertised ideals.[29] Hayakawa's attention to the power of television, which he called the most "revolutionary force in communication since the invention of movable type," was prescient, for it foreshadowed his own masterful use of the medium.[30] Although Hayakawa had published books, articles, and newspaper columns and had even produced a radio show titled *Hayakawa's Jazz Seminar,* it was not until his reign at San Francisco State College that he burst onto television screens across the nation.

On Strike! Shut It Down!

From 6 November 1968 to 21 March 1969, students at San Francisco State College mounted the longest student strike in U.S. history. The strike was led by the TWLF, whose constituent organizations included the Black Student Union (BSU), Latin American Student Organization (LASO), Mexican American Student Coalition (MASC), Pilipino American Collegiate Endeavor (PACE), and Asian American Political Alliance (AAPA), as well as Intercollegiate Chinese for Social Action (ICSA).[31] Strikers demanded the establishment of an autonomous school of ethnic studies in which Third World people would control faculty hiring and curricula, along with open admissions for blacks, Latinos, and Asian Americans.[32] Strikers engaged in bloody and violent clashes with the police, hundreds were arrested, and the San Francisco Police Department's Tactical Squad became an occupying army on campus. The strike eventually resulted in the establishment of the first and only school of ethnic studies in the United States.

The strike at San Francisco State College was the culmination of a period of mounting radical activity on campus. Beginning in 1966, students had mounted campaigns against censorship of campus newspapers, the presence of military recruiters and an ROTC company on campus, and the firing or disciplining of several non-tenure-track faculty members. The most proximate cause of the strike was the suspension of George Mason Murray, a graduate student in English and part-time instructor in the Educational Opportunity Program who was also the minister of education of the Black Panther Party. Murray had drawn fire from conservative politicians and the trustees of the California State Colleges for visiting Cuba and for making a controversial speech at Fresno State College in which he had made statements interpreted by some as calls for violence and political assassinations.[33] On 6 November 1968, the BSU called a campus strike to protest Murray's suspension and issued ten demands. The TWLF joined the strike on 8 November and issued five additional demands. Once underway, the strike was led by the TWLF, of which the BSU was a member organization.[34] The fifteen "nonnegotiable" demands included the establishment of an autonomous school of ethnic studies, the curriculum and faculty of which would be controlled by Third World people; the hiring of fifty ethnic studies faculty (twenty for black studies); open admissions for nonwhite students; and amnesty for strikers.

Asian Americans participated extensively in the Third World strike. Indeed, three of the TWLF's member organizations were composed of Asian Americans: ICSA, PACE, and AAPA. ICSA had been established in November 1967, and by the time of the strike it included about a hundred members. Initially, it focused on connecting students with social problems in San Francisco's Chinatown. Members volunteered at various social service agencies, taught English to immigrant youth, and ran a youth center that served as a drop-in center for immigrant youth, some of whom were associated with Wah Ching, a loosely organized Chinatown gang. During the strike ICSA taught courses in Chinese American history at the youth center in a subversively acronymed program called the Free University of Chinatown Kids, Unincorporated. ICSA joined the TWLF in late spring of 1968, despite worries that joining a coalition might jeopardize their programs and concerns about the militancy of the BSU. ICSA chair Mason Wong was instrumental in convincing the group to ally with other students of color. Spokesman George Woo was another important leader in ICSA and had gained a reputation among Asian Americans and others alike for his fiery and fearless invective. One Chinatown group that supported ICSA and the strike was Leway, which ran the pool hall that was a gathering place for some of the youth who would form the Red Guard Party, a primary subject of the next chapter of this book.[35]

Like ICSA, PACE was concerned with the link between campus and community. Its membership of around seventy was comprised primarily of immigrants but also included native-born Pinoys with family backgrounds including military and farm work. PACE members recruited and tutored Filipino American college applicants and were highly concerned with the eviction of elderly manongs from the International Hotel, an issue discussed in the introduction to this book. Leaders such as Ron Quidachay and Pat Salavar sought to radicalize Filipino American students by raising issues of racism and colonialism. Quidachay served as TWLF chairman the year before the strike, an indication of the extent to which Asian American participants in the coalition played influential roles.[36]

The San Francisco State branch of AAPA was started in the summer of 1968 by three Japanese American women who had met at a Berkeley AAPA meeting and agreed on the need for a chapter at their school. AAPA stressed the connections between the histories of various Asian ethnic groups and the need for multiethnic unity. Members met in study groups, where they read Mao's Red Book, Frantz Fanon, and the Black Panther newspaper. One AAPA member, Janice Mirikitani, became a leading Asian American poet (her poetry is a subject of chapter 5 of this book). The first AAPA had been founded at University of California–Berkeley by Yuji Ichioka, who had noticed that Asians were participating in new left activities as individuals but wanted to establish a group "behind an Asian American banner" to radicalize other Asians. Potential members were drawn from the Peace and Freedom Party roster; Ichioka "went down the list and picked out identifiably Asian names."[37] Thus, from its Peace and Freedom Party roots, AAPA supported Black Power and opposed the war in Viet Nam. Unlike the Berkeley AAPA, which was composed chiefly of Chinese Americans, the San Francisco State branch was primarily Japanese American.[38]

Acting President Hayakawa

Hayakawa's opposition to the Third World strike at San Francisco State was consistent with his liberal faith in the ability of assimilation to ameliorate racial injustices. A self-described "liberal Democrat" (at the time), he seemed in some senses to be ideally suited to preside over the fractious campus.[39] Hayakawa styled himself an expert on race relations and proclaimed sympathy with blacks, even chiding his fellow Japanese Americans for what he perceived as their antiblack prejudice. He professed support for a department of black studies in principle but lamented that the rational demands of black radicals were unfortunately mixed up with the notion that force and intimidation were appropriate tactics by which to attain their goals.[40] In some measure, Hayakawa's actions backed up his words, for he offered to settle the strike by proposing the establishment of a black studies department, albeit on terms that were unacceptable to the BSU. Despite his purported sympathy, Hayakawa acted decisively to end the strike.

Upon being named president on 26 November, he closed the campus one day early for the Thanksgiving break. However, he quickly reversed course and announced that the college would reopen at 8:00 a.m. on Monday, 2 December. He ordered all faculty to report to class as of that date and threatened that unauthorized absences for five working days from that date would be considered the equivalent of resignation. He threatened students who did not "conduct themselves with propriety and dignity" or who engaged in "creating disturbances interfering with the work and study of others" with suspension, expulsion, or other discipline. Finally, and perhaps most significantly, he promised to ensure a police presence on campus "to the fullest extent necessary to maintain and restore peace."[41]

Hayakawa declared a state of emergency, the rules of which prohibited students, faculty, staff, and the public from carrying firearms on campus but pointedly allowed police officers to do so. More important, it suspended use of the Speakers Platform and amplification equipment, except with approval from the administration, and prohibited "interference with classes or administrative processes." It promised that violators would receive immediate temporary suspension followed by "due process within 72 hrs."[42] The ban on amplifiers in particular was aimed at preventing the large-scale rallies that had galvanized strikers and their supporters, and it was this dictum that provided Hayakawa with the stage for his most noteworthy public performance.

The scene that made Hayakawa a household name occurred on 2 December 1968. Students had parked a sound truck on the border of the campus, near the corner of Nineteenth Avenue and Holloway Avenue, and were using the amplifier to exhort a crowd of about two hundred picketers chanting, "On strike, shut it down!" At about 8:10 a.m., Hayakawa emerged from the administration building and advanced toward the strikers. His trademark tam-o'-shanter firmly fixed upon his head, Hayakawa clambered aboard the truck and ripped the wires from its speakers. A shoving match ensued, but no one was injured. The *San Francisco Chronicle* praised Hayakawa for his "bravura performance."[43] The image of the feisty president physically confronting rowdy protesters made numerous evening newscasts and catapulted Hayakawa into the national consciousness.[44] This incident proved an iconic moment that defined Hayakawa in the public mind for years to come.

Hayakawa's hard line on campus radicals gained him immense popularity and acclaim, and did so with stunning rapidity. He immediately began receiving thousands of pieces of fan mail from across California.[45] Within months of his appointment, he was mentioned as a potential candidate for political office in California.[46] A May 1969 poll assessing the political viability of various public figures found that 89 percent of Californians "knew something about" Hayakawa, giving him higher visibility than even former California governor Edmund "Pat" Brown. A total of 82 percent of the respondents rated their impressions of him as "strongly favorable" or "somewhat favorable," while only 4 percent each rated him as "somewhat unfavorable" or "strongly unfavorable."[47]

Hayakawa's newfound fame brought him many speaking engagements with groups eager to hear from the man who had cracked down on the

Hayakawa, in his trademark tam-o'-shanter, disconnected a sound system at San Francisco State College, 2 December 1968. His action of tearing loose the wiring of this sound truck parked at the school's entrance catapulted him to national prominence as an opponent of campus militants. Photograph copyright Bettman/Corbis.

radicals. At one trade convention, Hayakawa was asked the correct way to wear tam-o'-shanters. He demonstrated various possibilities, including how it might be worn by a minister preaching, a curling team member keeping warm, and a girl trying not to mess up her hair. He concluded, "But the correct way to wear them is in the Scottish culture, of course. If you are a member of a fighting regiment, . . . you wear them on the side of your head with a jaunty angle like that (indicating), *and this is how you keep colleges open.*"[48] At this point the audience rose and gave him a standing ovation. Hayakawa's choice of images is telling. I do not think it is too much of an interpretive stretch to read his application of the fighting spirit of Scotsmen to the fracas at San Francisco State as a comment on his own racial politics, for in the remainder of his speech he made explicit his alliance with conservative whites.

Racializing Hayakawa

The racial position of Asian Americans was a vital point of contention in the controversy at San Francisco State, and much of the discourse on Asian Americans centered on Hayakawa and his actions. Four divergent positions emerged. First, Hayakawa styled himself a racial middleman who was neither black nor white and was therefore able to act as a neutral arbiter in racial conflicts. Second, strike opponents pointed to him as a person of color whose nonmilitancy constituted an implicit rebuke to campus radicals. Third, some white strike supporters attacked Hayakawa in racialized and racist ways. Finally, striker supporters assailed his authenticity as a "Third World" person, claiming that he thought and acted like a white man. All four depictions of Hayakawa—as racial middleman, nonmilitant minority, Asian dictator, and inauthentic Asian—highlighted his race.

In positioning himself as a racial middleman, Hayakawa necessarily emphasized his Asianness, balancing himself tenuously between black and white. On the one hand, he expressed sympathy for the plight of blacks and claimed familiarity with black culture. But on the other, he distanced Asian Americans from blacks by portraying Asian Americans as assimilated, like white ethnics, rather than permanently racialized, like blacks. At his first press conference after being named acting president of the college, he offered his services as a mediator between blacks and whites: "In a profound sense I stand in the middle. I'm not white and I'm not black. I'm appealing to my Oriental friends that I might be a channel to bring black and white together."[49] Beyond offering himself as a nonblack, nonwhite individual, by referencing his "Oriental friends," Hayakawa also positioned Asian Americans, as a group, between black and white. His racial middleman quip became part of the general discourse around the strike, appearing in a *Time* magazine profile of the acting president and the unrest at San Francisco State.[50] Campus radicals also took notice of the statement. They published a clever parody of Chairman Mao Tse-Tung's popular Red Book titled *Quotations from Chairman S. I. Hayakawa*, which was composed of some of Hayakawa's most outrageous statements and contained the racial middleman quote in a section headed "On Color."[51]

Hayakawa professed to understand the black perspective because he had personal friendships with African Americans and was intimately familiar with their culture. As evidence he pointed to his tenure as a *Chicago Defender* columnist and his expertise on jazz and art (Hayakawa was an avid collector of African art).[52] At one meeting he insulted a roomful of African American community leaders with his assertion that he knew black people because he "had often slept in the homes of black folks in Chicago."[53] On another occasion he claimed that he was more familiar with black culture than were white supporters of the strike:

> None of them have slept in Negro homes, as I have; attended Negro churches, as I have; traveled through the Deep South, as I have; gone into Negro bars and talked to Negro working men, to find out what they really think, as I have; or listened to Negro blues on the South Side of Chicago at six o'clock in the morning, as I have.[54]

His repetition of the phrase "as I have" underscored Hayakawa's assertion of personal familiarity. However, Reverend Cecil Williams of Glide Memorial Church contradicted the semanticist's claim by demonstrating how he was linguistically out of touch, saying, "He may know the *colored* or the *Negro* community, but he doesn't know the *black* community."[55]

To counterbalance his claimed familiarity with black viewpoints, Hayakawa placed Asian Americans within the assimilation paradigm alongside white European Americans. Assimilation theorists often stated that immigrant groups benefited from building community institutions as a necessary prelude to undergoing incorporation into the host society. In an influential 1963 study of assimilation in New York City, Nathan Glazer and Daniel Patrick Moynihan argued that ethnic groups such as Jews, Italians, and Irish had achieved political power and lifted themselves out of poverty by building community institutions. They concluded that blacks continued to suffer from discrimination and privation because they had failed to accomplish this first step toward assimilation and that this failure was what distinguished blacks from white ethnics.[56] Hayakawa concurred with Glazer and Moynihan's position on black exceptionality. He asserted that a black studies department was more important than other ethnic studies departments because the "Negro needs this more than any of us."[57] Hayakawa believed that blacks needed ethnic studies more than any other group because they lacked cultural and historical memory.[58] Before the strike, he had argued that the worst consequence of slavery had been the systematic destruction of African cultures, folklores, and languages, which left blacks with no base upon which to build self-esteem and community institutions.[59] He had advocated that as recompense blacks should be given control of community institutions such as the police and fire departments, banks, and businesses to enable them to begin the process of assimilation that had, so far, eluded them.[60]

In contrast to blacks, Hayakawa said, Asian Americans possessed intact cultures and awareness of their histories.[61] This enabled them to build ethnic communities and resources to draw upon to survive in an unwelcoming environment. At the Athletic Club dinner in San Francisco, Hayakawa told his fellow Japanese Americans that they were more fortunate than blacks, saying, "We are a colored race of non-whites—we've been through the same thing but we've been able to come through it better than the Negroes have."[62] He argued that "the Negro" would benefit from mimicking Japanese, Chinese, Jews, Poles, and other minorities by strengthening their cultural and community institutions in order to prepare for assimilation. Having undergone assimilation, Hayakawa concluded, "I don't need the Japanese community any more—but there was a time when I did need it."[63] In aligning Japanese and Chinese with white ethnics, Hayakawa suggested that they had undergone the process of assimilation that had made European immigrants a part of the mainstream. Two decades later, in 1986, Hayakawa continued to insist that "racism in America is neither unchanging nor implacable." With each succeeding generation, he argued, assimilation dissolves prejudices against "damn dagoes," "dumb Polacks," "shanty Irish," "Chinky-chinky Chinaman," and the "sly Jap" until finally these images "dissolve into distant memories to appear no more."[64] His list of supposedly fading slurs once again included Chinese and Japanese Americans with white ethnics—Italians, Poles, and Irish—as a way to argue for Asian American assimilation.

While Hayakawa positioned himself and Asian Americans between black and white, opponents of the strike attempted to capitalize on his nonwhiteness to discredit strikers and their demands. Hayakawa's race may even have been a factor in his appointment as acting president of San Francisco State. In 1968, amid rising tensions on campus, President John Summerskill resigned, and as California State Colleges Chancellor Glenn Dumke embarked on a search for a successor, he announced that four or five "Negroes" were among the candidates under consideration.[65] The chancellor's attempt to find a black president failed; Summerskill's successor turned out to be the conspicuously white Robert Smith. When Smith in turn resigned under fire in November, Dumke immediately tapped Hayakawa. According to Smith, Hayakawa's appointment came as "a bolt from the blue," shocking both faculty and administrators. Prior to being named acting president, Hayakawa had only infrequently taught on campus and had never served on important university committees or held an administrative post. He was so unfamiliar with the San Francisco State administration that at the first meeting after his appointment he had to be introduced to many key administrators in the room.[66]

Despite his prior noninvolvement in campus affairs, as the crisis at San Francisco State escalated, Hayakawa had made his politics abundantly clear. Faculty member Leo Litwak recalled, "Hayakawa had preached the hardest of all lines. He was on record as favoring extreme measures to be rid of troublemaking faculty and students."[67] Furthermore, he was a prominent member of an antistrike group called the Faculty Renaissance and had communicated his views on campus disorder to Chancellor Dumke and the trustees of the college.[68] The appointment of an Asian American could hardly have been accidental, for it put into place a president whose race might immunize him from charges of racism even while he sought to quash the strike.

From the moment of Hayakawa's appointment, his supporters made much of the fact that he was not white. California governor Ronald Reagan reportedly said upon offering him the position of acting president that if Hayakawa took the job he would be forgiven for Pearl Harbor — a comment that clearly positioned Hayakawa as Japanese. Furthermore, Reagan's nickname for the dapper don was "Samurai."[69] Similarly, in December 1968, the *San Francisco Chronicle* published a political cartoon featuring a samurai suit of armor and a caption reading, "Complete suit of Japanese armor is what S. I. Hayakawa should find next to his Christmas tree."[70] The *Chronicle* consistently lauded Hayakawa's get-tough policies at San Francisco State, and the cartoon constituted an endorsement of Hayakawa in racial terms. It suggested that when attacked by campus militants, Hayakawa should sheathe himself in his status as a nonwhite person—specifically, as an Asian American, given the Japanese imagery—and that doing so would shield him from charges of racism.

The conservative journal *Seminar*, which exhibited an extreme aversion to campus radicalism and referred to Berkeley's Free Speech Movement as the "Filthy Speech Movement," clearly viewed Hayakawa as a problem for militant blacks. A telling cartoon shows two black radicals wearing "shades" and leather jackets, one with an ammunition belt slung over his shoulder, standing before Hayakawa, seated at his desk as the president of San Francisco State College. The two men look puzzled, and the caption asks, "How Does One Handle Non-Militant Minorities?" In the lower right-hand corner, a tiny head cries "Banzai!"[71] The cartoon makes antistrike arguments using Hayakawa's race in two ways. First, it highlights him as a nonwhite person who opposes the strike, thus delegitimating strikers' tactics and demands by asserting that reasonable minorities like Hayakawa do not support them. Second, the shout of "Banzai!" positions Hayakawa specifically as Asian. This reference tapped into the popular discourse of the model minority, which claimed that Asian Americans—in contrast to blacks—had overcome discrimination by working hard rather than protesting.

Some white strike supporters also racialized Hayakawa as Asian in ways that ranged from merely crude to racist. The *Strike Daily*, a paper published by the Strike Committee, a group of white students affiliated with Students for a Democratic Society (SDS), printed a cartoon titled "Camp Hayakawa (Formerly San Francisco State College)." It portrayed the campus as a concentration camp surrounded by a barbed wire–topped chain-link fence, with a guard tower looming above and an automatic rifle–toting soldier guarding the gate. While the image suggested that Hayakawa was tyrannical, even fascist, it also referred to American concentration camps in which Japanese Americans had been imprisoned during World War II, and hence underlined Hayakawa's status as an Asian American.[72] More directly, *Open Process*, a liberal student paper, published a poem titled, "Doctor Hayakawa's Next Duty as Samurai (a tanka: to be chanted)." As if referring to him as a samurai and using the Japanese poetic form of the tanka was not blatant enough, the poem piled up more stereotypes, including a reference to hara-kiri, the Japanese ritual of redeeming one's honor through suicide. In urging Hayakawa to "cut open [his] heart" in order to "wash out dishonor," this Orientalist pro-strike poem not only exoticized Japan but also racialized the acting president as inherently Asian.[73]

Even the prominent new left leader Todd Gitlin commented explicitly on Hayakawa's race. By 1968, the former SDS president was in the Bay area and serving as a member of the *Strike Daily* editorial board. Reporting for a local paper, Gitlin wrote an article titled "Samurai Strongman at State," a clear reference to Hayakawa's Japanese ancestry. He went well beyond criticizing Hayakawa individually to impugn Japanese Americans as a group. Hayakawa had designated blue armbands as antistrike emblems, and Gitlin sneered about a "squad of Japanese-Americans" wearing the armbands: "God, they must have authority problems!"[74] His comment played to the Orientalist notion of the east as dominated by antidemocratic despotism and of Asians as strictly obedient automatons, incapable of independent thought. Furthermore, by spotlighting the Hayakawa supporters as Japanese American while ignoring Asian American strikers and supporters, Gitlin reinforced the portrayal of Asian Americans as the model minority, apolitical and assimilated.

While Hayakawa's backers believed that his race should exempt him from criticism, strikers and their supporters vigorously assailed his racial authenticity. The Oakland African American newspaper, the *Sun Reporter,* called Hayakawa "Uncle Sam," a jibe adapted from the epithet "Uncle Tom" that positioned him as an inauthentic white-pleaser. The *Sun Reporter* explained, "He was chosen as a front man, to be that man of color who could deny black people's reasonable demands by beating them into accepting that denial was their due."[75] In a similar discursive vein, two Japanese Americans reporting on the Athletic Club dinner called him an "Uncle Tom of grade A class" and decried "his sneaky [usurpation] of the Japanese-American Community."[76] Strikers attacked Hayakawa as an "Oriental 'white racist'" and a "Tojo Tom," both terms implying that his politics were in contradiction with his skin color.[77] Similarly, a "Wanted" poster portrayed a photograph of Hayakawa against a backdrop of the Tactical Squad in riot gear and listed his aliases as "Paper Puppet, Bootlicker, Ruling Class Lackey." The poster insisted that though Hayakawa might be a Third World person, he served the interests of the "racist corporate policies of the Board of Trustees of San Francisco State College."[78] (Seven people, including three members of the Progressive Labor Party, were arrested for putting up these posters.)[79] Thus, the poster highlighted the distinction between identity based solely on racial characteristics and identity as an expression of political commitments. By calling Hayakawa a puppet and lackey of racists, the poster asserted that though he might be a member of the "Third World" in strictly racial terms, his political beliefs betrayed the interests of Third World people. Puppet imagery became a consistent feature of the anti-Hayakawa discourse and was deployed repeatedly. One cartoon on the cover of the left-leaning student paper *Open Process* portrayed Hayakawa as a wooden marionette suspended by strings, and another showed him as a doll peeking out of the breast pocket of a riot gear–equipped police officer.[80]

The white SDS-dominated Strike Committee similarly deemed Hayakawa's appointment a diversionary move. They alleged that by selecting Hayakawa, who was putatively "a member of the Third World," the trustees intended to "take any legitimacy away from the demands [of the TWLF] and counter the charge of racism." Comparing Hayakawa to non-white U.S.-backed right-wing dictators such as Viet Nam's Nguyen Cao Ky and Nguyen Van Thieu and Haiti's François "Papa Doc" Duvalier, the Strike Committee condemned the trustees for "slickly and snakily" using him in a desperate attempt to "break the struggle against racism on this campus."[81]

Outside of San Francisco, the larger Asian American movement also impugned Hayakawa's credentials as an Asian American. The Los Angeles–based movement newspaper *Gidra* called him a "banana" — yellow on the outside but white on the inside.[82] Pat Sumi charged Hayakawa with being sorely out of touch with Asian American communities because he was "living with his white friends up in Mill Valley, thinking that he's white." Her larger criticism was not just that he thought he was white but that he acted in the interests of white supremacy. "I consider people like Hayakawa traitors—that they sold out to becoming white racists themselves," she wrote. "The stand he took at San Francisco State was obviously the same stand any white racist would have taken; it's not even with an understanding that he himself is oppressed to the point where he hates himself and his own people."[83]

Japanese Americans Debating Hayakawa

S. I. Hayakawa was the object of considerable disagreement within the Japanese American community of San Francisco. Whether they admired or detested Hayakawa, Japanese Americans acknowledged that he had drawn national attention. The San Francisco newspaper *Hokubei Mainichi* went so far as to name him "Nisei of the Year" for 1968, declaring:

For good or bad, the noted Canadian born Nisei semanticist, by virtue of his appointment to the acting presidency of the embattled San Francisco State College, has stirred up Nisei awareness in today's campus struggles. His administrative actions, good or bad, have made this man a national figure. In that sense, both the supporters and dissenters alike would undoubtedly agree that the name Hayakawa has become a household word. And in that sense, Dr. Hayakawa may now claim the title, Nisei of the Year.[84]

Therefore, on the night of his speech at the Athletic Club, dinner attendees and protesters alike gathered to debate the actions of the most prominent Japanese American in the nation.

It is tempting to characterize the conflict over the San Francisco State strike in generational terms, with Nisei supporting Hayakawa and their college-age Sansei children opposing him. Indeed, many participants in the debate posited just such a division. However, such a reading significantly obscures a multiplicity of perspectives within both generations. In general, Hayakawa did enjoy greater support among Nisei than among Sansei, but a number of prominent Nisei—including Edison Uno, Raymond Okamura, Yori Wada, Lloyd Wake, and James Hirabayashi—threw their weight behind the strikers at San Francisco State and urged their fellow Nisei to do so as well.[85] Because Nisei and Sansei lined up on both sides of the issue, constructing the confrontation in terms of a youth rebellion or generational conflict is insufficient. Instead, thinking in terms of a political paradigm shift—what Jere Takahashi calls a change in "political style"—affords more nuanced and accurate analyses. Many Sansei and a significant number of Nisei assumed the paradigm of race and power, whereas others clung to the assimilation model.[86]

A sizable portion of San Francisco's Japanese American community stood behind Hayakawa. Support for Hayakawa coalesced in the Community Interest Committee of Nihonmachi (CICN), organized and cochaired by three former presidents of the Japanese American Citizens League (JACL): George Yamasaki, Dr. Clifford I. Uyeda, and Steven J. Doi. The San Francisco chapter of the JACL had invited Hayakawa to be the keynote speaker at its annual installation dinner, but community pressure forced the JACL to withdraw its invitation. In place of the installation dinner, the CICN organized another dinner featuring Hayakawa as the keynote speaker.[87] The organizers carefully constructed the dinner as a neutral occasion that would not "honor" Hayakawa but would offer the community a chance to hear from the best-known Japanese American in the nation. Emphasizing that it was not taking sides, the CICN invited everyone, including TWLF supporters, to attend.[88]

Although the CICN professed neutrality, two of its co-chairs, Uyeda and Doi, signed a pro-Hayakawa petition circulated by the Nisei Junior Chamber of Commerce. The petition, printed on a scroll emblazoned "Banzai Sam!" garnered two hundred signatures, including those of *Hokubei Mainichi* editor Howard Imazeki, *Nichibei Times* editor Y. W. Abiko, Masao Ashizawa of Japan Town Redevelopment Corporation, and Yone Satoda. Calling Hayakawa bashers "a minority within a minority . . . no more than 1/12 of the Japanese-American students at the college," a spokesman for the Nisei Junior Chamber of Commerce claimed that 85 percent of the community supported Hayakawa. The petitioners cautioned that while they were sympathetic to the demands of the BSU, they condemned any illegal tactics and wanted education to continue.[89]

Although *Hokubei Mainichi* had awarded Hayakawa its "Nisei of the Year" honor with a neutral declaration, its editor, Howard Imazeki, emerged as a visible supporter of Hayakawa. In addition to signing the "Banzai Sam!" scroll, Imazeki praised Hayakawa's decision to reopen the campus as being in line with the sentiments of the "silent majority" of students and faculty. While he claimed to be sympathetic toward the aims of the BSU, he deplored the "violent, disruptive and destructive tactics being used to force their demands." However sympathetic Imazeki was toward Hayakawa, though, he rebuffed Hayakawa's appeal for support from the Japanese American community. "It was stupid of him . . . to expect any sort of personal support from our community," Imazeki wrote, because "Dr. Hayakawa is not and has never been a man of our community." Because Imazeki did not view Hayakawa as a representative of the Japanese American community, he urged him to make his "appeals to a wider community," by which he presumably meant whites and other San Franciscans at large.[90]

While the CICN supported Hayakawa, a substantial portion of the community opposed his actions at San Francisco State. On the left, the venerable radical Karl Yoneda admonished Japanese Americans, "Let us not prostitute our heritage by becoming lackeys or spokesmen for the reactionary dominant racist power structure as has Samuel Ichiei [sic] Hayakawa."[91] James Hirabayashi, a Nisei professor of anthropology at San Francisco State, emerged as an important critic of Hayakawa. Hirabayashi had known him for several years before the strike, for they were not only the first two Asian American professors at the college but were also neighbors in Mill Valley. Hirabayashi had been a regular attendee at Hayakawa's New Year's parties and on these occasions had raided Hayakawa's supply of *takuan* (Japanese pickled radishes). Hirabayashi was initially drawn into strike politics when Penny Nakatsu asked him to be faculty adviser to the San Francisco AAPA; in addition, he was a charter member of the faculty union. He characterizes his involvement as having begun due to the "happenstance" of having been AAPA adviser and office mate of the faculty union founder, but his personal politics prior to the strike belie such a simple explanation. Hirabayashi had long been involved in civil rights. In Mill Valley during the early 1960s, he had been part of a group devoted to fair employment and housing that picketed the offices of realtors who were discriminating against African American buyers.[92] The presence of Hirabayashi, an Asian American faculty member, on the picket lines at San Francisco State and in anti-Hayakawa meetings in the community lent legitimacy to the demands of the strikers.

Even the normally staid JACL was split by the controversy. Although the CICN was chaired by three former JACL presidents, several renegade units broke ranks with the JACL hierarchy. Earlier, when Hayakawa had been slated to speak at the San Francisco JACL installation dinner, the Women's Auxiliary had urged the Board of Governors to rescind the invitation because it might "incur anger of the black community" and cause dissension within the organization.[93] After the CICN announced its Hayakawa event, the Women's Auxiliary, Junior JACL, and Civil Rights Committee used their JACL affiliation to obtain a meeting room from the Bank of Tokyo for a press conference announcing the formation of a coalition called Japanese Americans United Against Hayakawa Dinner. In response, Wesley T. Doi, president of the San Francisco JACL, publicly apologized for the groups' "misuse of the JACL name," which had occurred without his knowledge or approval.[94]

Dissent came from many quarters of the JACL; even the national JACL president, Jerry Enomoto, questioned the wisdom of feting Hayakawa. Enomoto refuted the idea that the CICN could be dissociated from the JACL, noting that of the three co-chairs two were current JACL board members and one was an ex-officio member of the board. Writing in the JACL's national organ, *Pacific Citizen,* Enomoto said, "I urge that the concept of the strike be not immediately written off as synonymous with violence and destruction, because the whole story is not that simple. JACL has a deep obligation to look at what is going on in depth, with compassion and understanding." Enomoto's nuanced stance insisted that studying the issues did not compromise the JACL's general "opposition to tactics of violence, used to forcibly take over any public institution."[95]

Hayakawa's detractors strenuously sought to dispel the notion that Japanese Americans as a group opposed the strike, for they worried that his actions would be seen "not as acts of an individual but of [the] whole . . . Japanese Community." These strike supporters believed that Hayakawa was performing the dirty work for whites. As one commentator asked rhetorically, "Isn't Hayakawa doing exactly what a certain segment of the White Establishment always wished they could do except that a White person could never have gotten away with it?"[96] Several students staging a pro-strike demonstration emphasized their ethnic, and therefore racial, basis for striking. Wearing kimonos and carrying signs reading "Japanese-Americans support this strike!!" three female members of AAPA conspicuously displayed their Japanese ethnicity and clearly sought to distance the Japanese American community from Hayakawa.[97]

Along with distancing themselves from Hayakawa, AAPA also sought to build support for the strike within the Japanese American community at large by holding a special forum. Inviting members of the community to the meeting, AAPA stated, "The Sansei students who are involved in the San Francisco State crisis are asking to be heard and are requesting the community's support." Members of AAPA and other Japanese American students, along with several Japanese American faculty members, participated in the forum. In seeking support from the Nisei, the students portrayed the strike as a "crisis" that "affects the Japanese American Community" and urged Nisei to "participate in this program and to bring your friends."[98]

In addition, a group calling itself the Ad Hoc Japanese-American Committee Concerned with the SF State Crisis, composed of Japanese American students at San Francisco State and some of their Nisei supporters, wrote letters to the editors of several local newspapers. The Ad Hoc Committee's two main points were that Hayakawa was not a representative of the Japanese American community and that the TWLF demands were reasonable. First, they took pains to "challenge [Hayakawa's] statement that he reflects the views of the Japanese American community regarding the issues in question at San Francisco State, and has their unqualified support." As they saw it, the appointment of Hayakawa, a "member of a minority group," was "an attempt by state officials to confuse the issues." Second, they claimed that having "discussed at great length with many Japanese American students and faculty the demands being made" by the BSU and TWLF, they were convinced that the demands were "justified" and should be "immediately accepted and implemented by the San Francisco State College administration and the State College Board of Trustees."[99] The Ad Hoc Committee did not focus narrowly on students but instead sought to build broad-based support for the strike within the Japanese American community in general. A flyer advertising the 6 December meeting was addressed to "Nisei and Sansei Students," but it urged all students to "BRING YOUR PARENTS."[100] The meeting, held at Christ United Presbyterian Church, was moderated by Reverend Lloyd Wake of Glide Memorial Church and included student panelists Penny Nakatsu and Francis Oka of AAPA. More than three hundred people crammed into the church's social hall in a gathering that community leaders deemed the largest of the postwar period—an indication of the community's sense of urgency in confronting the Hayakawa problem.[101]

Raymond Okamura, an important Nisei supporter of the Sansei activists at both San Francisco State and Berkeley, used the language of identity in urging his fellow Nisei to support the Sansei movement. In a letter to *Pacific Citizen* he wrote, "Our generation, the Nisei, has succumbed to the pressures of assimilation. The new generation, the Sansei, want to re-gain a lost ethnic identity, and are seriously challenging the blind acceptance of white middle-class values."[102] Okamura's letter contains two important ideas that form the key to understanding the debate over the strike. First, he impugned assimilation as a negative process. This stance directly contradicted the JACL and Hayakawa's ideal of assimilation as the primary process by which racial equality could be achieved. Second, he lauded the Sansei for rebuilding a "lost ethnic identity" that does not aspire to whiteness. Taken together, these ideas form the basis for resisting racial injustice that underpinned the strikers' beliefs. Creating a Japanese American identity or, more widely, an Asian American identity, amounted to rejecting a trajectory leading to increasing acceptance through whiteness.

Strike supporters also emphasized that Hayakawa was external to the Japanese American community, deeming him an outsider on three accounts. First, he was Canadian-born, having become a naturalized U.S. citizen only in 1954. Second, he was a relatively recent arrival, having moved to California only in 1955. Finally, and most important, Hayakawa had opted not to build ties within the community. He had chosen to live across the Golden Gate Bridge from San Francisco in Mill Valley, a suburban community in predominantly white and wealthy Marin County.

Furthermore, Hayakawa's critics recalled his public criticism of the Nisei for their insularity in his refusal to address CINO in 1955.[103] At least one person appreciated the irony of the situation, lamenting that "the one Japanese American who in the past chose not to claim the S.F. Japanese community as his would be the cause to bring about this needless division in the community."[104]

Another reason that some chose to oppose Hayakawa had less to do with their stance on his actions themselves and more to do with the fact that his actions reflected badly on the Japanese American community's relationship with the black community. In San Francisco, the Japanese American district, Nihonmachi, was surrounded by the heavily black-populated Western Addition. A story in *Time* magazine in January 1969 claiming that blacks in San Francisco saw Japanese Americans as their oppressors caused an uproar among Japanese Americans. *Hokubei Mainichi* called the article the worst slander Nihonmachi had received since the World War II evacuation and insisted that relations between blacks and Japanese were friendly. As examples of black–Japanese American comity it cited the fact that the San Francisco JACL had joined the Western Addition Community Organization and claimed that Yori Wada, the director of the Buchanan Street YMCA, was a respected leader in the black community.[105] Progressives worried that Japanese American support for Hayakawa would introduce friction between Japanese Americans and African Americans. Edison Uno asserted that although black resentment of Hayakawa did not extend to the larger Japanese American community at that time, if the situation were to change, "immediate steps should be taken to denounce and disassociate ourselves with Dr. Hayakawa to preserve harmony and understanding" with the black community.[106] Similarly, when the Women's Auxiliary of the San Francisco JACL declared its opposition to Hayakawa's invitation, it did so out of concern that the invitation might "incur [the] anger of the black community."[107] Thus, while conservatives like those at the helm of *Hokubei Mainichi* simply denied tensions between Japanese Americans and blacks, progressives like Uno actively sought to build alliances and sympathies with African Americans.

The model minority thesis, which held that Japanese Americans had become accepted and joined the middle class through hard work and avoidance of vocal protests, provided another subject upon which Hayakawa and his detractors disagreed. In narrating his life history, Hayakawa told a sympathetic, antistrike audience that when his father was a young immigrant in San Francisco he had worked as a houseboy "in the kitchen of the father or grandfather of some of you." When he visited his son's home in Mill Valley, the elder Hayakawa had said that that was the type of house he had formerly entered through the servants' quarters.[108] The younger Hayakawa then went on to fondly recall his education at the nonelite University of Manitoba. As Hayakawa related it, this vignette suggested that the path from the servant entrance to the front door necessarily goes through the schoolyard.

Whereas Hayakawa embraced the model minority thesis, his opponents explicitly rejected it. AAPA believed that the problems with the model minority thesis were twofold. First, it was factually inaccurate, for "the myth of 'Orientals having made it' is exactly that—a myth." Instead of being accepted members of American society, AAPA claimed, "Orientals . . . have been the victims of racial prejudice. We still are."[109] AAPA's insistence on the falsity of the model minority thesis was based on its adoption of a racial paradigm that focused on the continuing political and economic salience of racial categories. It constituted an explicit rejection of the assimilation model and its narrative of ever-increasing social acceptance and economic gains. AAPA's second objection to the model minority thesis was that it differentiated between Asian Americans and other Third World people. AAPA protested against the use of "Orientals" as a model that "the establishment has and is still using against other minority groups" and worried that blacks were being told, "Why can't you do as the Japanese—the implication being that orientals know their place."[110] Because the model minority thesis portrayed Asian Americans as silent rather than vocal and successful rather than oppressed, AAPA challenged its veracity in order to make common cause with blacks and other Third World people. AAPA believed that, left unchecked, the model minority discourse would drive a wedge between Asian Americans and other people of color, both by representing Asian Americans as accepted by whites and by fostering resentment toward them within other minority communities. Emphasizing the continued racialization of Asian Americans thus led AAPA to reject assimilation into whiteness and endeavor to build interracial alliances with other people of color.

Legacies of the Strike

On 21 March 1969, after four and a half turbulent months, the TWLF reached a settlement with President Hayakawa and the San Francisco State College administration. The agreement called for the establishment of the

School of Ethnic Studies—with departments of American Indian Studies, Asian American Studies, Black Studies, and La Raza Studies—which offered new classes and hired new faculty to address the needs of the various communities. In addition to the establishment of the School of Ethnic Studies, the agreement specified that disciplinary suspensions of students would not extend beyond the fall semester of 1969 and promised to allocate unused special admission slots to students of color. The settlement did not satisfy all TWLF demands, however: no specific personnel were singled out for retention or firing, the new school operated with considerably fewer than fifty FTEs, and students were not granted control of the school's faculty hiring, curriculum, or admissions.

According to James Hirabayashi, who served as dean of the School of Ethnic Studies from 1970 to 1976, the discipline of ethnic studies that emerged after the strike diverged sharply in its views from mainstream academics in that it considered communities of color proper objects of study and legitimate producers of knowledge. The Asian American studies curriculum was developed through close collaboration between students, faculty, and the community, and many courses were taught by community members without traditional academic credentials. Furthermore, as dean, Hirabayashi tried to keep "as much revolutionary spirit" as possible, extending the principles of self-determination on which the strike had been based into the administration of the new school. The departments enjoyed as much autonomy as possible with regard to curricular and personnel matters.[111]

In addition to giving rise to the establishment of the School of Ethnic Studies, social scientist Karen Umemoto found that the TWLF strike mobilized "a new generation of fighters" who served their campuses and communities, and she credited the strike with helping to forge their "basic values and beliefs."[112] Furthermore, as Glenn Omatsu notes, the strike was "the first campus uprising involving Asian Americans as a collective force." The San Francisco State strike in many ways marked a turning point in Asian American political activism. Omatsu characterizes the strike as presaging what would follow in that the Asian American students shared deep links with their communities, rooted their activism within interracial alliances, drew inspiration from "leaders and revolutions occurring in Asia, Africa, Latin America, and the Middle East," confronted the university's power structure in a way that highlighted the nature of oppression in the United States, and mobilized a mass movement for direct, militant action.[113]

The actions of the students at San Francisco State reverberated nationally, for the TWLF was widely admired and sometimes imitated. Across the Bay, students at the University of California–Berkeley followed their working-class peers at San Francisco State by forming their own version of the TWLF and successfully striking for ethnic studies. The militants at San Francisco State and Berkeley collectively inspired the formation of TWLFs at dozens of other campuses around the nation.[114] Furthermore, their actions had lasting repercussions, for three decades after the strike, there were Asian American studies programs at thirty-seven colleges and universities, and "many more institutions" offered courses.[115]

Hayakawa in the Senate and Beyond

After serving as president of San Francisco State for four years, Hayakawa went on to a career in politics, during which his belief in assimilation pushed him further from the mainstream of Asian America and closer to a group of ultraconservative whites. The former Democrat "switched the tassels on his tam o'shanter from the left to the right" and ran for United States Senate as a Republican.[116] As Senator, Hayakawa once again eagerly played the role of a nonwhite conservative, urging the Supreme Court to decide in favor of the white litigant Allan Bakke in his discrimination suit against the University of California–Davis, opposing redress and reparations for Japanese Americans incarcerated during World War II, and attempting to make English the official language of the United States.[117]

The issue of redress and reparations demonstrated how Hayakawa's politics diverged from those of the mainstream Japanese American community. Beginning in the mid-1970s, the redress movement, which sought a governmental apology and monetary compensation, included organizations from across the political spectrum, ranging from the JACL, which pursued a strategy of lobbying legislators, to the National Coalition for Redress and Reparations, a group composed largely of veterans of 1960s activism, which mobilized a grassroots campaign.[118] Contrary to nearly the entire Japanese American community, Hayakawa believed that the incarceration was "neither a mistake nor an injustice."[119] Furthermore, he claimed that incarceration was "perhaps the best thing that could have happened to the Japanese Americans of the West Coast," because it "forced them out of their segregated existence to discover the rest of America" and "thus resulted in the Americanization of the Japanese in one generation after immigration—a record for non-English-speaking immigrants of any color."[120] In opposing redress and reparations, Hayakawa allied himself closely with the white ultraconservative Lillian Baker, who was perhaps the most active and vociferous antiredress activist in the nation. Their collaboration lasted over a decade, and she aided him in multiple ways. Baker served as the Los Angeles South Bay chair for Hayakawa's Republican primary campaign for the Senate[121] and frequently furnished him with documents, photographs, court decisions, and testimonies to support their antiredress position.[122]

Hayakawa's major political effort of the 1980s was a campaign to establish English as the official language of the United States, and on this issue he again diverged from the Asian American political mainstream and made alliances with conservative whites. Hayakawa argued that bilingualism threatened the nation's ability to maintain a public sphere shared by all citizens and that without a "common language" the nation risked hopeless fragmentation.[123] In 1981, he introduced a constitutional amendment to make English the official language of the United States, which died in the Senate. After serving a single term in the Senate, Hayakawa retired from public office and turned his attention more centrally to the English language movement. In 1983 he cofounded U.S. English, and in 1986 he spearheaded the campaign for Proposition 63, which sought to make English the official language of California. Once again, Hayakawa referenced his own race and life history and emphasized that he was a Japanese American leading the English language movement. He said, "I want to extend a welcome to all immigrants, and make sure they have the same opportunities I had to become successful and be elected to the U.S. Senate. The first requirement is that they learn to speak English. I am so glad to see so many Asians and Hispanics coming to this land of opportunity. But they must learn the language." He specifically referred to his status as a Japanese American immigrant to deny that the proposal was racist and anti-immigrant. And, as at San Francisco State, he portrayed himself as representative of the Asian American community's position on the issue. "The support (for U.S. English) from rank and file Asian Americans has been very good," he claimed, adding that Chinese and Japanese Americans had been particularly sympathetic (although he did acknowledge opposition from the group Chinese for Affirmative Action).[124]

Although the measure passed statewide by a three-to-one margin, limited evidence suggests that it did not garner that amount of support from Asian Americans. The board members of the Golden Gate (San Francisco) chapter of the JACL were "appalled" by a presentation from

U.S. English director Stanley Diamond, who indicted ethnic organizations as separatist, according to Clifford Uyeda, who had co-chaired the pro-Hayakawa CICN in 1969.[125] Major Asian American organizations opposed to Proposition 63 included the Chinese Consolidated Benevolent Association, JACL, Asian Law Caucus, Asian American Bar Association, Chinese American Citizens Alliance, and Filipino Bar Association of Northern California.[126] In the largely working-class environs of San Francisco's Chinatown, the initiative was rejected by 72 percent of voters.[127] Despite Hayakawa's claim that U.S. English was not anti-immigrant, the organization shared numerous ties with the Federation for American Immigration Reform (FAIR), a group dedicated to reducing immigration. The two organizations shared numerous officers, supporters, and contributors, and the cofounder of U.S. English was FAIR founder John Tanton, who in 1988 came under withering fire for crude anti-immigrant remarks that many interpreted as racist and anti-Latino.[128]

The extent to which the political spectrum shifted beneath S. I. Hayakawa in forty years was remarkable. It would no doubt have shocked the young professor who so earnestly believed in the power of studying language to eliminate racial antagonism to learn that in his eighties his devotion to a common language would ally him with nativists and white supremacists.[129] Hayakawa's positions as a public intellectual remained remarkably consistent over the decades, but the context of his words and actions changed dramatically, as did the reactions of his audiences. What became abundantly clear at San Francisco State College was that the liberal assimilationism of midcentury America was in direct conflict with a new racially based understanding of the place of Asians in America. While Hayakawa clung to his faith in the falsity of racial distinctions, the Asian Americans who faced off against him at San Francisco State rejected assimilation as a solution to the problem of race. Instead, they drew together as a multiethnic bloc, allied themselves with other people of color in the United States, and drew inspiration from militant nonwhite peoples of Asia, Africa, and Latin America.

Three

Black Panthers, Red Guards, and Chinamen: Constructing Asian American Identity through Performing Blackness

On 22 March 1969, in Portsmouth Square, a public gathering place in San Francisco's Chinatown, a group of young Chinese Americans calling themselves the Red Guard Party held a rally to unveil their "10 Point Program." Clad in berets and armbands, they announced a free breakfast program for children at the Commodore Stockton School, denounced the planned destruction of the Chinese Playground, and called for the "removal of colonialist police from Chinatown." The Red Guard Party's style, language, and politics clearly recalled those of the Black Panther Party, with which they had significant contact and by which they were profoundly influenced.[1] At the rally, the Red Guards performed an Asian American version of black nationalism by adopting the Panthers' garb, confrontational manner, and emphasis on self-determination.

Many years later, the Asian American playwright and critic Frank Chin dismissed the Red Guards' rally as a "yellow minstrel show."[2] But although Chin rejected the Red Guards' performance as a vain attempt to imitate blackness, in 1971, just two years after the rally, he had offered his own dramatic take on the interplay between Asian Americans and blacks in his play *The Chickencoop Chinaman*. Widely acknowledged as a germinal work of Asian American literature, Chin's play explores the relationship between Asian American identity and blackness by featuring Chinese American and Japanese American protagonists who associate with, claim sympathy for, and exhibit speech and dress patterns most commonly associated with African Americans. Set in the late 1960s, *The Chickencoop Chinaman* chronicles the adventures of Tam Lum, a fast-talking Chinese American, and his Japanese American sidekick, Kenji, as they attempt to produce a film about the career of their childhood hero, the African American boxer Ovaltine Jack Dancer and his putative father, Charley Popcorn. As a story about the search for heroes, fathers, and a usable past, *The Chickencoop Chinaman* provides a powerful meditation on the relationship between masculinity, race, and Asian American identity.

Both the Red Guard Party and Frank Chin were key players in the Asian American political and cultural mobilization of the late 1960s and early 1970s. The Red Guards were among the first radicals to arise from Asian American communities, and in their later incarnation as I Wor Kuen constituted one of the two preeminent Asian American leftist organizations.[3] They built community programs, organized Asian American workers, fought for better living conditions, protested against the Viet Nam War, and became integrally entwined in the Marxist-Leninist-Maoist left. Chin was highly influential in his own right as a writer, critic, and activist. *The Chickencoop Chinaman* marked his emergence as a major figure. It won the 1971 playwriting contest sponsored by the East West Players, the prominent Los Angeles–based Asian American theater company, and became the first Asian American play to be produced off Broadway.[4] Chin published numerous works of searing criticism, fiction, and nonfiction; cofounded the Asian American Theater Workshop in San Francisco, one of the most important venues for Asian American dramatic productions; coedited *AIIIEEEEE!*, a foundational anthology of Asian American literature; and organized the first Day of Remembrance to commemorate the incarceration of Japanese Americans during World War II.[5]

Yet Chin is also a controversial figure who has leveled highly gendered criticism of authors—most notably Maxine Hong Kingston—whom he has accused of peddling "fake" depictions of Asian American culture for white consumption.[6] Critics charge that his attempts to create a heroic Asian American tradition inevitably "reassert male authority over the cultural domain by subordinating feminism to nationalist terms."[7] It is not my intent here to rehash these critiques; instead I want to point out that critical perspectives on Chin have thus far failed to locate his rehearsals of Asian American masculinity in the historical context of the black power period. Reading *The Chickencoop Chinaman* through a racial lens reveals the play's linkages of Asian American identity to blackness.

The Red Guard Party and Frank Chin engaged in divergent modes of performance. While rallies on the street and drama on stage constitute different genres, those of both the Red Guards and Chin were scripted with intentionality and visually constructed and displayed the politics and identities of their participants. Furthermore, the Red Guards and Chin exemplify the two distinct ideologies most commonly understood to have motivated the construction of Asian American identity: Third World internationalist radicalism and domestic U.S. cultural nationalism. Comparatively examining the performances of radicals and cultural workers thus provides a valuable register of competing visions of Asian America.

The Red Guards and Chin intervened in an Asian America that had not yet been constituted. Through the mid-twentieth century, despite scattered instances of interethnic solidarity, most organizing among Asians in the mainland United States proceeded along ethnic or national lines. Indeed, at times, Asian ethnic groups strategically distanced themselves from each other.[8] In the late 1960s, however, a loosely organized social movement known as the Asian American movement arose to protest anti-Asian racism and exploitation. Although the Asian American movement comprised a variety of organizations and individuals with competing ideologies, all agreed with two fundamental premises: first, that Asians of all ethnicities shared a common racial oppression in the United States, and second, that building a multiethnic, racially based coalition would provide an effective basis for resisting racism.[9]

Performances of blackness catalyzed the formation of Asian American identity. Far from being mere mimics, however, Asian Americans who began to consider their own racial positioning through contemplations of blackness went on to forge a distinct identity of their own. The Red Guards adopted the Black Panthers' language and style—two key elements of the Panther mystique—as a political statement that underlined their espousal of the Panthers' racial politics. Thus, they inserted Asian Americans into a racial paradigm, arguing that Asian Americans constituted a racialized bloc subject to the same racism that afflicted blacks. Chin also scripted performances that pointed to blackness as a model of racial resistance and identity. But, important for him, emulating blackness provided a way to recuperate Asian American masculinity.

Understanding the construction of Asian American identity through its performance of blackness has three major implications for scholars of race and the 1960s. First, the extent to which Asian American identity was enacted through performances of blackness indicates the thorough imbrication of multiple processes of racial formation. It is by now widely accepted that racial formations proceed in a parallel fashion; for instance, much of the literature on the social construction of whiteness argues that whiteness came to be defined in opposition to nonwhiteness (most often, blackness).[10] But the construction of Asian American identity through the performance of blackness demonstrates the interdependence of racial formations strictly among people of color.

Second, understanding the rise of Asian American identity in response to blackness answers charges that in the late 1960s the new left betrayed the promise of the early 1960s by descending into narrowly divisive identity politics. Historian David Burner excoriates black power for engendering a "narcissistic absorption in the group content of self-identity" and a "solipsistic examination" of the self, and former 1960s activist Todd Gitlin mourns the left's putative decline into parochialism.[11] However, Asian American mobilization powerfully refutes this narrative of declension. Asian American adaptations of black power's emphasis on race and racial identity not only contributed to the construction of Asian American identity but also provided points of conjunction around which African Americans and Asian Americans could connect political and cultural movements.

Finally, highlighting the importance of performances of blackness to the construction of Asian American identity helps to broach divergent histories of the category itself. The Red Guards and Chin offered dramatically different prescriptions for what ailed Asian America, as demonstrated in one striking skirmish. Chin recalls teaching a class in which he directed Asian American students to act out some anti-Asian stereotypes, and a group of Red Guards took exception to the repetition of the offensive imagery. The Red Guard leader knocked Chin to the ground, yelling, "Identify with China!" Chin countered, "We're in America. This is where we are, where we live and where we're going to die."[12] The exchange highlights a fundamental cleavage in understandings of Asian American identity. During the late 1960s and early 1970s, groups such as the Red Guard Party (later I Wor Kuen), Wei Min She, Asian Americans for Action, and the Asian American Political Alliance adopted frameworks that connected anti-Asian racism in the United States to western imperialism in Asia. Meanwhile, Chin and his cohorts argued that Asian Americans were bound by a common culture that was born and bred strictly within U.S. national borders.[13]

Discrepant genealogies of the origin of Asian American identity reproduce this tension: social histories and documentary collections of Asian American activism in the 1960s and 1970s tend to locate Third World internationalism as its central ideology, while literary and cultural histories generally privilege domestic U.S. nationalism.[14] That both the Red Guards and Chin turned to blackness suggests the power of mimesis to produce new subjectivities and identifications across ideological boundaries. It also suggests that these strange bedfellows were engaged in the shared project of racial formation and that neither anti-imperialist internationalism nor domestic nationalism alone can adequately account for the multifarious beginnings of Asian American identity.

Asian Americans and Assimilation

Asian American radicals and cultural workers turned to blackness as a model for Asian American identity as a way to resist assimilation into whiteness. At the Red Guards' initial rally in Portsmouth Square, David Hilliard, chairman of the Black Panther Party, castigated the audience for its lack of militance and called Chinese Americans the "Uncle Toms of the non-white people of the U.S." He went on to assert, "If you can't relate to China then you can't relate to the Panthers."[15] Hilliard's appeal for the Red Guards to relate to China was in part a call for political radicalism and commitment to the ideology of Mao Zedong, but, paired with an accusation of Uncle Tom-ism, it was also an admonition against assimilation. Locating Chinese Americans as insufficiently Chinese, Hilliard charged that they needed to reinvigorate themselves by renewing their relationship to Asia.

Hilliard's claim that Chinese Americans were overassimilated could not have been made prior to the 1960s. From the beginning of large-scale migrations to the United States in the mid-1800s through the beginning of World War II, Asians had faced legal barriers to assimilation in the form of immigration restrictions, bars to naturalization, and antimiscegenation laws. In addition, the Yellow Peril discourse positioned Asians as inherently inassimilable perpetual foreigners.[16] In the postwar era, however, U.S. responses to cold war imperatives opened the possibility of Asian American assimilation. Between 1952 and 1967, Asian Americans gained rights to naturalization, immigration, and interracial marriage. These legal changes accompanied a social shift that suggested the possibility of Asian American assimilation in the form of a discourse that has come to be known as the "model minority myth."

Discussions of Asian Americans' integration after World War II inevitably credited their putative assimilation to their status as a model minority.[17] In 1966, sociologist William Petersen claimed in the *New York Times Magazine* that Japanese Americans were following the steps of white ethnics who had initially suffered discrimination but "climbed out of the slums" to enter the mainstream. He praised Japanese Americans for their dedication to education, low crime rates, and strong family values.[18] *U.S. News and World Report* extended the claim of assimilability to Chinese Americans, who it said were "winning wealth and respect" through their "hard work," lack of juvenile delinquency, focus on education, and eschewal of welfare. Both articles compared Asian Americans favorably to blacks, arguing that unlike "Negroes," Asian Americans had overcome racial discrimination and were on the verge of achieving assimilation.[19]

At this moment when Asian American assimilation seemed possible for the first time, the Red Guard Party's performance of black radicalism constituted an emphatic rejection. While black power encompassed a variety of ideologies, its advocates generally adopted discourses emphasizing power and self-determination over integration and inclusion.[20] In 1967, Stokely Carmichael and Charles Hamilton explained that blacks needed to "redefine themselves," "reclaim their history, their culture," and "create their own sense of community and togetherness." They deemed "assimilated" and "integrated" blacks to be co-opted by whites and hence ineligible to participate in creating this new black community and identity.[21]

For Asian Americans, adopting black power's antipathy toward assimilation marked a significant departure from previous modes of political mobilization. In contrast to prior assimilationists like the members of the Japanese American Citizens League and S. I. Hayakawa (as discussed in chapters 1 and 2), Asian American activists viewed racial oppression as a systemic rather than aberrant feature of American society. They believed that the racial oppression of Asian Americans stemmed from and served to justify their economic exploitation, and they sought to build Asian American power and culture autonomous of white approval.

The Red Guard Party's programs generally sought to build and strengthen Chinatown's community institutions rather than to insert Chinese Americans into mainstream programs. To that end, they started the Free Breakfast program, sponsored cultural programs and movie nights, published the *Red Guard Community Newspaper,* and confronted the police. As minister of information Alex Hing said, "We're going to attain power, so we don't have to beg anymore."[22]

Like the Red Guard Party, Frank Chin rejected assimilation as a palliative to racism. *The Chickencoop Chinaman* features an assimilationist Chinese American character, Tom, whose very name positions him as the Uncle Tom that Hilliard had posited. He provides an unambiguous expression of the model minority discourse when he says, "We used to be kicked around, but that's history, brother. Today we have good jobs, good pay, and we're lucky. Americans are proud to say we send more of our kids to college than any other race. We're accepted. We worked hard for it."[23]

In contrast to Tom's assimilationism, the protagonists Tam and Kenji struggle against whiteness. The Lone Ranger (described in the dramatis personae as "a legendary white racist")[24] appears in a fantasy scene and proclaims that Asian Americans are "honorary white." When Tam and Kenji protest, he insists that this bestowal is not a blessing but a curse that they cannot refuse. The curse of whiteness mandates that Asian Americans refrain from vocal protest and remain "legendary passive." They must acknowledge their place in the racial hierarchy, for the Lone Ranger orders them to "kiss" his "ass" and "know . . . that it be white." And they must abandon attempts to create an independent Asian American culture, as symbolized by the Lone Ranger's shooting the writer Tam through the hand.[25] Tam and Kenji understand the Lone Ranger's curse as an attempt to buy Asian American compliance with a white-dominated social order; their refusal indicates the play's explicit rejection of assimilation via playing the model minority. Elsewhere, Chin has stated that aside from being "a strategy for white acceptance," the model minority discourse was dangerous because it encouraged Asian Americans to "denigrate" blacks and see them as deserving of their oppression.[26]

Asian Americans and Blacks in Common Struggle

Cross-identifications between Asians and blacks arose at various moments during the twentieth century. At times, African Americans drew inspiration from Asian resistance to western imperialism. During the 1930s, tens of thousands of blacks flocked to the Pacific Movement of the Eastern World, which proclaimed Japan the "champion" of the "dark and colored races." During World War II, Malcolm X proclaimed his eagerness to join the Japanese Army, mostly to avoid being drafted but also echoing a strand of black sentiment that admired Japan as a militarily powerful nonwhite nation opposed to Euro-American imperialism.[27]

Asia also figured prominently in the black imagination during the 1960s and 1970s. After fleeing the United States, the militant Robert F. Williams spent three years exiled in China. Black Panther political education prominently included Mao's Red Book. Indeed, Mao's writings were central to the ideologies and practices of an entire generation of black revolutionaries, some of whom went so far as to adopt Chinese peasant-style dress and aesthetics to signal their radicalism.[28] When Muhammad Ali refused to be inducted into the military in 1967, his declaration "Man, I ain't got no quarrel with them Vietcong" reflected the antiwar stance of black nationalists ranging from the Nation of Islam (in Ali's case) to the Black Panther Party.[29] Indeed, party chairman David Hilliard suggested the necessity of Asian-black solidarity when he declared to National Liberation Front representatives in Viet Nam, "You're Yellow Panthers, we're Black Panthers."[30] As these examples show, black identifications with Asians were primarily with those across the Pacific rather than with Asians in the United States.

Although Asian American and African American identifications were mutual, it would be an overstatement to deem them reciprocal. The black power movement's "*rearticulation* of racial ideology" in the 1960s clearly opened spaces for new subjectivities to emerge.[31] Within these spaces, Asian Americans performing blackness and African Americans admiring Asian radicalism shared in creating what Vijay Prashad has aptly called the "multicolored Left,"[32] a hybridized multiracial social movement with both Asian and black inflections.

Asian Americans and blacks crossed paths daily, especially in West Coast cities such as Seattle, San Francisco, Oakland, and Los Angeles.[33] During World War II, many African Americans migrating westward settled in areas vacated by the Japanese Americans who had been imprisoned in concentration camps.[34] Upon returning to those areas, Japanese Americans found their former neighborhoods transformed. Maya Angelou sensed the changes in San Francisco's Nihonmachi in the air: "Where the odors of tempura, raw fish and *cha* had dominated, the aroma of chitlings, greens and ham hocks now prevailed."[35] These wartime demographic shifts meant that urban Asian Americans and blacks increasingly rubbed elbows in the postwar period.

Frank Chin grew up in the mixed-race context of Oakland. He recalls, "In the sixties, [black culture] became a force in Asian-America. It always had a large presence in Oakland. I grew up with rhythm-and-blues, jazz." However, it was not just proximity but also politics that inspired

Asian American adoptions. Chin credits the "sixties and the civil-rights movement" with making Asian Americans "aware that we had no presence, no image in American culture as men, as people. . . . So a bunch of us began to appropriate 'blackness.' We'd wear the clothes, we'd affect the walk and we began to talk black. We'd call our selves 'Bro' and began talking Southern: 'Hey, man.'"[36] Chin's recollection highlights masculine modes of bodily expression—clothing, gait, and speech—as the means of racial identification.

Asian Americans also encountered blackness intellectually. Historian Gary Okihiro recalls that many Asian Americans "found our identity by reading Franz Fanon and Malcolm X, Cheikh Anta Diop and W. E. B. Du Bois, Leopold Senghor and Langston Hughes."[37] Indeed, the debt that the field of Asian American studies owes to black intellectual figures cannot be overstated. Steve Louie, a veteran of the Asian American movement, believes that it "owes a huge political debt to the black power movement." He points to Stokely Carmichael, Malcolm X, Huey Newton, Bobby Seale, and the Black Panthers as visionaries "who laid the groundwork that really brought . . . the Asian American movement out."[38]

Some Asian American individuals who felt they were not part of a larger group participated directly in black social movements. Prior to the heyday of black power, the Chinese American political activist Grace Lee Boggs enjoyed a long association with C. L. R. James and worked closely with her husband, James Boggs, who wrote about the role of black industrial workers in a Marxist-Leninist revolution. She was so closely identified with the black movement that the FBI mistook her as "Afro-Chinese."[39] Yuri Kochiyama, a Nisei (second-generation Japanese American) woman living in Harlem, was a friend of Malcolm X and famously cradled his head as he lay dying in the Audubon Ballroom; she was also associated with the black radicals Kwame Toure (formerly Stokely Carmichael) and H. Rap Brown.[40] A few Asian Americans even joined the Black Panthers. Guy Kurose, a Japanese American who had grown up in the black community of Seattle, joined the Panthers, though he recalls that most of his activities were of the "jackanape" variety.[41] In New York, Lee Lew-Lee, a Chinese-Jamaican, joined Asian Americans for Action and I Wor Kuen but eventually gravitated toward the Panthers.[42]

When Huey Newton and Bobby Seale founded the Black Panther Party, they turned to an Asian American to obtain the first of the weapons that would eventually make them famous. As Seale recalls in his memoir, *Seize the Time:*

> Late in November 1966, we went to a Third World brother we knew, a Japanese radical cat. He had guns for a motherfucker: .357 Magnums, 22's, 9mm's, what have you. We told him that we wanted these guns to begin to institutionalize and let black people know that we have to defend ourselves as Malcolm X said we must. . . . So he gave us an M-1 and a 9mm.[43]

The "Japanese radical" was actually a Japanese American named Richard Aoki who had grown up in West Oakland with the families of Seale and Newton and later "hooked up with Bobby and Huey at [Merritt] College." In addition to the guns that he donated to the Panthers, Aoki later sold them a .357 Magnum and two other pistols. Aoki went on to become a field marshal of the Black Panther Party. Although he had been a radical prior to his involvement with the Panthers, working with them enabled him to see the need for racially based organizing to address the concerns and needs of Asian Americans. In 1968 he cofounded the Asian American Political Alliance (AAPA) in Berkeley while continuing to report back to the Black Panthers on AAPA's progress.[44]

Steve Louie joined the black liberation movement in part because he could relate to discrimination in personal terms. In 1960, his Chinese American family had been unable to purchase a home in La Canada, a wealthy suburb of Los Angeles. Convinced that he "had more in common with black people" than with anyone else in the United States, in 1967 Louie began volunteering at a storefront operation in Watts, where he mimeographed materials, leafleted, passed out flyers, and did other odd jobs. Although he did not fully understand the politics of the group sponsoring the storefront (which he later found out was backed by Ron Karenga's U.S. organization), Louie felt it important to aid in organizing the black community because he had personally experienced racial discrimination.[45]

Political Theater on the Street

Although Asian Americans encountered blackness socially and intellectually and through direct participation in black struggles, it was the actual performance of blackness that was critical to articulations of multiethnic Asian American racial identity. The "political theater" of rallies, marches, proclamations, and social programs—along with literary and cultural productions—produced a novel form of Asian American subjectivity by highlighting parallels between the common racialization affecting both African Americans and Asian Americans of various ethnicities.

AAPA's support for the Free Huey movement provides an excellent example of the power of performance to consolidate multiethnic ties. The movement sought Huey Newton's release from jail on charges of killing a police officer. At a large rally held to commemorate Huey's birthday, AAPA members hoisted "posters with 'Free Huey' inscribed in Mandarin, Japanese, Tagalog, and English."[46] Asian American support for Newton was not in itself surprising, for radicals of all races were influenced by the Black Panther Party as the premier vanguard organization of the late 1960s. Puerto Ricans in the Young Lords Party and Chicanos in the Brown Berets adopted the language and style of black power, the American Indian Movement was initially inspired by the Panthers, and progressive whites supported and praised them.[47] Even white socialites sought the "radical chic" of associating with Black Panthers.[48] However, adopting and adapting the ideology of black power had a particular effect for Asian Americans: it enabled them to construct Asian American identity as a new subjectivity that rejected assimilation and consolidated multiple Asian ethnicities under the rubric of race.

The significance of AAPA's participation in the Free Huey movement can thus be found in the manner in which the organization displayed its

Members of the Asian American Political Alliance participated in the Free Huey movement, supporting jailed Black Panther Party leader Huey P. Newton. Photograph courtesy of Roz Payne.

presence. Carrying posters written in Asian languages was an important statement for a group composed chiefly of native-born Asian Americans whose primary language was almost assuredly English. The posters suggested that Asian Americans' support for Newton derived from their own identities as racialized people. Furthermore, pointing to the racialization of Asian Americans drew an implicit parallel between the travails of blacks and those of Asian Americans. Finally, AAPA's posters visually represented the linguistic and ethnic diversity of the organization and of the San Francisco Bay area's Asian communities. Seeking justice for Huey Newton in this forum thus brought together Chinese, Japanese, and Filipinos as Asian Americans.

Many other Asian Americans drew inspiration from the Black Panther Party's vision of militant blackness. Steve Louie recalls that he reveled in watching the televised spectacle of the Panthers marching into the California Statehouse armed with shotguns:

> I thought that was so great! Not because I thought that they needed to go and shoot somebody, but just the attitude. They're basically saying, "Fuck you!" up in your face. We're not taking this crap anymore, we're going to defend ourselves and we're going to do it by any means necessary. . . . I just thought that kind of militance was just fantastic.[49]

Louie found inspiration not only in the Panthers' self-reliance but also in their theatrically staged performance of militance; in short, he admired their political style.

The Red Guard Party was the Asian American group most directly and heavily influenced by the Black Panthers. It consisted primarily of disaffected American-born Chinatown youth who had been the subject of "some not too secret proselytization by Panther leaders."[50] The Red Guards drew their membership from the crowd surrounding a nonprofit community agency called Legitimate Ways (Leway). Leway was founded in 1967 to provide the youth of Chinatown—who faced substandard housing, poor schools, overcrowding, and endemic poverty—with alternatives to street life and petty crime. It provided job placement assistance and recreational activities and venues, the most popular of which was a pool hall. The Leway pool hall became a gathering place for young people, often attracting crowds of up to two hundred. However, it also became a focus of police harassment.[51]

Alex Hing, minister of information for the Red Guard Party, attributes the initial connection between the Leway youth and the Panthers to

Chinese American women who were dating Panther men. When a core of about ten Leway members discussed forming an organization similar to the Black Panther Party, these "sisters" who were already "really politicized," invited the Panthers to visit Leway. Bobby Seale and David Hilliard did so in late 1967 or early 1968 and found a surprising scene: "When they went into Leway, it was like a Black thing that they saw pretty much. The music that was played out of Leway was jazz, soul music, that was the kind [of] ambience it had. People wore dark clothes, field jackets, sunglasses in the middle of the night, shooting pool, smoking cigarettes."[52] The music at Leway echoed the preference of most Asian American urban youth of the time, who primarily grooved to rhythm and blues and soul music rather than rock and roll, which tended to be associated with whites, hippies, and college students.

The Panthers urged the radical core of Leway to build a revolutionary organization and invited them to weekly study sessions on revolutionary theory held at the Panthers' San Francisco headquarters on Fillmore Street, at their national headquarters in Oakland, and at Eldridge Cleaver's house. This core group returned to Leway armed with an ideological framework derived from reading Mao Tse-Tung, Frantz Fanon, Che Guevara, and Fidel Castro and began recruiting members. While forming, the new group stayed underground for several months and "took pretty much [their] directions from the Panthers."[53] Bobby Seale even named the new organization. While the Leway group wanted to call themselves the Red Dragons, in the manner of a street gang, Seale appreciated the value of the "Red Guard Party"—named after Mao's youth brigade—as a "more political" and provocative name.[54]

The influence of the Panthers on the Red Guard Party was unmistakable. The Red Guards adopted the militant rhetoric and style of their mentors across the Bay. They wore berets and armbands at rallies; called police "pigs" and whites "honkies"; used slogans like "All Power to the People" and "Fuck the Pigs"; and appointed "ministers" of defense and information à la the Panthers.[55] The *Red Guard Community Newspaper* publicized numerous incidents demonstrating the "brutal harassment" of Chinatown residents by "the racist pig structure."[56] The Red Guards' attention to police harassment belied the idyllic image of a quaint Chinatown and instead cast Chinatown as a ghetto under siege from "pigs." In focusing on police brutality, the Red Guards reproduced one of the Panthers' most successful strategies. At the Panthers' behest, the Red Guards also instituted a Free Breakfast program for Chinatown kids.[57]

The Red Guard Party adopted its 10 Point Program explicitly from the Panthers' program, even borrowing its "What We Want, What We Believe" format.[58] Indeed, many of the Red Guard points echo verbatim points from the Black Panther program, simply substituting the word "yellow" for "black" throughout. The main points of the Red Guard program that follow the Black Panther program include demands for "freedom" for "Yellow people," decent housing, education, exemption from military service, an end to police brutality, release of all "Yellow men" from prisons and jails, trial by jury of peers from the "Yellow communities" for every "Yellow defendant," and full employment.[59]

The translation of "black" to "yellow" in the program was highly significant for two reasons. First, it suggested a racial parallel between Asian Americans and African Americans by locating Asian Americans within a paradigm focusing on power and self-determination. It argued that racial oppression was a constitutive feature of American society and that Asians, like blacks, were racialized subjects. Second, it signaled that Asians of all ethnicities shared this relationship of subordination. Rather than demanding freedom only for Chinese or Chinese Americans, the program demanded freedom for Asians of all ethnicities under the rubric of "yellow people." Re-rendering the Panthers' program in yellow thus emphasized not only the racial nature of being Asian American but also the multiethnic nature of that category as well.

Asian Americans also performed their racial radicalism by displaying "the symbols of Asian resistance to imperialism, particularly those of the Cultural Revolution—the Mao jackets, the Red Book, the slogans."[60] Red Guard rallies melded stylistic elements borrowed from the Panthers with Asian elements alluding to Red China. While the Red Guards wore berets and armbands in Panther fashion, they also donned Mao jackets and waved Chinese flags as ways to highlight their racial linkage to the Asian leader.

In retrospect, Alex Hing describes the Red Guards' rallies as "political theater." His description of an event on 4 May 1969 shows the aptness of that label. "We came in blasting the 'East is Red,' marching in," he recalls. "We had these handmade Chinese flags and these handmade Red Guard armbands. We all wore field jackets. . . . We marched in and it looked like we took over the rally but it was actually agreed upon."[61] The Red Guards had planned the rally in conjunction with Chinese foreign students who wanted to commemorate the fiftieth anniversary of the May 4th movement, but the American-born Red Guards instead wanted to emphasize the current problems of poverty and racism in Chinatown. The spectacle of the Red Guards in military attire, marching to martial music and appearing to seize control of the rally, visually displayed the militance they sought to convey.

Though obviously influenced by and indebted to the Panthers, the Red Guard Party did not represent a mindless replication of the Black Panther Party. Instead, the Red Guards sought to apply the lessons of black power to the specific needs of Asian Americans. When they found that few children were participating in their Free Breakfast program, the Red Guards turned their attention to aiding Chinatown elders, instituting a Free Sunday Brunch program. Every Sunday at 1:00 p.m., the Red Guards would provide free food to the seniors who congregated in the public gathering space of Portsmouth Square. At its peak, the Free Sunday Brunch program fed more than three hundred people per week. The Red Guards' shift in focus from schoolchildren to seniors demonstrated the application of the principles of black power to the specific needs of Chinatown, in which many elderly men lacked familial support networks because of decades of gendered immigration restrictions. Like the rallies, the brunch program can be read as a kind of performance, for it enacted the "true spirit of practicing socialism" by providing free food to those who needed it in especially public and visible ways.[62] In addition to the Free Sunday Brunch program, the Red Guards developed an array of community service programs that included a legal clinic, a childcare center, and a women's health clinic.[63]

The Red Guards also performed their radicalism by holding community events such as movie nights. They screened the film *East Is Red,* which extolled the virtues of the People's Republic of China. Although the Red Guards had planned only a single showing, the community demand was so great that they "showed it three nights in a row to a packed house."[64] The screening of this pro-Chinese movie positioned the Red Guards on the left and highlighted their presence as a political force in Chinatown. The high-profile manner in which they conducted their political, social, and cultural programs was deliberately performative and intended to draw attention to their organization.

The tenth plank of the Red Guard Party's 10 Point Program stands out as distinct from any appearing on the Black Panthers Party's program: it demanded that "the United States government recognize the People's Republic of China" and asserted, "Mao Tse-Tung is the true leader of the Chinese people: not Chiang Kai Shek."[65] Locating Mao as their ideological leader, the Red Guards "openly advocate[d] patriotism to the People's Republic of China" and studied his writings assiduously. To demonstrate their avowed communism, the Red Guards unfurled the five-starred Chinese flag at their rallies in Portsmouth Square.[66] While radicals of all races studied and admired Mao, the Red Guards related to him specifically as an Asian proponent of the worldwide movement against western imperialism.

Declaring allegiance to the People's Republic of China and support for the Black Panther Party were courageous acts in a Chinatown dominated by the Chinese Consolidated Benevolent Association (CCBA), an organization of conservative business elites with close ties to the Kuomintang (KMT, Chinese Nationalist Party).[67] The Chinese American left had nearly disappeared during the 1950s, hounded by violence, harassment, and blacklisting from the CCBA as well as by McCarthyism.[68] Thus, it was audacious of the Red Guards to unfurl the five-starred Chinese flag in 1969, for such an act invited serious and possibly violent repercussions. By openly performing their radicalism, the Red Guards (who advocated armed self-defense) presented a countervailing force to the KMT and its allies. In fact, the foreign students who cosponsored the rally on 4 May 1969 invited the Red Guards to participate because they could provide a security force to prevent a feared KMT attempt to shut down the event.[69] According to Alex Hing and Harvey Dong, the major impact of these performances of Asian American radicalism was that they "opened up Chinatown to politics" by loosening the "KMT's grip."[70]

Although the Panthers clearly provided inspiration and guidance to the Red Guards, they did not create Asian American radicalism de novo. Before joining the Black Panthers, Richard Aoki had developed an oppositional stance to the war in Viet Nam during his service in the army and after his discharge had participated on the Vietnam Day Committee.[71] Similarly, Alex Hing was no political naïf. By the time he arrived at the Leway pool hall he had already racked up significant encounters with the new left, including participating in Stop the Draft Week and demonstrating for free speech at San Francisco City College. Eventually he went "back to Chinatown" to "hang out with my old gang, my old crowd and to try to politicize them." At Leway, however, he discovered that some of the people there (particularly the "sisters" who had been associating with Panthers) were already "miles ahead" of him politically.[72] Hence, although the Panthers' influence on the Leway youth is undeniable, a core of Asian Americans had already begun to radicalize and merely needed a framework within which to articulate their discontent with society.

"A Yellow Minstrel Show"?

Asian Americans' performing blackness raises the fascinating possibility of yellow minstrelsy. Like the Irish of the nineteenth century, who David Roediger argues had sought to resolve their ambivalent relationship to whiteness in part through practicing blackface minstrelsy, Asian Americans of the 1960s suffered from discrimination expressed in racial terms yet occupied a higher socioeconomic position than did blacks.[73] Furthermore, the Red Guards and Chin clearly explored Asian American identity by "playing in the dark."[74] Finally, they invested black male bodies with divergent types of potency: political, for the Red Guards, versus sexual, for Chin.

Frank Chin charged that the Red Guard Party's performances of blackness constituted "a yellow minstrel show." For him, it was the inauthenticity of the Red Guard Party's Panther-inspired rap of "brothers and sisters," "power to the people," and "fight the pig" that marked the Red Guards as minstrels. While acknowledging that blackness provided a lens through which to perceive the racial positioning of "yellows," Chin distinguished between the experiences of Asian Americans and those of African Americans: "We started talking about the sisters in the street and the brothers in the joint. I'd been in the joint and I didn't see any yellows there. I didn't see so many of our sisters walking the streets. That wasn't our thing."[75] Chin's comment reflects a suspicion of Asian American radicals who overly romanticized the revolutionary potential of the lumpen, a hallmark of Panther ideology.

While charging the Red Guards with inauthentic performances of blackness, Chin specifically denies that his characters in *The Chickencoop Chinaman* practice minstrelsy. Lee, the main woman in the play, accuses Tam and Kenji of deriding blacks by the way they walk and talk.[76] Kenji earned the nickname "Blackjap Kenji" during high school in postwar Oakland because of his full-fledged adoption of black style, fashion, and language. As an adult, he continues to identify with blacks, saying, "I live with 'em, I talk like 'em, I dress . . . maybe even eat what they eat." Although he is a dentist, he lives in the Oakland section of Pittsburgh, "right in the heart of the black ghetto," because it feels "just like home."[77] Like Kenji, Tam adopts black speech patterns to the extent that when Charley Popcorn first meets Tam, he cannot believe that the black-sounding voice he heard on the telephone belongs to the Chinese American standing before him.[78] Tam and Kenji deny being minstrels, because their performances express an identity that feels genuine and appropriate to them. "Maybe we act black," Kenji insists, "but it's not fake."[79]

Chin thus distinguished between a generative adoption of blackness—which highlighted Asian Americans as a racialized group, spoke directly to conditions in Asian American communities, and emerged from organic relations between Asian Americans and blacks—and a nongenerative, vulgar, and overly romantic imitation of blackness. The critical distinction for Chin was *political*. The Red Guard Party's rap constituted yellow minstrelsy for Chin because he rejected its emphasis on the Panthers' version of revolutionary nationalism as a way to "organize" and "get together."[80]

Asian American performances of blackness in the 1960s can be seen in contrast to the earlier minstrel performances of probationary whites in the mid-nineteenth to early twentieth centuries, when blackface provided a means by which the Irish could earn the "wages of whiteness" and Jews could establish a "conjunction between blackface and Americanization" in motion pictures.[81] If the essence of minstrelsy was the performance of blackness by whites and soon-to-be whites in order to partake in while simultaneously disavowing the pleasures thought to reside in unrestrained blackness, one could argue that Asian American performances of blackness did not constitute minstrelsy. Asian Americans fit only half of Eric Lott's definition of blackface minstrelsy as ambivalent—both desirous and anxious.[82] Covetous of black radicalism and masculinity but not fearful of being stained by blackness, they sought to connect Asian Americans to African Americans. The Red Guards sought political unity with blacks through radicalism, and in *The Chickencoop Chinaman* Chin covets the supposed (indeed, stereotypical) virility of black men, but neither the Red Guards nor Chin distanced Asian Americans from blacks. Rather than pursuing whiteness, these performances were intended to locate Asian Americans as a racialized group alongside blacks. The Red Guards and Chin argued that Asian Americans should share an affinity with African Americans based on their common subjugated racial position and that Asian Americans should consider the problems and possibilities—first explored by blacks—involved in mobilizing around a racial identity. Their performances of blackness thus signaled an explicit rejection of rather than an assimilation into whiteness.

Asian American mimesis was neither minstrelsy nor parody. Instead, following Homi Bhabha's suggestion that mimicry is always ambivalent,

東
FREE
HUEY

YELLOW
PERIL
SUPPORTS
BLACK
POWER

Supporting Black Power enabled Asian Americans to conceptualize themselves as racialized subjects as well. Photograph courtesy of Roz Payne.

I argue that these performances of blackness produced a "subject of difference" that was "almost the same, but not quite."[83] Rather than reproducing blackness, they constructed a new form of Asian American subjectivity, one organized around racial commonality among Asians.

Blackness and Asian American Masculinity

Both the Red Guard Party and Frank Chin enacted performances that articulated a black-inspired vision of Asian American masculinity as a form of resistance to racism. But whereas the Red Guards admired the radical politics enacted by black men, Chin sought the sexual potency that they embodied.

As Tracye Matthews has argued, the Panthers' early actions and statements created a "self-consciously masculine, 'lumpen' public identity for the Party" that equated resisting racism with black men's regaining their masculinity.[84] Over time, however, women in the Black Panther Party became increasingly visible, not only in the rank and file but also in leadership positions. Eldridge Cleaver's 1969 repudiation of "male chauvinism" in his statement of support for Erica Huggins reflected a new official ideology that sought the "liberation of women."[85] Of course, this shift was hardly seamless, for women in the party continued to struggle with sexism and barriers to leadership.[86]

The Red Guard's initial adoption of the Panthers' style and strategies reflected the Black Panthers' first phase of hypermasculinity in several ways. Donning berets and armbands and marching into rallies in formation cast the Guards as a paramilitary organization. Using confrontational language and terminology such as "pigs" and "honkies" also demonstrated a certain swaggering machismo. Finally, calling attention to police brutality as a main concern not only replicated a key Panther strategy but also framed the problems of Chinatown in primarily male-centered ways.

Although performances of masculinity were key to the Red Guard Party's initial phase, some evidence points to an uneven evolution in the gender ideologies and practices of its members. When the Red Guard Party disbanded in 1971, one faction merged with I Wor Kuen, a radical group based in New York City, to form National I Wor Kuen (IWK).[87] IWK explicitly advocated equality for women: its "12 Point Program and Platform" included a plank that demanded "an end to male chauvinism and sexual exploitation" and declared unequivocally, "Sisters and brothers are equals fighting for our people."[88] Women such as Carmen Chow played prominent, perhaps even preeminent, roles as leaders.[89] Furthermore, IWK (along with other Asian American organizations including Wei Min She) struggled for higher wages, better working conditions, and unionization for female garment workers and stressed the necessity of women's liberation as integral to national liberation.[90] Finally, IWK repudiated the Red Guards' prior "ultra-military line"—which advocated "armed struggle" and "violence"—as "narrow and incorrect" to the extent that it neglected to build class consciousness among workers.[91]

This shift in rhetorical focus from militarism to community organization indicates a reordering of the archetypal roles within the Red Guard Party–IWK imaginary. The bad-ass Chinatown cat, a role that could be played only by a man, was eclipsed by the dedicated community worker, which a woman could play just as well as a man. Thus, the transformation from the Red Guard Party (hypermasculine, militarist, male-led) to IWK (egalitarian in principle, vanguardist, female-led) suggests that the ideologies and practices of gender among Asian American revolutionaries were contested and dynamic.

Although the Red Guards initially performed masculinist blackness to express their political radicalism, Frank Chin turned to black masculinity to recover the lost virility of Asian American men. *The Chickencoop Chinaman* has been the subject of extensive literary criticism.[92] But remarkably little attention has been paid to its racial dynamics, and literary critics have generally failed to properly historicize the play as a product of the black power period. Reading the play within this context opens it to interpretations of its delicate intertwining of race, gender, and sexuality.

Finding Asian American masculinity lacking, the play's protagonists, Tam and Kenji, turn toward black men as role models. In particular, they idolize a boxing champion named Ovaltine Jack Dancer. Chin links Asian American men to black men specifically through their penises. At one point, Tam and Kenji fondly remember how they had once been driving with Ovaltine when all three of them stepped outside the car and began "pissing in the bushes." Amid this reflection, Kenji recalls the previous time he had urinated with a black man. While visiting New Orleans, he couldn't decide whether to use the segregated white or black facilities. A "black dishwasher," seeing his "plight," guided him to the black restroom, and they stood together pissing into adjacent urinals.[93] The dishwasher resolved Asian American racial indeterminacy by directing Kenji away from whiteness and toward blackness.[94]

Later, when Lee, the only Asian American woman in the play, insists that she is "just one of the boys," Kenji facetiously suggests that she "go out by the car and piss in the bushes."[95] Lee's inability to do so further emphasizes the phallic link between Tam and Kenji and the various African American men. Furthermore, Lee, who is only part Chinese and can pass for white, is thus granted only partial status as an Asian American.

Tam initially travels to Pittsburgh to track down Charley Popcorn, whom the boxer Ovaltine claims as his father, in order to make a movie exploring how this "mighty Daddy" made his son into a great fighter.[96] Ovaltine maintains that he was inspired to be a fighter when he saw his father's "mighty back ripplin [sic] with muscles" and covered with "whiplash scars." According to this genealogy, Ovaltine derived his own masculinity from his father's manliness, which was stymied by racial oppression, for even Popcorn's rippling muscles had not exempted him from the Jim Crow humiliation of whipping. Ovaltine goes on to assert that as an adolescent he had physically beaten a white boy, an act that symbolically redressed his father's degradation. Fearing the consequences, Ovaltine and Popcorn had fled in their automobile. When clear of danger, they had stopped, stepped out of the car, and stood "pissin [sic] by the roadside."[97] By partaking in the ceremonial urination, Popcorn had bestowed upon Ovaltine his masculinity—signified by his phallus and redeemed by his son's transgressive resistance—and Ovaltine does likewise with Tam and Kenji. Popcorn begets Ovaltine. Ovaltine begets Tam and Kenji. Masculinity and racial pride flow from the Adamic black father to his figurative Asian American sons.

This tidy story of masculine descent disintegrates almost immediately. Upon hearing Tam relate Ovaltine's story, Popcorn first denies that he is Ovaltine's father, then pulls up his shirt to reveal a smooth, scarless back.[98] Charley Popcorn, bearing no whiplash marks and being "nobody's father," fails to be the virile progenitor Tam has been seeking.[99] The revelation that Ovaltine's past is fictitious suggests Chin's ambivalence toward Asian American romanticization of blackness. Though he acknowledges that performances of blackness played an instrumental role in galvanizing Asian Americans' considerations of their racial positioning, Chin indicates that blind imitation will ultimately prove insufficient. Tam and Kenji begin by performing blackness to recuperate their masculinity but ultimately find blackness an unsatisfactory model for Asian American identity.

His dreams of masculine descent from blackness crushed, Tam turns to Asian American history as a source of manly endeavors. Earlier, Lee had expressed disapproval of people's trying to "make it on the backs of blacks,"[100] a metaphor that Chin enacts literally. In a soliloquy between scenes, Tam sits astride Popcorn's back as he recalls the day his white wife left him, a story emphasizing his emasculation at the hands of a white woman. He concludes with the Chickencoop Chinaman's lament, "Buck Buck Bagaw," the phrase recalling Chinese American male impotence.[101] At his lowest point, weak and humiliated by a white woman, Tam relies on a black man to hold him up. However, in the next scene the men reverse positions: Tam hoists Popcorn onto his back. As he carries Popcorn upstairs, Tam shouts, "We built the fuckin [sic] railroad. Moved a whole Sierra Nevada over."[102] This reversal signals Chin's departure from the model of black masculinity and a turn—expressed more fully in later works—toward excavating Asian American heroism in historical acts like that of building the railroad.[103]

In the play's final scene, Kenji announces that he and Lee are expecting a baby.[104] Impending fatherhood marks the end of his impotence, which is achieved only through establishing a phallic connection to black men, first in New Orleans with the dishwasher and later on the roadside beside Ovaltine. In *The Chickencoop Chinaman*, Asian American men regain their masculinity by taking hold of their phalluses alongside black men doing similarly.

Performances of black masculinity by the Red Guard Party and Frank Chin did not exhaust the range of possibilities for Asian American subjectivities. Instead, their late 1960s versions of Asian American power, which tended to marginalize women and homosexuals, were greatly contested. Women in the Asian American movement commonly confronted sexism within organizations and personal relationships. Like their sisters in the other segments of the new left, some Asian American women were relegated to menial tasks, struggled to be heard on matters of ideology and strategy, and faced opposition when they sought leadership positions.[105] Asian American women confronted men who sought control over the sexuality of "their" women and saw them simply as "legit lay[s] for the revolutionary" men.[106] But the Asian American women's movement was not separatist; instead it sought to make women's liberation central to the larger Asian American movement.[107] Indeed, the Asian American women's and antiwar movements opened new spaces for Asian American women to develop "sisterhood" with each other and to develop leadership skills.[108] Women like Pat Sumi, Evelyn Yoshimura, Carmen Chow, and Wilma Chan performed visible, key leadership roles within the Asian American movement.[109]

During the early 1970s, the gender ideologies and practices of the Asian American left underwent dramatic contestation. *Gidra,* the premier movement periodical, published a special issue on women and men in 1972. IWK and its chief rival, Wei Min She, organized female sweatshop workers in 1974–75.[110] By 1975, declarations linking women's oppression to U.S. imperialism and capitalism were obligatory. However, these changes in the Asian American left were not mirrored by Frank Chin, whose convictions about gender and sexuality remained steadfast.

Despite their divergent politics, in the late 1960s and early 1970s, both the Red Guard Party and Frank Chin performed blackness as a way to conceptualize Asian American identity, resist assimilation, and build multiethnic solidarity. Their racial politics stood in stark contrast to the liberal assimilationism of S. I. Hayakawa, which sought to alleviate racial discrimination against Asian Americans through assimilation and allying with whites. The Red Guards and Chin desired instead to ally Asian Americans with African Americans and with each other.

Four

"Are We Not Also Asians?"
Building Solidarity through
Opposition to the Viet Nam War

On 12 May 1972, the newly formed Bay Area Asian Coalition Against the War (BAACAW) announced its presence with a rally at Portsmouth Square in San Francisco. Unlike the Chinese American–dominated Red Guard Party rally held at the same location three years earlier, this gathering was multiethnic; rather than unveiling programs for Chinatown, this rally called for Asian Americans of all ethnicities and nationalities to oppose the killing of fellow Asians in Viet Nam. The five hundred people in attendance heard Chinese, Japanese, Filipino, and Vietnamese speakers condemn "the imperialistic, racist, genocidal nature of the war" and express support for the 7 Point Peace Program proposed by the Provisional Revolutionary Government of the Republic of South Viet Nam. United under the slogan "One Struggle, Many Fronts," BAACAW advocated opposition to U.S. imperialism both at home and abroad, and it connected the oppression of Asians in the United States to the prosecution of the war in Viet Nam.[1]

Like BAACAW, Melvyn Escueta argued that Asian Americans should oppose the Viet Nam war as anti-Asian. His 1975 play *Honey Bucket* has been called "one of the most successful and significant plays in Asian American theatre history."[2] It was the first Asian American play to tackle the war and remains the only one written by a veteran. *Honey Bucket* features a Filipino American veteran, Andy Bonifacio, who is guilt-ridden for having killed his fellow Asians in Viet Nam. Although he had joined the Marines as a gung-ho cold warrior, Andy has come to identify with the Vietnamese people as subjects of the same U.S. imperialism that colonized the Philippines and oppresses and exploits Asians in the United States. Understanding the war in terms of U.S. imperialism led Asian Americans like Escueta and members of BAACAW to declare racial commonality with the Vietnamese people, build multiethnic racial solidarity among Asians in the United States, and mark Asian American distinctiveness from the mainstream antiwar movement.

Opposition to the war in Viet Nam drew together a wide array of organizations and individuals whose diverse ideologies included pacifism, liberalism, cultural nationalism, and Marxism-Leninism.[3] While the mainstream antiwar movement was predominantly white, the left segment included African Americans, Asian Americans, Latinos, and Native Americans along with whites. Leftists opposed the war on the basis of a racial and economic analysis undergirded by three interlocking frameworks. First, they viewed the war as an imperialist effort by the United States to further its geopolitical dominance through conquest. Second, they decried the war as racist in that it killed disproportionate numbers of nonwhite American soldiers. And finally, they identified with the Vietnamese people as oppressed by U.S. power. Stokely Carmichael's characterization of the draft as "white people sending black people to make war on yellow people in order to defend the land they stole from red people" captured all three of these sentiments, for it made an analogy between the war and the invasion of North America, noted the lopsided involvement of black soldiers, and implied sympathy between the "black" and "red" people of the United States and the "yellow people" of Viet Nam.[4] Similarly, Huey Newton explicitly voiced the Black Panthers' support for "the self-defense of the Vietnamese people" because he believed that the people of Viet Nam shared a position of subjugation with people of color in the United States.[5]

Elizabeth "Betita" Martínez, a Chicana journalist and activist who traveled to North Viet Nam in 1970, used the language of the Chicano movement to describe the Vietnamese as "campesinos," or peasants, as a way to emphasize their similarity to the rural New Mexico readers of her newspaper, *El Grito del Norte*. The paper published three pairs of photographs juxtaposing Vietnamese and New Mexicans: smiling children, Vietnamese with their water buffalo and New Mexicans with their horses, and Vietnamese and New Mexican women in "outdoor, rudimentary" kitchens with their "long dark hair tied back."[6] On 29 August 1970, some thirty thousand Chicanos gathered at the Chicano Moratorium in Los Angeles, shouting slogans such as "Chale no! We won't go!"[7] Protesters linked the war in the jungle to the war in the barrio. The Brown Beret newspaper *La Causa* charged, "The Vietnam War is the ultimate weapon of genocide of non-white people."[8]

While Asian American radicals protested against the war along with their white, black, brown, and red comrades, doing so had the singular effect of strengthening their own multiethnic racial identity. Asian Americans were uniquely positioned by the war in Viet Nam, for unlike every other racial group, they were conflated with the enemy because they bore faces that looked like those of the enemy (at least according to the racial order in place in the mid- to late twentieth-century United States). The dehumanization of Southeast Asians—who were portrayed variously as suicidal fanatics, premodern primitives, cowardly ingrates, and hypersexual prostitutes—directly affected the experiences of Asian Americans in the military and structured Asian American antiwar discourses. Asian Americans' understanding of U.S. Asians as racialized people, on the one hand, and their horror at the genocide of Vietnamese people, on the other, reinforced each other dialectically. One Japanese American veteran remembered his moment of epiphany: "I saw how Whites were treating the Vietnamese, calling them Gooks, running them over with their trucks. I figured I am a Gook also."[9] Relating to the Vietnamese people as fellow Asians helped to construct a multiethnic Asian American antiwar movement that included Chinese, Japanese, and Filipino Americans working in concert with Vietnamese émigrés in the United States.[10]

The central feature of Asian American antiwar discourse was an understanding of the war as yet another instance of U.S. imperialism in Asia, prior examples of which included the colonization of the Philippines, the atomic bombings of Hiroshima and Nagasaki, the occupation of Okinawa, and the Korean War. Articulating racial commonality between Vietnamese people and Asian ethnics in the United States connected the prosecution of the war in Southeast Asia to the exploitation and oppression of Asians in the United States as dual effects of U.S. imperialism. Deploying this understanding of Asian commonality strengthened multiethnic solidarity among Asian Americans. Furthermore, understanding the war not just as imperialist but specifically as anti-Asian distinguished Asian Americans from the larger antiwar movement.

Asian Americans both fought the war and opposed it. More than

Asian American antiwar activists expressed particular revulsion at indiscriminate killing of their fellow Asians in Viet Nam. This banner, carried through New York City in 1971, decried the My Lai massacre, in which more than three hundred unarmed civilians had been murdered by U.S. soldiers in March 1968. Photograph by Bob Hsiang; copyright 2008.

88,000 Asian Pacific Islander Americans served in the military during the Viet Nam era.[11] Moreover, estimates place approximately 34,600 Asian or Pacific Americans in the Viet Nam theater of operations, and at least 250 Asian or Pacific Islander names appear on the wall of the Vietnam Veterans Memorial.[12] Asian Americans also actively participated in the antiwar movement across the nation. Asian contingents marched in many of the largest events, including the 24 April 1971 mobilization in San Francisco and the 20 January 1973 Inaugural Day demonstrations in Washington, D.C. BAACAW organized numerous antiwar activities in 1972 and 1973, and the progressive groups Asian American Political Alliance (AAPA) and Asian Americans for Action, along with the explicitly communist groups I Wor Kuen and Wei Min She, made opposition to the war central to their programs. Two Asian Americans participated in the Winter Soldier Investigation sponsored by Vietnam Veterans Against the War in Detroit in early 1971. Lance Corporal Scott Shimabukuro served as a panelist in a session examining racism in the military and was joined by Mike Nakayamo in a discussion of the experiences of "Third World" soldiers.[13]

Despite their presence in both the war and the antiwar movement, however, Asian Americans are largely absent from historiographical, journalistic, and literary depictions of the era. As Renny Christopher notes, "Ethnocentrism and nationalism have marked U.S. discourse about the war in Viet Nam," ensuring that both contemporary and post facto American constructions of the war commonly represent it as a conflict of the United States against itself, thus ignoring Vietnamese perspectives and the war's impact on Vietnamese people.[14] The ethnocentric amnesia that Christopher describes has similarly excised Asian Americans from memories of the war and antiwar resistance.[15]

Asian American invisibility contrasts with the recognition in the war literature of the importance of blacks and Latinos. Historians such as Richard Moser stress the salience of race to soldiers of color, citing instances of resistance by black and Latino soldiers motivated by antiracism, including organizing antiwar groups, refusing combat orders, and "fragging" particularly racist or incompetent officers in the field. Furthermore, they note that black soldiers bonded as "bloods" or "brothers" and Latinos as "la raza."[16] Two collections of veterans' oral histories, Wallace Terry's *Bloods* and Charley Trujillo's *Soldados,* have attained canonical status within the Viet Nam corpus, and the literature on African American and Latino experiences of the war and resistance is healthy and growing.[17]

The Asian American Antiwar Line

Asian Americans mobilized performances that displayed their affinity with the Vietnamese as fellow Asians both in the theater of the streets and in formally staged theatrical productions. BAACAW was probably the largest and most prominent Asian American antiwar organization. Though short-lived, it mobilized hundreds of Asian Americans in antiwar activities, including demonstrations, marches, study groups, educational efforts, and fundraising drives. Formed in May 1972 in response to the bombing of Hanoi and the mining of Haiphong Harbor, BAACAW consisted of seven regional chapters. Though the regionals were somewhat autonomous, according to Coordinating Committee chairman Nelson Nagai, BAACAW was highly organized, holding biweekly ninety-minute meetings of the Coordinating Committee at which each regional would submit detailed reports and action plans.[18] It drew from a wide range of the Asian American left, including staffers from the San Francisco–based radical newspaper *Rodan,* student leaders in Asian American student unions, members of I Wor Kuen and the Asian Community Center (associated with Wei

Min She), activists involved in the I-Hotel struggle, the J-Town Collective and Japanese Community Youth Center, and so on. Because it was comprised of people with various left-of-center political tendencies, it organized around two "principles of unity": opposition to the Nixon Administration and support for the Provisional Revolutionary Government's 7-Point Peace Program of July 1971.[19] BAACAW functioned as an umbrella organization. It coordinated antiwar activities—including demonstrations, study groups, fundraising drives, and teach-ins—among Asian Americans across the region, provided speakers, and assembled and disseminated antiwar printed materials and films.

Although Melvyn Escueta was not a member of BAACAW, his play *Honey Bucket* similarly argues that the war unjustly harmed fellow Asians. A two-act play set in San Francisco in 1973, *Honey Bucket* narrates the story of Andy Bonifacio's dawning Asian American racial consciousness as he reflects on his experiences in Viet Nam. Failing college, his marriage falling apart, and descending into madness, Andy is clearly a man in crisis. Throughout the play he interacts with the ghosts of his buddies from Viet Nam, reminiscing, laughing, arguing, and reliving combat. Frank Abe, who garnered praise for his "convincing performance" in the lead role of Andy,[20] was more experienced than most of the crowd involved with the play. A Sansei (third-generation Japanese American), he had trained in drama at the University of California–Santa Cruz and the American Conservatory Theater and had already appeared on television in *Farewell to Manzanar*.[21] In trying to puzzle out Andy's emotions and motivations, Abe mused that Andy "creates the play, the stage, and the soldiers" in "his mind," and "he brings the soldiers back to satisfy his need for punishment and atonement."[22] Indeed, the play takes place primarily in Andy's head. Although Andy and the audience can see and hear the ghosts, his wife and parents are altogether unaware of them. In contrast, Andy never looks at his wife and parents; it is as if they are the invisible specters. Thus, Andy's interior life with the ghosts feels more real than his conversations with his wife and parents, who seem intrusive and out of place by comparison.

Honey Bucket was developed by Escueta in the Asian American Theater Workshop (AATW) and produced by AATW in 1976. AATW, cofounded by Frank Chin in 1975, sought to generate an authentic Asian American theater by developing acting and writing talent—a sort of self-determination in the theatrical realm. Although many scholars have noted tensions between Chin's cultural nationalism and the radicalism of the Asian American political left, his nurturing of *Honey Bucket* demonstrates the extent to which Asian Americans of varying political stripes found common ground in opposing the war. The play was not only the testimony of the Viet Nam veteran Escueta but, as a product of extensive revision in AATW, it was also a representation mediated by the Asian American discourse on the war. In 1976, Chin selected *Honey Bucket* to open AATW's new stage in the Richmond District of San Francisco in a production that he directed himself.[23]

Born in 1945 in the Philippines and raised in San Francisco, Mel Escueta was, as Chin called him, "an unlikely playwright." Gung-ho to fight communism, he enlisted in the Marines, served in Viet Nam in 1966 and 1967, and spent a total of "five years, eleven months, and 23 days" in the Corps. Upon returning to San Francisco, Escueta did not join the Asian American movement but instead felt alienated by the hostility of antiwar protesters, one of whom gave him "the finger" while he was attending Easter mass in uniform with his family. He had dropped out of college and was working as a mail carrier when he delivered an announcement of AATW's training program. Intrigued, he stopped in at the workshop despite having no real interest in acting, writing, or the technical side of theater. AATW clearly met a need for Escueta; he began taking acting classes and eventually became an instructor in AATW's Script Development Program and a member of its board of directors. Although he had begun to ponder questions about the war much earlier, AATW gave him a forum in which to crystallize his thoughts as he wrote and revised. As he recalled, "It took six years for the questions to come and for me to start answering them," but "nothing made sense until I got to AATW."[24]

Honey Bucket began as a short story that Escueta wrote for a creative writing class at City College of San Francisco; before it was produced, however, it underwent a year and a half of rewriting and polishing in AATW rehearsal workshops and conversations with Chin "in restaurants, walking to restaurants, and walking from restaurants."[25] The play was originally scheduled to run for four weeks in October 1976, but a strong audience response extended its run for two additional weeks. It garnered nearly $2,200 in ticket revenue in October alone, more than recouping its budgeted expenditures of only $1,700.[26]

Recognizing Fellow Asians

For Asian Americans, identifying with Vietnamese people was a significant way in which they rejected assimilation and strengthened their imaginary ties to Asia.[27] To recognize the Vietnamese as fellow Asians was to locate oneself as a subject of a racial regime that acted upon Asians in the United States and Asians in Asia in parallel ways. The Asian American antiwar movement articulated Asian Americans' racial commonality with Vietnamese people in two distinctly gendered ways: identification based on the experiences of male soldiers and identification by women.

Asian Americans in the U.S. military often experienced what I term "common racialization," that is, being identified with the enemy because of their race. This common racialization was performed by non-Asian U.S. officers and enlisted men, Vietnamese people, and Asian American soldiers themselves. Asian American veterans frequently recall that they were visually equated with the enemy, beginning in basic training. At the Winter Soldier Investigation of Vietnam Veterans Against the War, Scott Shimabukuro testified that his first experience as a Marine was stepping off the bus at boot camp and having his drill instructor exclaim, "Oh, we have a gook here today in our platoon." Throughout basic training, instructors pointed to Shimabukuro, saying, "He [the Viet Cong] looks just like that, right there."[28] Mike Nakayamo similarly testified that he was called "Ho Chi Minh" as soon as he got off the bus and referred to as a "Jap" and a "gook" throughout basic training.[29] Other veterans corroborate the reports of the Winter Soldier witnesses. Larry Silvestre was called racist names including "gook" all through boot camp.[30] G. Akihito Maehara was singled out by his Marine Corps drill instructor, who told the entire unit, "This is what the enemy looks like! We kill people who look like him." From then on, Maehara was referred to using racial terms: "a friendly gook, Charlie Chan's cousin, Slant Eye, Yellow Belly and Zipper Head."[31] Similarly, "Raymond Imayama" and the only other Asian American in his unit were targeted by their drill instructor as examples of what "the Viet Cong looks like, with slanted eyes."[32] Don Mitsuo was even ordered to don loose black clothing and a conical straw hat and paraded before his platoon as an example of a "gook."[33] Ron Chinn was called a gook so often during basic training that he became simply "Private Gook." As Chinn noted, non-Asians could retain their individual identities, while he became a nameless enemy simply because of his race.[34]

Common racialization did not cease at the end of basic training. But although being labeled a "gook" was insulting on a base in the United States, it was downright dangerous "in country." Nakayamo continued to be "constantly referred to as 'gook'" in Viet Nam and frequently had his identification papers checked on base because he was "yellow."[35] Mike

Muromoto was also called a gook in Viet Nam and was very careful not to leave base alone for fear that if he lost his I.D. he would need someone to vouch for him in order to return to base.[36] Similarly, Silvestre worried that because he was an "Oriental" who looked "exactly" like a Vietnamese villager, it would be "easy to get killed" mistakenly; hence, he returned from patrols only in broad daylight and did so waving and yelling, "I'm coming in, I'm coming in!"[37] Jose Velasquez recalls having American GIs pull their guns on him for looking "just like a Viet." His sergeant ordered him to tell them who won the 1967 World Series, but Velasquez, who was not a baseball fan, could only guess, "Uhh, was it the Yankees or the Dodgers?" Fortunately, the Americans took the word of his sergeant, who vouched, "He's one of us. Don't . . . shoot him."[38] Postwar research on Asian American veterans substantiates these soldiers' stories. While just one-fifth of respondents to a 1992 study reported that their physical characteristics were equated with those of the enemy, more than half reported that they were mistaken for Vietnamese. Most tellingly, a majority believed that their ethnicity affected how they were treated by their commanding officers and fellow GIs.[39]

Vietnamese people also recognized Asian American soldiers as fellow Asians. Don Woo recalls that a group of Vietnamese children asked him, "Hey, G.I.; you same-ee, same-ee me?" to which he replied, "Yeah, I'm same-ee, same-ee you."[40] While being identified as Asians by Vietnamese people could generate goodwill, it could equally lead to hard feelings or danger. Velasquez was detained at the post exchange in Da Nang by a Vietnamese sentry who pointed at him, insisting, "He Vietnamese," and would not let Velasquez pass until his buddies raised their weapons and corrected, "No Vietnamese."[41] Fully four-fifths of Asian American veterans surveyed believed that their ethnicity affected how Vietnamese people treated them.[42]

At the 8 October 1976 premier of *Honey Bucket,* the play began with two standing figures surrounded by dangling cargo nets and wooden crates on a starkly lit stage. A woman in Vietnamese peasant garb reached out to stroke the black hair of a man clad in combat fatigues and haltingly inquired, "Same-same, Viet-me?" The protagonist, Andy Bonifacio, replied, "Filipino. Uh, Philippines." "Filotan," the woman mused, then concluded, "Same-same, Viet-me."[43] The play thus captured the experiences of many Asian American veterans in finding that Vietnamese people perceived them as co-racials. However, in the opening scene Andy rejects this assertion of commonality and seeks instead to differentiate himself by insisting that he is Filipino, not Vietnamese.

The evolution of Andy's racial consciousness constitutes a major theme of *Honey Bucket*. He initially employs the commonplace and racist GI practice of calling the Vietnamese "gooks." But his sympathies evolve as he meets them as human beings rather than faceless enemies, and through a series of encounters he eventually comes to identify with them as fellow Asians. While on patrol, Andy sees a farmer and his water buffalo and remarks, "Reminds me of the Philippines. . . . There but for the grace of God goes Grandpa and his carabao."[44] While acknowledging that the farmer may well be Viet Cong by night, Andy believes that Vietnamese peasants, like his own grandparents, should have the right to grow their crops and live in peace. On another patrol, Franklin, a white member of the squad, kills an old Vietnamese woman who, he reports, was chewing some "red crap." The old woman again reminds Andy of the Philippines, and he counters, "My grandparents chew that 'crap.' It's called betel nut."[45] Like the fictional Andy, Chinese American Marine Larry Wong found that elderly Vietnamese people reminded him of his grandparents. The sight of an old woman dressed in black, cooking rice over a fire, conjured images of his own "Grandma Wong," who had always worn black while "out at the farm in Yakima."[46]

In addition to portraying similarities between the elderly in Viet Nam and the Philippines, *Honey Bucket* inscribes Asian commonality upon the bodies of the most innocent—infants. In one scene, Andy (who is nicknamed Mug) and a buddy discuss a baby that had been killed on patrol that day:

MUG: The one with the birthmark on his ass?
GEORGE: All Asians are born with it. It's called a Mongolian birthmark.
. . .
MUG: My mother told me why all Filipinos are born with it. We're God's favorites and he gives each of us a loving slap on the "puit" (slaps George's ass) before he sends us down.[47]

The "Mongolian birthmark" is a temporary blemish that reputedly marks all Asian newborns. Although Andy believes that it marks only Filipinos, George's comment expands the scope of the birthmark to all Asians. The similarities between Vietnamese and Filipinos, from infant to elderly, and Vietnamese people's recognition of him as a fellow Asian eventually force Andy to exclaim, "Same-same, Viet-me."[48]

Because of his newfound racial understanding, Andy renounces the term "gook." In his apartment in San Francisco, he becomes enraged when he believes that his wife has used the slur, shouting, "Don't call them gooks!"[49] Likewise, Asian American soldiers often refused to apply dehumanizing racial epithets to the Vietnamese. Whereas many servicemen called the Vietnamese "gooks, slant-eyes and slopes," Mike Higashi recalls that Asian American soldiers "had more empathy in talking to them. . . . We wouldn't talk about them that way. . . . To us, they were just people." Higashi attributed Asian Americans' empathy to the fact that "we were Asian and didn't lump them in a category."[50] Furthermore, he said, "I didn't use those terms because [they] could have easily been used on me."[51]

BAACAW eagerly incorporated veterans' perspectives into its programs. An Asian American Viet Nam veteran addressed one meeting on his experience "with the racist United States Army."[52] Similarly, an announcement of a demonstration promised that a veteran would "talk about war atrocities and the contradiction he faced as an Asian forced to fight against other Asians."[53] The J-Town regional organized a meeting of Asian American veterans to discuss their military experiences. One former soldier reported, "I know now that the Vietnamese are really our courageous brothers and sisters fighting the common enemy—the U.S. government and its policies of exploitation at home, aggression abroad and in particular racism and genocide directed against all Third World people."[54] Another meeting featured a short skit by a BAACAW offshoot, Asian Vets Against the War, which portrayed "how GI's became friendly with the Vietnamese people and refused to destroy a village."[55] All of these activities reinforced the idea that Asian Americans shared an identity with the Vietnamese by virtue of their Asian commonality.

BAACAW sought to strengthen the bond between Asian Americans and the Vietnamese people through charity. For one fundraiser they produced an antiwar calendar for the year 1973, with proceeds earmarked for the Asian American Medical Supply Drive, which aimed to send medical supplies to Viet Nam. For $2.00 plus 20 cents postage, buyers received a calendar in which "photos, dates and poems of political significance to the war relate the desire for peace and the right of self-determination of the Indochinese people." The supply drive was a national effort initiated by the Los Angeles–based Asian Movement for Military Outreach, with participation from BAACAW, the New York Asian Coalition Against the War, and the Los Angeles Asian Coalition. The gift of medical supplies was intended to "demonstrate support for the Vietnamese people" and "strengthen ties of friendship between Asians in the United States and Vietnam." However, it also served the purpose of promoting a "greater unity of the Asian anti-war movement."[56] The supply drive's emphasis on racial commonality between Asian Americans and the Vietnamese thus also reinforced ties between Asian Americans of various ethnicities and regions.

The veterans' accounts and Escueta's portrayal of how participating in the war provoked internal conflict for Asian American veterans clearly foreshadowed Philip Kan Gotanda's treatment of the subject in his play, *Fish Head Soup,* in which a Japanese American character named Victor relives the war in a series of flashbacks.[57] In the first flashback, Victor's drill sergeant singles him out, ordering him to stand on a chair in front of his unit and barking, "Boys, pay close attention. This is the gook enemy. Black hair, yellow skin, slanty eyes."[58] The attention to racial markers—skin color and eye shape—in identifying "the gook enemy" make it clear that Asian Americans also counted as the enemy. In the second flashback, Victor laments that when he was hit by mortar fire, "they wouldn't pick me up, the medics. I was lying there, bleeding all over, they were picking everyone else up. I kept screaming, 'I'm an American, I'm a Japanese American, I'm not VC.' But they wouldn't pick me up. They walked right past me."[59] Finally, in a scene that haunts Victor (he flashes back to it three times), he recalls an incident in which a Vietnamese soldier spared his life:

> And this young VC is coming towards me. He's all out of control, shooting everything—Bam! Bam! Bam! Wounded GIs, dead bodies—Bam! Bam! Bam! He's totally jacked up. I see him coming towards me and I can't move, my leg . . . Bam! Bam! He hits Jackson, blows half his body away. He looks at me. Our eyes lock. He raises his gun. He's terrified. He's looking at me. His gun is aimed right at my face. He's going to shoot, he's going to blow my fucking head off . . . *(Beat)* He lowers his gun, still looking at me, staring at me, at my face. My face. He runs off. He didn't shoot me. He didn't kill me . . . *(Pause)* I am not the enemy. I am not the . . . enemy. I am not the enemy.[60]

Victor believes that the Vietnamese soldier spared him because he was Asian, as shown by his repetition of the phrase "my face." This realization, along with his sergeant's labeling him as a "gook" and the medics' assumption that he was Viet Cong, causes Victor to question the extent to which he can claim status as an American. He repeats "I am not the enemy" as a mantra to ward off his Vietnamization, trying to reassure himself that he is indeed an American. But paradoxically it also reinforces his Asian-ness by reiterating that he is not the enemy of the Vietnamese by virtue of his face.

Although *Fish Head Soup* was written well after the war ended, it clearly revisits issues critical to the Asian American antiwar movement. Gotanda had come of age during the late 1960s, and even while a high school student in Stockton had been opposed to the war.[61] At the University of California–Santa Cruz in 1969, he had "participated to a limited extent in the then newly formed Asian American Political Alliance" and shared its antiwar politics.[62] His dramatic representation of Asian American veterans' experiences—being seen as the enemy by Americans and being recognized as fellow Asians by the Vietnamese—demonstrates the extent to which veterans' narratives suffused the Asian American antiwar movement's consciousness.

Victor's conflict over whose enemy he constitutes echoes Andy Bonifacio's pain and confusion. Andy's downward spiral derives in no small part from his having been, as he says, "a gook killing gooks."[63] Even after returning to the United States, Andy is so remorseful that he cannot bring himself to discuss the war with his therapist: "I can't tell the good doctor that I was Asian killing Asian."[64] Haunted by the memories of his actions and the ghosts of his comrades, Andy drifts toward insanity, living a postwar nightmare of guilt and regret.

Psychologists who treat Asian American veterans recognize that, like the fictional Andy, many were susceptible to "race-based stress" induced by being perceived as the enemy, by witnessing the dehumanization of Asians who resembled them, and by "race-based remorse" over killing fellow Asians.[65] Nearly three-fifths of Asian American vets perceived the Vietnamese to be "very similar" or "similar" to themselves.[66] The psychic stress of killing fellow human beings is often diminished in soldiers by strategies of dehumanizing the enemy, but for Asian American soldiers who identified with the enemy on racial grounds, dehumanization was a less effective means by which to mitigate their feelings of guilt. Furthermore, the dehumanization of the Vietnamese by fellow GIs also took its toll on Asian American soldiers. Ron Chinn attributes his posttraumatic stress disorder "one hundred percent" to "being treated like garbage before I went over and then when I got there same thing. I can hear them say when I walked into the compound, 'Damn, the gook survived.'"[67] Finally, some Asian American veterans came to regret not standing up more explicitly to oppose the use of terms like "gook," which only exacerbated their postwar stress.[68]

The Asian American movement's press also portrayed racial commonality between Asian Americans and Vietnamese people. *Gidra* was the best-known and most influential newspaper of the Asian American movement, with a circulation of approximately five thousand.[69] In 1970, it reprinted an interview with a former GI named Sam Choy, who related the racism of his fellow soldiers. On his tour of duty in Viet Nam, the other GIs "started making comments about me looking like the Viet Cong." The harassment was the worst when they got back from patrol: "They started asking me where I was born, where my parents were born, if I was a Communist. They even asked me what I thought about China. They thought I could turn traitor at any time." Because his fellow soldiers didn't trust him, Choy was made a cook. Then, one day, his mess sergeant called him a "chink." Enraged, Choy threw his knife on the floor, and when he ignored orders to pick it up, the sergeant "kept yelling all kinds of remarks, like slant-eyed Chinaman, gook, chink, and he went on and on." Choy grabbed a rifle and held off the sergeant and others, and eventually the military police, even firing a couple of warning shots. Faced with the overt racial hostility of his supposed countrymen, Choy admitted, "By this time I was near the perimeter of the base and was thinking of joining the Viet Cong. At least they would trust me."[70] This tale reinforced the idea that the anti-Asian racism that fueled the war in Viet Nam also affected Asian Americans. Choy's fellow soldiers' suspicion of him exemplified the American tendency to lump together all Asians, regardless of their race or nationality. Furthermore, Choy's own belief that the Viet Cong would accept him conveyed the idea that Asian Americans should identify with the Vietnamese people because of their common experience of U.S. racism.

Also writing in *Gidra*, Viet Nam veteran Norman Nakamura argued in 1970 that many GIs in Viet Nam were "racist bullies" and cited instances of random GI violence against civilians, including women and children. He attributed GI racism to military indoctrination that encouraged the use of the epithet "gooks," which he believed cast the Vietnamese as "inferior, unhuman animals" and thus justified barbarism toward them. He also noted that Vietnamese women were subject to obscene treatment, because "many G.I.s believe that all Vietnamese women are whores."[71] Nakamura's indictment of the war concluded that the racism mobilized by the military against Vietnamese people would inevitably apply to all Asians.

Asian American women in Viet Nam confirmed Nakamura's fears. For Army nurse Lily Adams, being Asian American afforded critical insight into how GIs treated Vietnamese women. She recalls, "As far as the issue about my looking Asian, when I was in civilian clothes and walking around the compound with a guy, the other guys would just assume I was a whore." This made her "very angry," primarily because she realized that that was the way they saw all Vietnamese women.[72] Similarly, Debbie Wong remembers being taken for a prostitute because of her race: "A lot of times, because of my Oriental face, my situation was really rough. Just walking down the street I'd get derogatory comments from the GIs. They thought I was a Vietnamese bar girl—only bar girls wore Western clothes, and I was always in blue jeans."[73] Being repeatedly mistaken for prostitutes reinforced for Adams and Wong that U.S. soldiers viewed them as Asians and opened their eyes not only to the prevalence of anti-Asian racism but also to its gendered nature.

Honey Bucket vividly portrays the intertwinings of racialization and gendering and decries the war's warping effect on Asian American gender relations. In a somewhat hostile review published in *East/West* magazine, Genny Lim particularly objected to the play's treatment of women, whom she believed were present only "to be screwed."[74] Some audience members apparently concurred with Lim in finding the play's treatment of women offensive, as evidenced by a male attendee's letter to AATW defending the play against charges of "sexism."[75] To be fair, the women characters are fairly one-dimensional, and the staged production did display violence against women. In one scene, a despondent and drunk Andy turns to Loida, his Filipina ex-girlfriend, to talk about his wartime experiences—which he never discusses with his white wife, Irene. As he recounts the death of his buddy George, the ghosts emerge and scream, "Fuck the bitch! She killed George! Fucking gooks killed George!" The script's stage directions read, "Andy starts on pants. Lights out."[76] In the staged version, however, the lights stay on, and the ghosts encircle Andy as he crouches over the shrieking Loida; they rhythmically thrust themselves on the couple for several moments before the lights dim. The amplified portrayal of the rape was in keeping with director Frank Chin's penchant for ferocity. (At one rehearsal in which Chin had specified that "anything goes," an actor pulled a real switchblade to heighten the scene's intensity. Frank Abe was cut on the wrist, and although he was bleeding and wanted a break, the rehearsal continued. That night he wrote in his journal, "I want to leave the stage and just fuck it. But Frank [Chin] doesn't stop the rehearsal, so I go on.")[77] It is significant that the ghosts urge Andy to rape Loida rather than Irene, for they hold her, as an Asian, responsible for George's death. The imbrication of race and gender are clear as the ghosts inflict sexual violence on Loida as retribution for her race.

Part of *Honey Bucket*'s depiction of sexism derives from its portrayal of a macho American military culture that objectifies and devalues women, particularly Asian women, as experienced in real life by Lily Adams and Debbie Wong. Tim, a minor character who was stationed with "MAC-Vee, Saigon," attends a party at Andy and Irene's apartment and casually reveals that he had fathered and abandoned a child in Viet Nam. After meeting Loida, he remarks, "Nice woman. Nice personality. . . . Looks like the kind of person who would enjoy fine things. . . . Whether you pay it straight out or buy her dinner, pussy costs money."[78] Tim represents white soldiers for whom Vietnamese children were the disposable products of their liaisons and Vietnamese women were no more than "pussy." Though he has been flirting with the white Irene throughout the party, it is the Filipina Loida that Tim objectifies.

While decrying the sexism of GIs toward Vietnamese women, *Honey Bucket* also laments its deleterious effects on gender relations between Asian Americans. Prior to Andy's enlistment in the Marines, he and Loida had shared romantic feelings for each other. She had urged him not to enlist, but as a believer in "dominoes" he had been too eager to become "a small cog in huge war machinery" to save the world from communism. Her entreaties unsuccessful, Loida had pleaded, "Andy . . . touch me . . . make love to me."[79] The tenderness present between Andy and Loida before his tour in Viet Nam contrasts sharply with the savageness of the rape after the war, in which he engages at the urging of the ghosts. The transformation from Andy's prewar gentleness to his postwar cruelty illustrates the idea that the crude sexism spawned by the military in Viet Nam bore real consequences for Asian American women.

In addition, Andy's rape of Loida forecloses any possibility of reconciliation between them. Andy has married the white Irene over the objections of his parents. His mother, Fely, hints that she would like to see him reunite with Loida, and the tension between Fely and Irene is palpable. Irene does not keep rice stocked in the kitchen (Fely complains that Uncle

Ben's does not count), nor does she know how to cook it. In contrast, Loida feeds Andy rice and adobo and even lets him eat Filipino style with his fingers, a practice that Irene finds barbaric.[80] Loida thus represents Andy's opportunity to reconcile with his Filipino American identity. Furthermore, she holds the promise of healing, for Andy confides in her while refusing to discuss the war with Irene. Andy's brutality against Loida signifies the war's warping effect on Asian American gender relations and the necessity of overcoming this distortion in order to attain healing and closure.

The relationship between the war in Viet Nam and the sexual objectification of Asian women was a key issue for segments of the Asian American antiwar movement, just as Escueta portrayed it in *Honey Bucket*. In a *Gidra* article Evelyn Yoshimura noted that the U.S. military systematically portrayed Vietnamese women as prostitutes as a way of dehumanizing them, for if Asian women had "slanted eyes and slanted vaginas," they were "much easier to kill." Furthermore, the sexualization of Vietnamese women affected Asian American women by conditioning GIs to see all Asian women as subservient and hypersexual. Thus, Yoshimura wrote, "We as Asian American women cannot separate ourselves from our Asian counterparts. Racism against them is too often racism against us." Yoshimura ultimately found U.S. imperialism responsible for creating the interlinked stereotypes of "Suzy Wong, Madame Butterfly and gookism."[81]

As early as 1969, several Asian American groups were keenly aware of the importance of ending the type of sexism experienced by Lily Adams and Debbie Wong as a part of eradicating racism. *AAPA Newspaper* attributed sexism among Asian Americans to the legacy of a "two-fold history of oppression of women—one from the Asian homelands and the other from the United States." AAPA maintained that women were "still sexual objects" and that Asian American men's attempts to control Asian American women's sexuality had to end. Therefore, it derided as hypocritical a situation in which "a Third World brother might beg [an Asian American woman] not to let 'whitey' exploit her (let him do the job instead)!" Because AAPA saw sexism as integrally connected to racism, it refused to pit Asian American women against Asian American men, arguing, "If Asians really care about freedom, we must concern ourselves with the women's liberation struggle."[82]

Asian American women understood the liberation struggle as including Southeast Asian women. In April 1971, a delegation attended the

Indochinese Women's Conference in Vancouver (organized in part by Pat Sumi), where they met with women from Viet Nam, Laos, and Cambodia. They returned greatly inspired by the struggles these women were enduring with strength and commitment. The Asian American antiwar movement idealized, even romanticized, the figure of the courageous Vietnamese woman freedom fighter. Indeed, the image of a Vietnamese woman, often toting an assault rifle, functioned as an icon of commitment and resistance, appearing in numerous leaflets, flyers, and newspaper articles.[83] Thus, understanding Vietnamese women as fellow Asians enabled Asian American women to see their own antiwar activities in San Francisco, Los Angeles, and New York as an extension of the actions of Vietnamese women fighting in Hanoi; furthermore, this viewpoint portrayed opposition to the war as opposition to sexism.

Asian American opposition to the war not only connected racialization to sexual exploitation but also opened spaces for women to act as leaders. Although ending the war was a serious matter, participating in the antiwar movement fundamentally reordered activists' multiple senses of identity in encounters that were also playful. Pam Tau Lee recalls:

> We would go to people's houses. . . . The women are cooking the food and the men are talking. Then we get to sometimes talk, too. . . . It was really filling a gap in terms of our identity and who we were. And there was just that kind of brotherhood that was going on. And there was a sisterhood that was going on in the kitchen.[84]

The importance of that "sisterhood" in the Asian American antiwar movement cannot be overemphasized. Although Lee represents it as beginning "in the kitchen," a woman's place in the Asian American antiwar movement was also in the leadership of an organization, at the head of a march, on stage behind a microphone at a rally, and as an iconic representative of resistance.

Women participated in the Asian American antiwar movement in various capacities ranging from rank-and-file members to members of cadres to leaders. Key leaders included women such as Pat Sumi, Evelyn Yoshimura, Wilma Chan, and Carmen Chow. As I mentioned in the introduction, in 1970 Sumi, who had a long history in the new left and antiwar movements prior to her involvement in the Asian American movement, traveled with Alex Hing as part of an antiwar delegation to North Korea, Viet Nam, and China. She returned to the United States, where she traveled around the country and became highly visible for her efforts to educate Asian American communities about the war.[85] Although the Asian American antiwar movement was not perfectly egalitarian, participating in the movement opened spaces for Asian American women to exercise leadership and develop consciousness about gender as well as racial oppression.

One BAACAW fundraiser, an all-star basketball tournament, provides an excellent example of how women transformed gender practices within the Asian American antiwar movement. Because of the sport's popularity in Asian American communities, which frequently sponsor basketball leagues, the tournament was conceived of as a way to reach people who did not normally participate in antiwar activities. The plan was initially to invite male players only. However, as BAACAW chairman Nelson Nagai recalls, this choice provided a lesson in "sexism," for a struggle quickly arose and women demanded equal treatment as athletes and as members of the antiwar movement. So the tournament was revised to feature both a men's game and a women's game. Including a women's game recognized not only the importance of women in the antiwar movement but also the importance of athletics to Asian American women, many of whom played in Asian American women's leagues. The tournament brought in athletes who, though perhaps not politically active, were "the heroes of the Asian American community." Because they starred in ethnic- and region-specific leagues, the tournament was their first opportunity to play with and against each other. The composition of the tournament was therefore the product of political considerations, for it brought together players of various ethnicities (Japanese, Chinese, and Filipinos), from different regions (San Francisco, the East Bay, and San Jose), and both women and men.[86]

The tournament was conducted by the J-Town Regional on 8 July 1972 at Lincoln High School in San Francisco and raised funds to rebuild Bach Mai, a Vietnamese hospital destroyed by U.S. bombing, and also to cover BAACAW's operating expenses. It was attended by an "enthusiastic crowd" of some six hundred. A BAACAW speaker discussed the purpose of the benefit at halftime, and educational materials on the 7-Point Peace Program were distributed. After the tournament concluded, attendees took advantage of the sound system and empty gym floor by dancing until midnight. Because many attendees were community members who would not otherwise have participated in antiwar activities, the J-Town Regional deemed significant "the expressions of anti-war feelings by the wide cross section of people from the community."[87] Without the intervention of Asian American women, that cross-section would undoubtedly have been narrower.

Asian American women were not alone in being transformed by protesting the war. Just as Asian American women staked their claim to equality through their antiwar activities, Chicanas "stop[ped] making tortillas" for the movement and gained self-confidence through opposing the war. Furthermore, they built an indigenous Chicana feminism in part through identifying with Vietnamese women, who, though feminine, were fierce independent fighters.[88]

Articulating Anti-Imperialism

Beyond developing an identification with Vietnamese people as fellow Asians, both Escueta and the Asian American antiwar movement interrogated the connections between U.S. imperialism abroad and domestic racism. In *Honey Bucket*, Andy belongs to the "Bravo Co.'s Gook Squad," so named by its members because it includes "a Jap, a Chink and two Flips."[89] Initially, Andy refuses to accept the appellation "gook" and insists instead that he is fully American:

> GEORGE: You Flips have trouble identifying. Now Sandy
>   knows he's a Chink and I know I'm a Jap.
> ANDY: I'm an American.
> SANDY: We know we're gooks. I don't know about Filipinos. . . .
> GEORGE: We're Bravo Co.'s Gook Squad. All from the same
>   side of the Pacific Ocean.[90]

George and Sandy's acknowledgement that being "from the same side of the Pacific Ocean" binds them all together as indistinguishably Asian points to the legacies of migration induced by U.S. neoimperialism and the unequal relations between the United States and Asia, as discussed in chapter 1. Furthermore, by using the epithets "Jap" and "Chink" to identify themselves, they point out that American racism is what conflates them with Vietnamese people as "gooks."

Andy's Filipino American sergeant, Ed Vega, appreciates the irony of Filipino Americans' fighting for the United States in a war against "gooks." When Andy ("Mug") calls a Vietnamese farmer a "gook," Ed inquires:

> ED: Gook? . . . Do you call Pilipinos "googoos"?
> MUG: Googoos? What?

ED: Pinoys are googoos. No, you wouldn't know. You're too young.[91]

Ed's comment that Andy is "too young" to comprehend the offensiveness of the term signals the playwright's understanding of the war in its historical context. As the old-time sergeant points out, the term "gook" originated as an anti-Filipino derogation during the Filipino-American War but during the Korean and Viet Nam wars was extended into a general dehumanizing term for all Asians.[92]

Escueta further locates his anti–Viet Nam War critique within the context of western imperialism through the naming of his protagonist. Andy's full name is Andrés Bonifacio, after a famous Filipino anti-imperialist leader who had founded Katipunan, an armed independence movement that fought first against Spain, then against the United States.[93] Bonifacio is a nationalist hero in the Philippines, and Filipino American leftists considered him a "working-class hero."[94] Yet *Honey Bucket* is not a Filipino nationalist work; instead it shows how racialization has operated in parallel ways on various Asian groups to produce a multiethnic Asian American cohesion. Escueta invokes Bonifacio as an Asian anti-imperialist rather than a Filipino nationalist in order to show why Asian Americans ought to oppose the war in Viet Nam.

One critical response to *Honey Bucket* chided it precisely for its eschewal of Filipino nationalism. Writing in the *Philippine News*, community editor Ed Diokno lauded the play's portrayal of Filipino culture and "Filipino spice," claiming that the production made the smell of *bagoong* (an aromatic Filipino dish) practically palpable. However, he found that the "Filipino perspective the work was supposed to give is, actually, the perspective of any Asian who might have had to fight in that war." Diokno, writing for an ethnic-specific newspaper, was disquieted by the play's multiethnic Asian American racial politics and wanted the play to focus on Filipino exceptionality rather than Asian American solidarity. But despite his reservations, Diokno labeled *Honey Bucket* a "triumph."[95]

In contrast to Diokno, Genny Lim, writing for the Asian American periodical *East/West*, found much to criticize. She argued that the play did not explore the racism of the war sufficiently:

> Andy makes no real attempt to understand the people who he calls "gooks." . . . He and his friends are really no different from the non-Asian soldiers who went to Vietnam. Andy's consciousness begins with

his yellow skin and remains there. He is never able to make the transition from question to self-awareness and there lies his madness.[96]

Lim's review was unfair in two ways. First, Andy abandons the word "gook" after learning its origins from Ed, and afterward he uses it only to refer to himself and other Asian Americans as a gesture of solidarity with the Vietnamese. Second, the play is rife with references to the horror of Asians' committing anti-Asian violence. That indeed constitutes its central theme, so Lim's assertion that Andy is no different from non-Asian soldiers rings false. Andy's madness results not from his inability to attain "self-awareness" as an Asian (as Lim claims) but from his racial awakening, for he is guilt-ridden over having killed his fellow Asians.

Escueta went beyond expressions of sympathy for Vietnamese people to mount a critique of the war in Third World liberationist terms. When one of the ghosts ironically laments, "We wiped out entire villages for democracy . . . but, from a business point of view, it isn't too bad a war," Escueta opened space for a political economy analysis.[97] Although the play does not pursue this line of reasoning further, its implication that the war served class interests clearly connects with broader critiques such as that of Students for a Democratic Society, which focused on the benefits accrued by the military-industrial complex. Furthermore, Escueta widened the term "gook" to refer to all people of color:

> ANDY: My country 'tis of thee. Same-same, Viet-me. I was a
> gook killing gooks.
> LOIDA: You're not a gook. You're a human being. Don't let . . .
> ANDY: Anyone not white is a gook. . . .
> GEORGE: A Jap . . .
> FRANKLIN: Nigger . . .
> SANDY: Chink . . .
> ED: Googoo . . .[98]

By broadening "gook" to refer to "anyone not white," Escueta transformed it from an exclusively anti-Asian epithet to a rallying point for opposition to the war and resistance to all racism in American society. Although a more in-depth exploration of Third World liberation remains beyond the play's scope, it alludes to the ideology of anti-imperialism that motivated Asian American antiwar activists throughout the late 1960s and early 1970s.

Like Escueta, Filipino American writer Sam Tagatac connected U.S.

imperialism in the Philippines, Viet Nam, and the United States in his modernist short story "The New Anak."[99] Constructed as a pastiche of movie scenes spliced together by the onomatopoeic whirring of a projector, the story cuts back and forth between images of Pinoys in California, fighting in the Philippines during the 1898 Filipino-American War, and combat in Viet Nam. Doming, an elderly Pinoy living alone in the International Hotel in San Francisco, remembers the Philippines of his youth, replete with carabaos pulling plows. He recalls villagers silencing children with hands over mouths while fleeing from American soldiers and a young girl "baring the wounds in her chest, clear as day where the bayonet entered."[100] Doming's memories of the Filipino-American War are interwoven with the experiences of Elpidio, a "Pilipino" American soldier in Viet Nam. In a letter home, Elpidio writes that he is positioned on a bridge "frequented by . . . carabaos." Ordered to guard it with his life, he opens fire on a black-clad person crossing the bridge on a bicycle only to discover that he has torn "great wounds" in the "chest" of a "little girl, teen-ager, a woman."[101] The repeated details of carabaos and a girl with a punctured chest underline the parallels between the Philippines and Viet Nam, both of which are understood to be tropical Asian venues for U.S. imperialist wars. Underscoring this point, a "husband and wife" viewing television coverage of Viet Nam remember the Philippines as the site of "the fire and color of another Asian war" that "blue eyes" (American soldiers) "refused to leave."[102]

Beyond establishing equivalences between the Philippines and Viet Nam, Tagatac also compared the war in Viet Nam with the travails of Filipinos in the United States. The barbed wire surrounding Elpidio's position in Viet Nam echoes the barbed wire around his farm in California.[103] Furthermore, Tagatac wrote cryptically that "Nam is created" for Filipino children who "leave to seek their ancestry."[104] This comment can be understood to suggest that Filipino youth discovered their "ancestry" in Viet Nam because the modern war reinstantiated American imperialism in Asia, the 1898 version of which colonized the Philippines and led to the subsequent migration of Filipinos to the United States. By going to fight in Viet Nam, young Filipino Americans retraced their families' immigration in reverse and revisited the prior war in Asia. Their ancestry was thus intimately bound up in American imperialism. Finally, by locating Doming as a tenant of the embattled International Hotel, where, as I mentioned in chapter 1, many impoverished, formerly migrant laborers settled, Tagatac drew parallels between the American colonization of the

Philippines and attempts to evict elderly bachelors from the last remnant of San Francisco's Manilatown.

The Asian American antiwar movement took a squarely anti-imperialist stance. BAACAW opposed the war in Indochina as only the latest instance of U.S. imperialism against Asians.[105] Its newsletter proclaimed, "The war cannot be explained in any other way than in the context of U.S. imperialist aggression against the people of Indochina whose only desire is for peace and independence. Therefore, our goal is to build a solid, broad-based anti-imperialist movement of Asian people against the war in Vietnam."[106] BAACAW's anti-imperialist politics typified the position adopted by many other Asian American groups. As early as 1969, AAPA declared that it opposed the Viet Nam War, not for reasons of pacifism or because Americans were being killed, but because the Vietnamese people were "struggling for independence, democracy, peace, and neutrality" and were "resolved to drive out any imperialist forces from Viet Nam."[107] Thus, AAPA's position on the war was fundamentally founded on sympathy for the Vietnamese people in their struggle for self-determination. Indeed, anti-imperialism was one of AAPA's central tenets: An "AAPA Perspectives" column declared, "We Asian Americans oppose the imperialistic policies being pursued by the American government."[108]

Organizing against the war as an instance of anti-Asian U.S. imperialism brought together Asians of various ethnicities and strengthened racial solidarity. BAACAW was a multiethnic group comprised of "Asian students from various campuses and Asian organizations and individuals from the Chinese, Pilipino, Vietnamese and Japanese communities of the Bay Area."[109] At a meeting held on 27 May 1972 at Glide Memorial Church in San Francisco, BAACAW was structured as a collection of seven chapters or "regionals": San Jose and the Peninsula, San Francisco Student (covering San Francisco State, San Francisco City College, and the University of California Medical School), San Francisco Chinatown, Manilatown, San Francisco Japan Town, Oakland, and Berkeley.[110] The establishment of separate regionals for Chinatown, Manilatown, and Japan Town marked not only the multiethnic makeup of the organization but its explicit aim to organize in various ethnic communities.

On 29 July 1972, BAACAW sponsored a picnic in Menlo Park that was attended by two hundred people from different regionals. Under a National Liberation Front flag, gatherers enjoyed "Chinese songs of struggle by the Chinatown Progressive Association, a magic show, guerilla theater skits by members of the San Jose regional . . . , [and] a performance

Protesting the war in Viet Nam helped to strengthen multiethnic ties within the Asian American movement. The Asian American Political Alliance, members of which are shown protesting in Washington, D.C., in 1971, was an early and important organization that expressed anti-imperialist politics. Photograph by Bob Hsiang; copyright 2008.

by Taiko drummers from the Japanese community." In the afternoon, the picnic guests played games of "tug-of-anti-war" and volleyball, ran potato sack races, and threw sandbags at an effigy of President Richard Nixon.[111] It is significant that the entertainment was multiethnic: Chinese songs and Japanese taiko drumming were brought together to express attendees' solidarity with the Vietnamese people, all in the context of a good old-fashioned American picnic.

The multiethnic nature of the antiwar movement found expression in Asian Contingents—ad hoc coalitions assembled for specific occasions—that marched and rallied at numerous events across the nation. On 24 April 1971 in San Francisco, Asian Americans participated in a gathering of approximately a quarter million protesters that has been deemed "the largest antiwar demonstration ever on the West Coast."[112] At that event, an Asian Contingent comprised of Filipino, Chinese, Korean, and Japanese Americans marched together en route to Golden Gate Park waving Red Books and carrying flags of the People's Republic of China, North Korea, and Viet Nam. The flags symbolized the identification of

Asians born in the United States with those in Asia, and the variety of nations represented demonstrated the multiethnic solidarity that had been created. Recalling the spirit of togetherness and unity engendered by the Asian contingent, Pat Sumi said, "It was good!"[113]

In 1973, Asian Americans joined together on both coasts for demonstrations against Richard Nixon's 20 January inauguration. In San Francisco, the Asian Contingent was sponsored by the multiethnic BAACAW, the predominantly Chinese American groups I Wor Kuen and Wei Min She (which had more than their fair share of political differences in other arenas), the Japanese American group J-Town Collective, and the Filipino anti-Marcos group Kalayaan.[114] In Washington, D.C., the Asian Contingent drew some two hundred Chinese, Japanese, Filipino, Korean, and Indian Americans of various ages from New York, Washington, Philadelphia, Boston, Ohio, and small colleges all over the East Coast.[115] Together they marched to the Washington Monument, where they joined a throng estimated at a hundred thousand people.[116] After the rally, the Asian Contingent retreated to a church where they "got a chance to eat, thaw out, and get to know the different Asians from the East Coast." The respite was brief, for a Filipina "sister" mentioned that Imelda Marcos was attending Nixon's Inaugural Ball just a block away. Ferdinand Marcos had declared martial law in the Philippines on 21 September 1972 to fend off leftist militancy and was widely considered a puppet of U.S. capitalism by the left. The Asian Contingent quickly decided to act collectively and boarded buses to Marcos's hotel. Once there, Chinese, Japanese, Korean, and Indian Americans "linked arms" with Filipino Americans and joined in chanting "Makibaka!" (Tagalog for "Struggle!") outside the hotel. As one participant wrote, "I felt the unity, strength and power of the people in the deepest of my bones. We were indeed motivated by a fighting spirit!"[117] The ease with which this ad hoc coalition could turn from protesting the war in Viet Nam to calling for Marcos's overthrow shows the importance of anti-imperialism in connecting different struggles, and the conjoinment of Chinese and Japanese Americans to shout in Tagalog with Filipino Americans demonstrates the power of anti-imperialism to foster racial solidarity.

Marking Asian American Difference

In addition to building multiethnic solidarity, the Asian American line on the war also marked Asian Americans as distinct from the mainstream antiwar movement. Indeed, the Asian American antiwar movement emerged from a belief that the mainstream peace movement was racist in its disregard for Asians. In 1972, Paul Wong noted in *Bridge* magazine that the Asian American antiwar movement objected to the mainstream's emphasis on "bringing the troops home." Instead, Asian Americans stressed the need to end the genocide by using slogans such as "Stop killing *our* Asian brothers and sisters" to emphasize the racial link between the Vietnamese and Asian Americans.[118]

BAACAW itself grew out of an incident at the massive 24 April 1971 moratorium in San Francisco. Some people of color grew dissatisfied with the moderate politics being projected from the speakers' platform, and a coalition of people of color, led by Latinos including Brown Berets, staged a takeover. The Asian contingent, which was about three hundred strong, had been refused speaking time at the microphone, so the takeover provided an opportunity to present their point of view. A squadron of Asian Americans physically bulled their way onto the platform, shoving and elbowing aside anyone in their way. Once in place, they formed a protective barrier around Patsy Chan, who addressed the enormous crowd for about five minutes.[119] These Asians Americans were mainly dismayed by the antiwar movement's hostility toward the Asian American line against the war. A *Rodan* commentary on the event asserted, "Most of the anti-war sentiment in this country is still clearly racist. The reality that the worst thing about the war is that Asian people are being uprooted and murdered daily is still far from the consciousness of the majority of Americans, who are only concerned about American deaths." Because most of the antiwar movement was still motivated by a desire to end U.S. casualties, it glossed over the death and injury inflicted upon the Vietnamese people, who "surely suffered from this war more than any group in this country."[120] BAACAW thus grew in part out of Asian American disdain for the mainstream antiwar movement's unwillingness to take on the issues of anti-Asian racism and genocide.

BAACAW devised a strategy for visually representing Asian American distinctiveness. When a leader called out, "Snake dance!" scores of individuals broke out of the crowd. Wearing matching headbands, they linked arms and formed a single-file line that undulated through the surrounding throng. As their block-long procession weaved its way down the street, the dancers chanted in unison, "Ho Chi Minh, Ho Chi Minh, NLF is gonna win!"[121] The snake dance emblematized the position of Asian Americans in the antiwar movement. It joined protesters of various ethnicities—Chinese, Japanese, and Filipinos—together into a cohesive Asian

American alliance, and it also differentiated Asian American protesters from the mainstream antiwar movement.

Although Asian Americans deemed racist the mainstream antiwar movement's blindness to the killing of Asians, they also objected to its inattention to Asian Americans and their domestic problems.[122] For example, a *Gidra* article reported that an "Asian brother" had been invited to speak at an event organized by the Student Mobilization Committee. He was brought to the mike three times, but each time was asked to sit back down and allow someone else to speak first. The group Asians Against Fascism commented, "Okay, we understand there were many speakers, but the point is, are we (Asian Americans) being taken seriously? Why is it when people say Third World, they are referring to the Blacks, the Chicanos and the native Americans? What about the Asians?" Because Asian Americans understood the war and domestic anti-Asian racism as ineluctably intertwined, they took exception to others who, while adoring the Vietnamese, "refuse[d] to take seriously the Asian struggle in Babylon. They [did] not recognize the fact that Asians in Southeast Asia and Babylon share[d] a common oppressor."[123]

Steve Louie remembers that while the white antiwar movement had "this moral thing about no killing," Asian Americans sought to bring attention to "a bigger issue: . . . genocide. So the broader movement had a hard time with the Asian movement, in some ways. Because it broadened the issues out beyond where they wanted to go, beyond what a lot of people wanted to deal with: the whole question of U.S. imperialism as a system, at home and abroad."[124] For Louie, U.S. imperialism provided the conceptual link that made the Viet Nam War and racism within the United States part of a larger whole. Thus, the movement's interpretation of U.S. imbroglios in Asia served to build Asian American identity by highlighting the war's specifically racial features. While whites and others protested a war that may have been racist because it killed black and brown Americans disproportionately, Asian Americans mobilized against the war because it was specifically anti-Asian. In protesting the Viet Nam War, Asian Americans linked the war in Asia with a system of anti-Asian racism in the United States. As the Asian American authors of one article asked rhetorically, "What are we really doing when we protest the war in Viet Nam? Are we protesting the war in Viet Nam or the war at home?"[125]

In a similar vein, after having walked out of the 20 January 1973 Inaugural Day demonstration, the Los Angeles Asian Coalition (AC) released a statement outlining its position on the white antiwar movement.

AC was dismayed by the "racism and paternalism that exists within the white anti-war movement" in terms of both ideology and practice. Vowing to boycott events sponsored by the white National Peace Action Coalition (NPAC), AC denounced "NPAC's racist line of 'Bring our boys home'" because it was concerned only with American lives, not Vietnamese. Furthermore, it did not properly link the war in Viet Nam to the oppression of Asians in the United States, which included problems with drug abuse and inner-city redevelopment in Asian American communities. Thus, AC claimed, "Vietnam is not only an issue that affects us from across the sea, but is also a war within our communities." Besides ideological differences, AC charged NPAC with "racism" in their "work style and relationships with Third World groups," not confronting their own "white skin privilege," and "tokenism." AC believed that NPAC sought the support of white liberals without "educat[ing] them as to the nature of racism in this country" and therefore "reinforce[d] it." AC's statement concluded that the "movement to fight against U.S. imperialism abroad must also confront white racism in all its aspects at home and especially within the movement."[126] The AC statement makes clear that it was not enough to withdraw U.S. troops; instead it was necessary to connect militarism in Viet Nam with racism in the United States. While it is vital to understand AC's critique of NPAC in the context of the heated rivalry between the Socialist Workers Party–led NPAC and the People's Coalition for Peace and Justice, it is also important to note that AC tapped into a current of thought that decried NPAC's refusal to broaden its antiwar message to include antiracism.[127]

People of color were not immune to criticism, either. A *Rodan* article admonished a Chicano member of the Brown Berets who had said, at the 24 April 1971 demonstration, "To Hell with Vietnam!" While denouncing the "high proportion of black and brown troops in the combat zones," the *Rodan* article insisted that even though many of the American soldiers bore Spanish surnames, they were still invading troops, and the Brown Beret speaker's attitude discounted the misery visited upon the Vietnamese people. Despite this contradiction, however, the article concluded that it was of paramount importance to build unity among Third World people.[128]

BAACAW disbanded after the signing of the Paris Peace Accords in 1973, and Asian Americans, along with the larger antiwar movement, demobilized with the withdrawal of U.S. troops from Viet Nam. But opposing the war had an impact that outlasted the war itself. For Chinese, Japanese, and Filipino American radicals, conceiving of themselves as part of a global community of Asians opposed to U.S. imperialism contributed to the building of a multiethnic, racially based coalition within the United States. The snake dancers emerged from the crowd as individuals but linked arms, declared solidarity with left Asia, and coalesced into a unified force opposed to anti-Asian imperialism abroad and to racism at home. For these snake dancers and many others like them, opposing a race war contributed vitally to the production of the category known as "Asian American," a racial formation that continued to unfold far after the cessation of hostilities in Viet Nam.

Five

Performing Radical Culture: A Grain of Sand and the Language of Liberty

From 1970 to 1974, the Asian American folk music trio A Grain of Sand performed across the United States from New York to Los Angeles and all points between in "basements, churches, community centers, storefronts, rallies, campuses," traveling "wherever there were events, people, or organizations that might be receptive to 'the news.'"[1] JoAnne (later "Nobuko") Miyamoto, Chris Iijima, and William "Charlie" Chin came together as a result of their Asian American activism and played music that was an organic expression of the core ideologies of the Asian American movement. The personal and political journeys of the members of A Grain of Sand illustrate more general patterns within the Asian American cultural field of the 1970s, for the trio's cultural productions paralleled those of other Asian American artists and revolutionaries. The "news" that Miyamoto, Iijima, and Chin spread through music was that Asian Americans should empower themselves and reach out in support of other people who were oppressed. They strove to create politically aware art, not propaganda, with the hope that the music they performed would touch hearts and souls and portray a positive vision of love, beauty, and community.[2] The community they sought to build was predicated on building multiethnic solidarities, interracial alliances, and transnational sympathies.

The late 1960s and early 1970s witnessed an unprecedented flowering of Asian American culture. Institutions like Kearny Street Workshop in San Francisco and Basement Workshop in New York City fostered Asian American artists and writers; Janice Mirikitani published poetry exploring Asian American experiences and politics; and the germinal anthology *Aiiieeeee!* gave voice to Chinese, Japanese, and Filipino American writers.[3] In discussing the black power movement, historian William Van Deburg claims that its most lasting and powerful effects were cultural.[4] A similar claim may plausibly be made for the Asian American movement, for the texts produced and institutions established during the movement period became some of its most enduring and influential legacies.

Focusing on the music and performances of A Grain of Sand dispels two myths about Asian American cultural production and political activism. First, scholars have often succumbed to the mistaken notion that Asian American activism began as a nationalist enterprise that only later graduated to more egalitarian and inclusive forms.[5] In particular, the cultural field is frequently portrayed as especially narrow and chauvinistic, best understood under the rubric of "cultural nationalism."[6] However, the cultural productions from the inception of Asian America were ideologically varied. My aim in this chapter is to delink culture from nationalism by highlighting antiracist and anti-imperialist cultural expressions. Second, some scholars have envisioned Asian American cultural work as primarily interested in building self-awareness and racial pride, an interpretation that vitiates the political potency of this work.[7] To the contrary, I argue in this chapter that the cultural productions of the movement period must be understood more broadly in the context of crucial ideological debates over the nature of Asian American identity.

Asian American artists of the movement period agreed that a new wind was blowing—that Asian people in the United States were rethinking their identities and relationships to each other, to America, and to Asia. But while they concurred that something new was in the air, they differed on its exact meaning. Franklin Odo perceptively noted the ideological diversity of the Asian American movement, commenting in the preface to the germinal 1971 anthology *Roots: An Asian American Reader* that the movement included "'back to Asia' types" alongside those who held "a strictly Americanist, localized, point of view."[8] The multiplicity of the movement itself was mirrored in the cultural arena, which provided a vital stage upon which artists struggled to define Asian American identity. Cultural workers who explored the theme of Asian American identity may be properly thought of as part of the Asian American movement, regardless of whether they actually joined movement organizations or participated in extraliterary movement activities, because they self-consciously explored theoretical issues underpinning the movement. In poems, plays, music, and debates over aesthetics, they pondered issues such as Who is Asian American? Does Asian American identity inhere in culture or politics? What is the relationship between Asian Americans and Asia? What is the relationship between Asian Americans and other nonwhite people in the United States?

Three paradigms of Asian American identity competed in the cultural arena.[9] First, the cultural nationalism of the "strictly Americanist" point of view defined Asian Americans as American-born people of Asian ancestry who shared a common culture and sensibility that was distinctly American yet different from that of the white mainstream. This definition built a common identity for native-born Asian Americans of multiple ethnicities but excluded Asian immigrants, who were thought to be culturally distinct. Second, the diasporism of the "'back to Asia' types" viewed Asians in the United States as part of the global diaspora from Asia and argued that these Asians retained inherent links to their ancestral Asian homelands. Although it did not differentiate between native-born Asians and immigrants, its singular ethnic or national perspective did nothing to build multiethnic and interracial connections in the United States. Finally, anti-imperialism focused on the role that American racism, capitalism, and imperialism played in engendering Asian migrations to the United States and the continued exploitation of Asians after their arrival. It encouraged unity among Asian Americans regardless of their ethnicity or immigrant status because American capitalism exploited all Asians in comparable fashion; it sought solidarity with blacks, Latinos, and American Indians because these groups, like Asian Americans, were exploited and subject to racial discrimination; and it expressed camaraderie with left Asia in its struggle against U.S. imperialism, especially in Indochina. A Grain of Sand provided one of the clearest cultural articulations of the anti-imperialist position.

From Grains to Pearls

The members of A Grain of Sand came to the group through divergent paths. Miyamoto was a performer who had danced professionally on Broadway and in films before becoming politically involved, Iijima had been raised by a musician father and a radical mother, and Chin had been a successful musician who eventually came to wonder why he knew more about Anglo-American music than about that of his own people. Exploring the personal journeys of the members of A Grain of Sand reveals how their conceptions of race evolved over time as they drew upon the surrounding context of the antiwar and black power movements to build an understanding of what it meant to be Asian American. The notion of Asian American identity that they ultimately advocated was a political marker rather than an ethnic descriptor, and it represented opposition to racism in the United States and imperialism abroad. However, as Miyamoto emphasized in recalling their history, A Grain of Sand also strove to build a culture that empowered Asian Americans to realize their full potential as human beings by throwing away Orientalist stereotypes and recognizing their commonalities with other oppressed people.[10]

JoAnne Nobuko Miyamoto, a Sansei (third-generation Japanese American), was born in Los Angeles in 1939 to parents with a love of music and dance.[11] Her father was a truck driver with a "passion" for classical music who dreamed of being a pianist, and her mother had wanted to be an artist. During World War II, the family was imprisoned at the Santa Anita Assembly Center before they were released to harvest sugar beets, initially in Montana and later in Idaho; they spent most of the war in Ogden, Utah. After the war they returned to Los Angeles and lived in a mixed-race neighborhood with Japanese and African Americans, though her parents told JoAnne "not to play with the kurochan" (a somewhat derogatory term for blacks). She began taking ballet lessons around the age of seven, when her family moved to the famously diverse environs of Boyle Heights, which contained Jewish, Russian, Mexican, and Japanese communities, and went on to attend the Los Angeles Conservatory of Music and Art.[12] She was talented enough to earn a scholarship to the American School of Dance, where she trained in ballet, modern dance, and various ethnic dances.

By the time she was in junior high, Miyamoto began to understand that her artistry would always be affected by her race. The American School of Dance was directed by the esteemed choreographer Eugene Loring, who took her aside and said, "JoAnne, in order to be a dancer, you have to be twice as good as everybody else."[13] Loring's comment challenged her to strive harder, and by the time she was fourteen, she was auditioning for films, television shows, and musicals. After trying out for Red Skelton's television show, she was told, "You're very good, but we can't use you because you'd stick out." This comment made her even more determined to "cross the color line."

Miyamoto's breakthrough into professional dancing involved less crossing of the color line than conforming to it. The strikingly beautiful girl was cast in nonwhite roles that played to her seeming exoticism. She first caught the eye of the eminent choreographer Jerome Robbins, who offered her the role of the Indian princess Tiger Lily in the Broadway musical version of *Peter Pan*. JoAnne's father flatly refused to allow his fourteen-year-old daughter to go to New York unaccompanied. Two years later, Robbins again called on Miyamoto when he choreographed the film version of Rodgers and Hammerstein's musical *The King and I*. At the time she danced in the movie, Miyamoto did not understand the depths of its Orientalism, which envisions the east, represented by the King of Siam, as being modernized through the instruction of the intrepid white woman Anna.[14]

Asian-themed plays were popular on Broadway during the 1950s, and one of the most successful was *Flower Drum Song*, which was touted as the first musical with an all-Asian cast despite the fact that some key roles were played by non-Asians in yellowface. Miyamoto's first Broadway role was the lead dancer in *Flower Drum Song*. Cultural historian Christina Klein argues that this musical played into Cold War attempts to place Chinese Americans on the path to whiteness by casting them as assimilable and erasing the history of their racialization, and her point can easily be extended to include Asians of all ethnicities, given the diversity of the cast.[15] As when she had danced in *The King and I*, the teenaged Miyamoto was not fully aware of the play's racial politics, but dancing in it thrust her into a world of Asian American performers, including the dancer Yuriko Amamiya, who had taught ballet at the Gila River Relocation Center in Arizona during the war and studied in New York with Martha Graham; the actor Jack Soo, who was born as Goro Suzuki but took a Chinese stage name to avoid anti-Japanese discrimination;[16] and the singer Pat Suzuki, who played the role of the seductive, Americanized Linda Low in the Broadway show. Amamiya took Miyamoto under her wing and, "like a mother hen," protected the seventeen-year-old girl from the dangers of the big city.

Performing in a predominantly Asian American cast further opened JoAnne's eyes to the color line that circumscribed their opportunities. During a matinee performance of the famous "Chop Suey" number, which includes a parodic mishmash of Asian and western forms, she looked out at the audience and realized what they were seeing on stage: "I looked out at this audience . . . and I knew that they didn't have a clue. They just thought that we were just so cute and exotic. And I just felt this feeling of discomfort. It was a bitter taste in my mouth." She wondered, "How come I can only do these kinds of musicals and these kinds of shows? How come I can't just be a plain person?" While most of the cast stayed on to take full advantage of the opportunity to work on Broadway, Miyamoto left the show after one year because she "just couldn't stand it."

After leaving *Flower Drum Song*, Miyamoto returned home to Los Angeles, where she auditioned for the film version of *West Side Story*, little knowing that the movie would mark a turning point in her performing career. Although she was aided by her prior relationship with the film's director, Jerome Robbins, Miyamoto also made it through auditions by being able to pass as Puerto Rican—clear confirmation of which side of the color line she inhabited. In addition to dancing, JoAnne sang in the chorus, which she enjoyed. After the group parts were recorded, she was taken to a sound stage and placed alone in a booth to record an individual part. "I was so petrified to sing by myself!" she remembers. But she realized that singing could provide new opportunities, so she began serious vocal training. At first she was incredibly shy, to the point that she would stop singing if anyone entered the room, but her teacher, Dini Clarke, drew her out of her shell and helped her to build self-confidence. The African American Clarke not only introduced JoAnne to the world of black music but also opened her eyes to the racism that blacks endured.[17]

The year 1967 saw Miyamoto mature both musically and politically. She was invited to sing at the Colony Club, where Pat Suzuki had gotten her start in Seattle. She spent eight months performing intensely, singing two shows a night during the week and three shows a night on weekends. JoAnne sometimes hung out with students from the University of Washington who stopped by the club, and from them she began to become acquainted with the counterculture and the antiwar movements, both of which were heating up during this period. She also began to worry about what might happen to her draft-age younger brother, Bob. Her dawning political awareness made her wonder, "What am I doing singing in a nightclub?" When her singing stint ended, she returned to Los Angeles and resolved to get involved in the movement somehow.

Miyamoto's first political act outside of show business was to volunteer for Eugene McCarthy's presidential campaign, and doing so led her deeper into the world of radical politics. An acquaintance on the campaign introduced her to Antonello Branca, an adventurous Italian filmmaker who was making a documentary about the Black Panthers.[18] JoAnne and Antonello promptly fell in love, and she agreed to join him in his project. They traveled around the country filming wherever the action happened to occur, from People's Park in Berkeley to protests of Nixon's inauguration in Washington, D.C. At People's Park, JoAnne was hit by the police for the first time while just standing on the street. During this period, she recalls, "I was beginning to really become political myself. I was seeing what oppression was really about, how they were trying to control people's freedom of speech."

Shadowing the Panthers, mostly in Los Angeles but also in the Bay area, radicalized Miyamoto further, for she came to sympathize with their perspective and understand their racial politics. During this period she read Malcolm X and Eldridge Cleaver's *Soul on Ice*. She also met a number of Panthers, including Geronimo Pratt, who were "trying to feed children, trying to get organized, trying to fight against police repression, trying to deal with housing and health issues." While she came to see the Panthers as devoted and effective community organizers, she also observed how many of them were imprisoned on various charges and wondered, "Why are they being oppressed like this?" Although she was personally disinclined toward armed self-defense and was shocked when someone brought a firearm into her apartment, she also understood the frustration that arose from police harassment. JoAnne's experiences with the Black Panthers also debunked the idea that the organization was racially separatist. On the contrary, working with the Panthers opened her understanding of her own racial identity. As she put it, "They really welcomed me. They knew I was Japanese, they knew about [internment] camp. They looked at me like a sister and they called me 'sister.' And that blew my mind." Building camaraderie with black people went against what her parents had taught her, for they had discouraged her from making friends with black children, probably in an attempt to climb the ladder of assimilation to whiteness by maintaining distance from blackness.

Although Miyamoto entered radical circles by observing the black struggle, she soon connected her politics to her own racial identity. She traveled with Branca to New York to film at a church in East Harlem that had been taken over by the Young Lords, a Puerto Rican organization, for their community programs.[19] There, in the midst of an intense Puerto Rican struggle, a "little Japanese lady" tapped her on the shoulder and grilled her, "Who are you? What's your name? What are you doing here?" The "little Japanese lady" was Yuri Kochiyama (who went by "Mary" at the time), a longtime activist in Harlem. Kochiyama asked JoAnne, "Have you hooked up with Asians in New York?" Miyamoto recalls, "I hadn't hooked up with Asians, period. I was in the black movement with all these black movement people." But Kochiyama insisted, "You have to come to this meeting of Asian Americans for Action." That moment marked the beginning of Miyamoto's immersion in the Asian American movement, but she always retained her devotion to multiracial organizing, which she had learned from observing and supporting the black and Puerto Rican movements.

At the meeting of Asian Americans for Action (AAA), Miyamoto met Chris Iijima, who would become her partner in music and political struggle, and his remarkable parents, Kazu and Takeru ("Tak") Iijima. Like Miyamoto, Chris Iijima had inherited a love of music from his parents, particularly his father, who was a pianist and music teacher.[20] But whereas Miyamoto's parents had been apolitical, Chris had been a "red diaper baby" born to radicals. His mother, Kazu, had been a member of the small but vital Japanese American left before World War II.[21] She had joined the Young Communist League while in college at Berkeley and, as one of an estimated two hundred Japanese American communists, understood the red baiting and ostracism that befell radicals.[22] She also belonged to the most prominent Nisei (second-generation Japanese American) progressive group, the Young Democrats, which included both communist and noncommunist students and workers who participated in electoral politics, formed discussion groups, and supported the CIO.[23] Throughout this period, Japanese American radicals took principled but unpopular stances. For example, at a time when Jimmy Sakamoto of the *Japanese American Courier* defended Japan's annexation of Manchuria, Karl Yoneda and other communists condemned it as imperialist.[24] The Young Democrats, with chapters in Oakland and Los Angeles, were also the only group to openly oppose the forced removal of Japanese Americans from their homes during World War II. In early 1942, Iijima and other Oakland Young Democrats wrote a letter condemning the so-called evacuation, which all of the community newspapers refused to publish.[25] The Young Democrats in Los Angeles wrote to "congressional representatives and city council officials urging them to oppose the forced removal."[26] While Japanese American communists remained true to their convictions, the U.S. Communist Party (CPUSA) purged them upon the outbreak of war with Japan. While some party members, like Karl Yoneda and Elaine Black, personally blamed CP general secretary Earl Browder for this betrayal, Iijima criticized the party more broadly.[27]

During the late 1960s, Kazu Iijima came to admire the black power movement and "its emphasis on ethnic identity and pride," which she viewed as in stark contrast to the cultural amnesia that had befallen the Sansei youth. In late 1968, she and another radical Nisei woman, Minn Matsuda, discussed forming a Japanese American organization, but Iijima's son Chris convinced them to include Asians of all ethnicities. Iijima and Matsuda recruited individuals they knew and Asians they approached at antiwar demonstrations to attend a meeting held on 6 April 1969. This was the start of AAA, which brought together a remarkable set of elders—including, in addition to Iijima and Matsuda, Iijima's husband, Tak; Aiko Herzig-Yoshinaga; and Yuri ("Mary") Kochiyama and her husband, Bill—along with younger people, many of whom were Chinese American students from the Asian American Political Alliance at Columbia University who had been politicized through participating in black power, student, and other new left movements.[28] The intergenerational alliance of AAA framed itself as antiracist, anti-imperialist, and particularly opposed to the war in Viet Nam.[29]

Although elders like Kazu and Tak Iijima provided a link between Asian American radicalism in the 1970s and its predecessor in the prewar period, the next generation took it in entirely new directions. Chris Iijima was a talented musician and ardent radical in his own right who passed away on 31 December 2005 at the age of fifty-seven. In his far too brief life, he deeply affected thousands of people across the nation with his heart, mind, and voice. His family and friends fondly remember his combativeness and willingness to argue over nearly anything, but always with an attitude of camaraderie. They also remember the total joy with which he embraced life, which was epitomized by his passion for finding the best food, especially Chinese, wherever he went. Iijima's activism stretched from the 1960s, when he participated along with his sister and parents in the 1963 March on Washington and led antiwar demonstrations at Columbia University, to the twenty-first century, when as a law professor he continued to advocate for racial justice and solidarity.[30] His Asian American–focused activism began with AAA but extended to Basement Workshop, a grassroots arts and community organization in New York City's Chinatown, and I Wor Kuen, the radical Asian American group that had begun in New York, eventually went national, and later merged with the Red Guard Party, as discussed in chapter 3.[31]

Miyamoto and Iijima circulated in a New York City environment in which radicals of varying races constantly crossed paths. Miyamoto recalls eating with Black Panthers who included her in their "Feed the People" programs, saying, "You're part of the people too, you know." She also remembers being stared at intently by a member of the Young Lords who finally recognized her from *West Side Story,* which he had seen seventeen times. Young Asian American radicals strove to defy the "model minority" stereotype with their appearance: rather than dressing respectably, they sported long hair, wore army jackets and berets, and generally looked like "movement people." In this milieu, Miyamoto came to know Iijima first as a strident and militant activist; only later did their musical partnership emerge from their common politics.

In 1970, Miyamoto and Iijima drove to Chicago on what would prove to be the first leg of an extended and transformative journey. The two were part of a contingent of progressive Sansei who were going to the Japanese American Citizens League (JACL) national convention in order to pressure what they saw as a hidebound organization toward greater political relevance. In Chicago they met with Black Panthers who greeted them warmly as brothers and sisters. They toured the building where the charismatic Panther leader Fred Hampton had been assassinated by the FBI and Chicago police and viewed the holes made in the walls of the Panther office by incoming bullets.[32] At Wrigley Field, they also joined Native Americans demonstrating for better housing. The Indians welcomed the Asian Americans into their story circles that night and told them the prophecy of the Warriors of the Rainbow: five thousand years of evil would be followed by five thousand years of good when warriors of all colors of the rainbow came together. Miyamoto recalls how powerful it was to hear the story and realize "and there we were: the Panthers, the Native Americans, Asian Americans." The trip to Chicago was an important moment for the two young Sansei, for it marked their adoption of interracial solidarity and their explicit rejection of JACL-style assimilationism, which was also rejected by many involved in the controversy over S. I. Hayakawa at San Francisco State.

It was on this trip that JoAnne saw Chris for the first time not simply as a "heavy politico" but also as a musician. She had glimpsed his guitar on the westward drive but did not think much about it until he took it out in Chicago and began to play and sing. Only later did she learn that Chris had attended the High School of the Performing Arts in New York and that his guitar playing and singing had been deeply influenced by studying the blues. By then Miyamoto had more or less relinquished performance in favor of activism, but she joined Iijima in song and in doing so melded music with political action. She came to deeply admire Iijima's songwriting skill, for "Chris could write a song like that" (she snaps her fingers) and "had the ability to translate complicated ideas into simple and poetic forms." They wrote collaboratively, bouncing ideas about both words and music back and forth in a way that was "sort of magical." Nobuko's recollection is that they never disagreed about music but argued about everything else, including how much rehearsal was necessary: "Even though Chris didn't like to practice, we did practice. I think that was a lot of our argument, because I came from more of a performing background and I was pushing to try to give it some polish."[33]

Iijima was never shy about pressing for what he thought was right, and because he believed strongly that gender equality was an essential part of overall liberation, he urged Miyamoto to grow personally in that area. When they first began performing, she felt too shy to speak between songs. Chris pushed her to be more vocal, saying, "JoAnne, there are a lot of sisters out there who expect you to speak. You have to speak." He was concerned that it was sexist that men spoke on stage while the only woman remained silent. JoAnne eventually became comfortable speaking and credits Chris for helping her to grow in that regard.[34]

Iijima and Miyamoto wrote their first song in Chicago, a number called "People's Beat," which was inspired by the words of Fred Hampton, and they performed it the next day at the JACL convention.[35] After singing for an "all Asian audience" a song that had come from their hearts, Chris and JoAnne "knew that something powerful had happened." That performance proved to be a pivotal moment in their lives. The JACL convention was marred by the tragic murder of Evelyn Okubo, a young Sansei woman from Stockton, California, and the vicious assault of another, Ranko Yamada.[36] The violence impressed upon JoAnne that "this was a serious struggle," and she and Chris decided to go to California to do a fundraiser for the Yellow Seed, Evelyn's organization, and meet with more Asian Americans.[37] First, though, they returned to New York City, where they wrote five songs and arranged several others. They held a fundraiser at the Japanese Buddhist Church on the Upper West Side and raised enough money to fly to California. They played their first concert in Los Angeles and from there traveled to Stockton, Fresno, Sacramento, and San Francisco, singing at every stop along the way.

Although Miyamoto and Iijima channeled their politics through their songs, music drew Charlie Chin into Asian American politics. Chin had been born in 1944 to a father who was a laundryman originally from Toisan, China, and a mother from New York with roots in Trinidad.[38] He remembers that musicality suffused his childhood: "At house parties," where family and other West Indian Chinese gathered, "everybody played and sang. Musical instruments were abundant." The first instrument he learned to play was the cuatro, a four-stringed guitar common to Venezuela and the West Indies. At the age of eighteen, Chin headed for Greenwich Village to escape his father's ultimatum of college, a job, or the military, but he admits that he was also drawn by rumors that the beatnik women who hung out there were "easy." The naturally talented musician soon established himself on the folk music scene and even taught himself to play several new instruments simply by picking them up and studying their forms and histories. Within a few years he was even teaching traditional Anglo-American musical performance. In 1967, while he was a banjo instructor at a music camp called Pinewoods in Cape Cod, an advanced player asked Chin for a lesson on a particular technique. After the lesson, Chin's roommate made a piercing comment on the irony of a Chinese guy from New York City teaching a white guy from Kentucky how to play his own kind of music. Chin recalls: "It struck me, because he was right. What dug away in the back of my mind . . . was that I knew everything there was to know about *them* and *their music,* but I didn't know anything about *my own.*"

The idea that Chin needed to learn more about his own music took three years to germinate, but when it finally did, he was transformed. By the late 1960s, Chin sensed that the rock and roll scene was growing more vibrant than the folk scene, so he electrified, grew his hair, and joined a band. Although they were not headliners, the band toured and played with famous acts. However, the hard-driving life of a rock musician took its toll, and eventually Chin decided to "bail." At that point, he found himself divorced, burned out physically and mentally, "staying alive by bartending in Greenwich Village," and "wondering what to do next." The answer came unexpectedly: Chin recalls that one day in 1970 a "Chinese guy" walked into the bar where he worked "with some flyers under his arm, and said, 'This is a place where a lot of musicians hang out, right?' I said, 'Yeah.' He said, 'Any Asian musicians here?' I said, 'Whoa, I kind of play a little.'" The visitor gave Chin a flyer, told him about a concert and conference at Pace College several blocks away, and invited him to bring a musical instrument so he could "jam."

Chin grabbed a guitar and headed to Pace, where he was startled to find that "the conference was all Asians, or that's what they called themselves. I had never really heard people call themselves Asians before. We were Orientals before that." He observed groups from several colleges and various areas of the city participating in seminars, workshops, and cultural presentations. The musical portion was scheduled last, and while waiting backstage Charlie met a Japanese American duo by the name of Chris and JoAnne. The program ran late, leaving too little time for both Charlie and the duo to perform. He urged them to take the slot, but JoAnne insisted that they should all perform together.[39] Chin went onstage that night with Miyamoto and Iijima, having never once heard them play. He backed them up on their songs, and they backed him up on his. As Charlie listened to the music, he also listened to the words and began to think, "Something's going on here." That "something" gnawed at him; he had been fairly cynical about discussions at the conference earlier in the day, but as he recalls, "I couldn't swallow it, but I couldn't spit it out."

The performance at Pace in 1970 not only marked what Miyamoto calls "the beginning of us as a trio"—within a week or two Chris and JoAnne invited Charlie to perform with them at another venue, and their collaboration blossomed from there—but it also launched Chin's political transformation. He immersed himself in New York's Asian American artistic scene; participated in Basement Workshop; joined a commune on Division Street in Chinatown, where he underwent a process of "reeducation" to deal with sexism and materialism; and spent six months exclusively within the confines of Chinatown in order to undo his "whitewashing."[40]

A Grain of Sand performed a simple style of music produced by two acoustic guitars and three voices: JoAnne's dulcet leads, Chris's throaty tenor, and Charlie's resonant baritone. Their music is best categorized as folk, a form popularized at the time by artists like Bob Dylan, Joan Baez, and Joni Mitchell. The trio's adoption of the folk genre had material benefits, making their performances eminently portable and easy to set up. Free of elaborate amplifiers or electronics, Chin recalls, "we just had to grab them [the guitars], get in the car, and go. . . . It allowed us to set up and play anywhere: college dorm lounge, major hall, hallways sometimes, in a community center."[41] Beyond its tactical advantages, however, the trio's employment of folk music was strategic as well. As Oliver Wang argues, A Grain of Sand tapped into a long tradition of using folk music to advocate for "social justice, working-class concerns, and communal struggle."[42]

Throughout the early 1970s, A Grain of Sand performed for Asian American organizations from coast to coast and in between. The three "revolutionary minstrels" traveled on bare-bones budgets and were seldom

Charlie Chin, Nobuko JoAnne Miyamoto, and Chris Iijima recorded the album *A Grain of Sand* in 1973. Their music encapsulated much of the ethos of the Asian American movement, and their performances enabled connections to be built across the nation. Photograph by Bob Hsiang; copyright 2008.

if ever paid.[43] Chin remembers, "If you could get us there, we would play." Most of their performances were intimate, staged before small audiences in storefronts, dorm lounges, and basements. They slept on floors, ate whatever their hosts fed them, and were driven from one venue to the next. When they had to drive themselves, JoAnne took the wheel, because neither of the New Yorkers had a license at the time, but Chris and Charlie kept her awake with movie trivia.[44] The two points of this itinerant, spartan lifestyle were to spread the message of Asian American collectivity and to create networks of like-minded people. "We were trying to bring this message to other Asians in the country," says Chin.[45] The music was a tool to engage people without lecturing to them and was meant to instigate discussions that sometimes lasted all through the night. In addition to proselytizing, Chris, JoAnne, and Charlie also built connections between disparate elements of the Asian American movement. Wherever they went, they told of what they had witnessed elsewhere, listened to stories of what was happening locally, and relayed those stories to others at their next stop. By weaving the fabric of the Asian American movement together through music and stories, Miyamoto says, "We became like griots, like Asian American griots."[46]

The three members of A Grain of Sand were not, as they have sometimes been described, "the Peter, Paul and Mary of Asian American folk
music."[47] In retrospect, Chris Iijima rankled at that characterization because he never enjoyed Peter, Paul, and Mary's music. Moreover, Iijima
felt that such a description depoliticized A Grain of Sand's message about
Asian American identity. For him, Asian American identity was a tool by
which to advance antiracist and anti-imperialist causes, "a means to organize other Asians for political purposes, to highlight aspects of racism,
to escape the hegemony of whites in progressive movements, to support
other progressive racial formations, to establish alternative forms of looking at society/history, etc."[48] This notion of Asian American identity as a
marker of progressive politics rather than a descriptor of ethnicity was
commonly understood within the Asian American movement during the
1970s. Although the members of A Grain of Sand expressed these sentiments in a particularly artistic and effective way, their views on the matter were typical rather than exceptional. Nobuko Miyamoto explains that
the trio drew upon and expressed the ideas of the Asian American movement and indeed the larger new left movements arising across the globe:
"The power of the music was the context which it came out of. We happened to have these skills to be able to get it out, but it really came through
this movement. We absorbed these ideas and it came out, and we had an
audience for it."[49] Chris Iijima agreed: "We were simply responding to
what was going on around, about, and within us."[50]

The trio recorded their album *A Grain of Sand* in 1973 for Paredon
Records, a label specializing in liberation music from around the globe
that had been established by the socially conscious blues and jazz singer
Barbara Dane, whom they had met through singing at antiwar events. By
then they were receiving more invitations than they could accommodate,
and committing their music to vinyl enabled them to reach a wider audience.[51] They recorded the album on a shoestring budget "in a few days—
often in one take as if in live performance."[52]

The twelve tracks of "A Grain of Sand" examine three components
of Asian American identity: multiethnic unity, interracial solidarity, and
anti-imperialism, expressed particularly as opposition to the war in Viet
Nam. The members of A Grain of Sand believed that adopting all three
of these ideas was integral to what it meant to be an Asian American. Far
from being exceptional, this belief typified the politics of many cultural
workers within the Asian American movement.

Multiethnic Unity

The first theme of the album is that Asians of all ethnicities share a common identity that is new and different from what they had known before. It argues that this new Asian American identity coheres because of the systematic, undifferentiating nature of American racism; in other words, Asians of all ethnicities share common experiences of exploitation and discrimination. The trio's ethnic composition—including the two Japanese Americans Iijima and Miyamoto and the Chinese American Chin—stressed the importance of building solidarity among all Asian ethnic groups. The album begins with one of their most powerful works, "Yellow Pearl," which explains the group's name:

> A grain,
> A tiny grain of sand
> Landing in the belly
> In the belly of the monster
> And time is telling
> Only how long it takes
> Layer after layer
> As its beauty unfolds
> Until its captor
> It holds in peril
> A grain,
> A tiny grain of sand.
> . . .
> [chorus]
> And I am a yellow pearl
> And you are a yellow pearl
> And we are the yellow pearl
> And we are half the world
> And we are half the world.[53]

According to this metaphor, Asians, who comprise but a minute percentage of the U.S. population, are the "tiny grain of sand" trapped in the "belly" of the monstrously racist United States. Yet in resisting racism they construct an identity that is as beautiful as a pearl and much more significant than a solitary grain of sand. The phrase "yellow pearl" reclaims and revises the anti-Asian epithet "yellow peril," transforming it from something loathed to an object of beauty. The chorus insists on the collective nature of the yellow pearl: "I," "you," and "we" form it together. Furthermore, Asian American identity includes all Asians. The pronoun "we" in the phrase "we are half the world" refers not to any particular ethnicity or nationality but to Asians across the globe. Similarly, another line, "I see signs of myself/Come drifting in from the East," references the entirety of Asia as opposed to any particular nation.

In another of the group's songs, "Wandering Chinaman," the narrator is forced by poverty to leave his family in China for America, where sixteen-hour workdays and a migrant's "lonely and lonely" life awaits him. Finally able to marry and raise children, his story ends unhappily, for his daughter leaves home to be with a "red-haired man," one of his sons becomes a drug addict, and the other dies in Viet Nam.[54] The song highlights the racism and exploitation that befell many Chinese immigrants, but the album does not focus exclusively on Chinese Americans. Instead, it draws parallels between their experiences and those of other Asian ethnic groups. "We Are the Children" argues that Asian Americans comprise a litany of ethnicities, including Japanese American "offspring of the concentration camp," Chinese American "sons and daughters of the railroad builder," and Filipino American "children of the migrant worker."[55] Their common subjection to exploitation and discrimination binds these diverse groups together as Asian Americans.

This new recognition of multiethnic Asian American identity as a "yellow pearl" is presented as something to be celebrated. "Something about Me Today" records the emergence of the narrator's racial pride, which begins with individual self-acceptance and leads to the building of a group identity and a deep sense of community:

> I looked in the mirror
> And I saw me . . .
> And I didn't want to be
> Any other way . . .
> Then I looked around
> And I saw you.
> And it was the first time I knew
> Who we really are . . .[56]

The key transformation is from the individuated "I" and "you" to the collective "we." Once the narrator recognizes a collective identity, she can "feel us growing stronger" as "we" go about "building something new."

Like A Grain of Sand, the Japanese American poet Janice Mirikitani explored the idea of a new and unified Asian American culture. Mirikitani was a pivotal figure in the Asian American literary scene and actively participated in a multiracial coalition centered at Glide Memorial Church in San Francisco. She edited the first Asian American literary journal, *Aion,* which took its name from a Japanese word meaning "a new state of mind, a new psychic era," and whose ideograms signified "wholeness, totality, universal harmony, the self."[57] She also coedited the landmark collection of multiracial poetry *Time to Greez! Incantations from the Third World.*[58]

Mirikitani's poem "Firepot" appropriates the trope of the melting pot, long a symbol of assimilation, and transforms it into an emblem of multiethnic Asian American racial solidarity. Instead of various Asian ethnicities and nationalities being subsumed into an unraced (read "white") America, Mirikitani posits them as remaining "unassimilated" vis-à-vis the American whole yet becoming alloyed together to form a new Asian people. Koreans, Japanese, Chinese, Samoans, Filipinos, and Southeast Asians all hail from "different shores," speak "different dialects and languages," and are "born from different roots." However, these distinctions ultimately prove false, for

> we have been fractured
> made to look at each other
> as though we are
> divided
> but if we see with clear eyes, we know we are bound by common
> shackles[59]

These false distinctions are imposed from without, though by whom is not clear from these lines. The vagueness and passive voice of "we have been" and "as though we are" are replaced in the next line with active certainty: "we see" and "we know" that all Asians are "bound" by the anti-Asian racism signified by "common shackles."[60] A multiethnic hybrid cuisine symbolizes the new Asian identity and culture being built, for the firepot is "a collective soup of many tastes and ingredients" comprised of foods from various Asian cultures:

> Rice
> Adobo
> sashimi
> imo
> juk
> gai lon
> kim chee
> chicken feet
> a pickled sea
> choy sum & mango trees[61]

The poem performs a fundamental intervention in the trope of America as melting pot by refiguring the process of assimilation for Asians. Long denied entry into the American polity by virtue of their supposed inassimilability, in Mirikitani's vision Asians bridge boundaries of ethnicity and nationality to form a new collective identity for themselves. Instead of assimilating toward whiteness, Asians assimilate toward "yellow/brown."

Interracial Solidarity

While A Grain of Sand's album is clearly concerned with Asian American identity, it argues that being Asian American should mean actively pursuing interracial solidarity with blacks, Latinos, and American Indians. One song, "Jonathan Jackson," honors a seventeen-year-old man who was killed while trying to free his brother, George Jackson, from prison. It praises Jonathan as a martyr who opted for a meaningful death over a "living dying."[62] Lauding Jackson signaled A Grain of Sand's advocacy of black power, for George Jackson was a black radical and served as a field marshal of the Black Panther Party. This musical statement of solidarity with African Americans was backed up through the trio's performances and personal lives. Miyamoto recalls, "We were taking our stories and using the music to exchange" with black communities and organizations. Music provided a source of camaraderie across racial boundaries, because through music "you touch people's souls." A Grain of Sand played for the Republic of New Africa (RNA), a black nationalist organization dedicated to establishing an independent black nation in the American south. Yuri Kochiyama was so involved with RNA that she was conferred citizenship, one of few nonblacks to be so honored. Both of Kochiyama's daughters married black activists and bore biracial children, and it was she who introduced JoAnne to the man (a follower of Malcolm X) who would become the father of her son Kamau. These actions, although they may not have been typical, nevertheless forged a "blood link" between the black and Asian American movements.[63]

In addition to expressing the trio's solidarity with African Americans, *A Grain of Sand* demonstrates their support for American Indians. "Warriors of the Rainbow" derives from the Indian prophecy that Miyamoto and Iijima had heard from Native Americans in Chicago, foretelling a day when warriors of all colors of the rainbow would come together to triumph over evil,[64] and in "We Are the Children" Asian American children playing "cowboys and Indians" cheer not for the white cowboys but for the Indians—"ride, red-man ride!"[65] Asian American contacts with

American Indian activists, although rarer than those with blacks and Latinos, did exist. In 1970, about twenty Japanese Americans visited Indians involved in the multitribal takeover of Alcatraz Island in the San Francisco Bay, bearing gifts of food and clothes and a banner reading "Japanese Americans Support Native Americans."[66] In 1973, a contingent from Los Angeles traveled to Wounded Knee, South Dakota, to show their solidarity with the Indian takeover there and smuggled food and medical supplies past federal officials to the besieged members of the American Indian Movement.[67] The fourteen Asian Americans who made it inside Wounded Knee surprised the Indian occupiers, who thought they were representatives from the People's Republic of China! Asian American supporters of the Wounded Knee takeover drew analogies between the removal of Japanese Americans from their homes during World War II and the forced displacement of Indians from their native lands onto reservations and expressed the desire of both groups for "self determination and sovereignty for our people, here and overseas."[68]

The most notable multiracial commitment of A Grain of Sand is expressed in "Somos Asiáticos" (We are Asians), sung entirely in Spanish. This song was released as a single in Puerto Rico, and its lyrics point to the shared interests of Asians and Latinos:

> Nosotros somos Asiáticos (We are Asians)
> . . .
> Hablamos la misma lengua (We speak the same language)
> Porque luchamos por las mismas cosas (Because we struggle for the same things)
> . . .
> Podemos hablar juntos (We can talk together)
> Podemos cantar juntos (We can sing together)
> Podemos pelear juntos, siempre juntos (We can fight together, always together)
> Yo para tu gente (Me for your people)
> Tu para la mia (You for mine) . . .[69]

This song envisions the unity between Asians and Latinos as being built in social action, because "we struggle for the same things" and "fight together, always together." Group identities enable this solidarity, with "me" and "you" exchanging support not for each other as individuals but for "your people" and "mine." Perhaps most important, the song emphasizes love and common humanity as the basis for unity and struggle, for it characterizes music as the "language of liberty, lyrics of love."

"Somos Asiáticos" emerged from a burgeoning relationship between A Grain of Sand and Latino activists. JoAnne lived on New York's Upper West Side in an area with an active squatters' movement. Neighborhood denizens, mostly Dominicans and Puerto Ricans, would appropriate buildings that had been left vacant and abandoned, jury-rig electricity and plumbing, and live as squatters in apartments. Confrontations with the police were inevitable. Chris and JoAnne lent their support by singing at squatter sites, and Chris was even arrested. When JoAnne and her brother Bob decided to open a drop-in center for Asian Americans, they turned to El Comité, a Puerto Rican organization, which identified an abandoned storefront on Eighty-eighth Street and Amsterdam Avenue. One night they "liberated" the building and nervously waited for the police to arrive. When it became apparent that no one would interfere with their plans, they cleaned and fixed up the space as a gathering place. Miyamoto recalls that they wanted a name that was strongly revolutionary and finally settled on Chickens Come Home to Roost, after Malcolm X's revolutionary dictum that American violence would return to haunt the nation. Later, El Comité nicknamed the people of the Asian American movement who hung out there "the Chickens." The Chickens and El Comité took over another building on Ninety-first Street that had a large open space that they converted into a coffeehouse called The Dot. Charlie Chin remembers that the place was named for a giant circular dot painted on one wall, and Nobuko Miyamoto recalls that large construction cable spools served as tables. The Dot became a performance space where musicians from Cuba, Peru, and the Dominican Republic played and sang "the most fantastic music."

Chris and JoAnne decided that they needed to write music in Spanish, and of course Charlie had grown up playing the cuatro and singing Trinidadian music. "Somos Asiáticos" was just one of their Spanish numbers; in fact, they could play almost an entire set in Spanish. Asians singing in Spanish was a unique phenomenon, so Puerto Ricans and Dominicans invited A Grain of Sand to perform at many of their demonstrations and events.[70] Miyamoto recalls, "We did more gigs for Puerto Ricans and Dominicans in New York than for Asian Americans. They were so pleased we could sing in Spanish. Our biggest audience was when we played for the Puerto Rican Liberation Day in 1973 or 1974, to a packed house in Madison Square Garden."[71] In retrospect, Chin is less sanguine than Miyamoto in his assessment of interracial cooperation. According to his view, cooperation between Asian Americans and Latinos occurred primarily between "progressive elements" of each community, rather than within the rank and file, because the communities did not overlap geographically and had different class dynamics. And, as he points out, no one sang "We are Puerto Ricans" in Chinese.[72]

Although "Jonathan Jackson," "Warriors of the Rainbow," and "Somos Asiáticos" connect Asians to the struggles of other individual races, the song "Divide and Conquer" argues for unity in general. It begins by questioning why people are alienated and isolated, then proposes a solution: "By yourself, you are just by yourself. Together, we can all take a stand." In this scheme, unity does not just come about but rather is built through action, for it is in taking a stand that we can all begin "walkin' hand in hand."[73] A Grain of Sand thus sought to build solidarity between Asian Americans and blacks, Native Americans, and Latinos through its musical content and its social practice. Rather than viewing Asian American identity as a category that separated Asians from other groups, they argued that the solution to the problem of racism could be found only through building multiracial alliances.

Transnational Sympathy

The political sympathies of A Grain of Sand were not constrained by national boundaries but rather asserted that Asian Americans must act in solidarity with Asians in Asia, particularly the Vietnamese people who were resisting U.S. imperialism. They argued, like the antiwar Asian Americans who were discussed in chapter 4, that the exploitation of Asian Americans in the United States was integrally intertwined with American imperialism in Asia.

The song "War of the Flea" draws inspiration for Asian Americans from the struggles of the Vietnamese people, suggesting that even an overpowered group can prevail if they fight with conviction for freedom:

> War of the small
> War of the flea
> Where the strongest bomb is human
> who is bursting to be free.[74]

On the one hand, the flea may represent Asian Americans, who comprise a tiny fraction of the American population. On the other, the flea may stand for the Vietnamese, who face the overwhelming military superiority of the United States. Natural images of "the jungle," the "moon," "sunshine," "rain," and a "cave" are interspersed throughout the song, suggesting guerilla warfare rather than the technologically advanced weap-onry deployed by Americans. This interpretive ambiguity serves to link the oppression of Asian Americans in the United States to the American mil-itary bullying of the Vietnamese. Both face overwhelming odds but find their most effective weapon in the "human/who is bursting to be free."

Several Asian American poets underscored the linkage between Asian Americans and Vietnamese people in ways similar to those used by A Grain of Sand in their lyrics. Mirikitani's poem "Jungle Rot & Open Arms" further builds identifications between Vietnamese and Americans. Its narrator, an Asian American woman, hears an American GI describing a raid on a village in which his Vietnamese lover was killed. Speaking to the narrator, the soldier recalls, "Her hair was / long and dark—like yours," thus positioning the narrator as a stand-in for the Vietnamese woman. After hearing his story of sorrow and loss, the narrator concludes,

> i stood amidst
> his wreckage
> and wept for myself.[75]

The weeping Asian American woman clearly imagines herself as a sur-rogate for the Vietnamese woman. The poem establishes equivalencies between Vietnamese and Asian American women, blurring the distinc-tions between them and implying that, as fellow Asians, both are targets of American racism.

Similarly, Wing Tek Lum's poem "Chinese New Year" links Asian Americans to Vietnamese people. It describes the holiday festivities in New York City's Chinatown, but the sound of firecrackers bursting on Mott Street evokes the Tet offensive of 1968. The juxtaposition of celebratory fireworks in New York with armaments exploding across the Pacific is a sobering reminder of the war still raging in Vietnam and suggests that Asian Americans should not forget their compatriots abroad.[76]

In "I can understand . . . ," Brenda Paik Sunoo not only identifies with fellow Asians in Vietnam but protests against Asian Americans' fight-ing against them. Like Mirikitani, she posits an original state of Asian unity shattered by migration and exile. Sunoo wonders how Asian Amer-icans have become so estranged from their extended Asian family that they can kill people who share their surnames.[77]

In his poem "Bach Mai," George Leong recognizes that the process of building a multiethnic Asian American identity will be slow and painstaking, for it will have to overcome a prior history of Asian ethnic antagonisms.[78] He points to the grief his mother still suffers from having lost a son in China during World War II to atrocities committed by Japanese soldiers. Yet Leong remains hopeful that his mother can someday come to terms with her hatred for Japanese, because American racism against Asians of all nations in the United States is far more powerful, lasting, and salient than the mass murder of Chinese by Japanese decades ago. The poem's title refers to Bach Mai Hospital, a civilian facility in Hanoi destroyed by U.S. air strikes (though the military initially denied hitting the hospital).[79] Using the bombing of civilians as an emblem of anti-Asian racism, Leong argues that because American racism does not discriminate between Asians on the basis of nationality, the struggle against it should eclipse historic nationalistic antagonism between Asians, even if healing intra-Asian resentments takes a long time.

Together, these poems suggest that because American imperialism does not distinguish between Asians in Vietnam and Asians in the United States, Asian Americans should relate to the Vietnamese people as fellow Asians and use that relationship as a basis for opposing the U.S. war in Viet Nam as an anti-Asian war.

"A Sharp Weapon"

A Grain of Sand's musical performances of anti-imperialism were only one facet of the political actions of the trio's members, who were also directly involved in the radical segment of the Asian American movement to varying degrees. Iijima, the most explicitly political of the three, was a member of I Wor Kuen, AAA, and many other organizations; Miyamoto was a member off AAA and the Chickens Come Home to Roost, and Charlie Chin was a member of Basement Workshop. Other hard-left Asian American organizations such as Wei Min She also took culture seriously, viewing it as a tool in the struggle against imperialism and capitalism, even if they did not invest their songs, poems, and plays with the same level of artistry as did A Grain of Sand. The cultural productions of radical groups like Wei Min She and the leftist criticism of cultural workers they deemed politically insufficient reveal the importance of cultural struggle to activists spanning the entire spectrum of Asian American politics.

In 1975, Wei Min She, which termed itself an "anti-imperialist" organization, criticized the literary wing of the Asian American movement for being overly concerned with the question of identity. The occasion was the Asian American Writers Conference held in March at the Oakland

Museum, which the group criticized for lacking a "political focus" and instead emphasizing "'self-expression' to promote 'good vibes' about being Asian American. . . . In a word," the group continued, "the Conference itself was hungup [sic] on identity—What is Asian American?"[80] Wei Min She's critique is not surprising, given that the conference had been sponsored by the Combined Asian American Resources Project, an organization co-founded by Frank Chin, who was decidedly not a radical. Participants included pioneering Asian American writers such as Hisaye Yamamoto, Toshio Mori, Wakako Yamauchi, Jade Snow Wong, Momoko Iko, Yoshiko Uchida, and Jeanne Wakatsuki Houston, none of whom displayed much in terms of radical politics. The major theme of the conference was reclaiming the legacy of Asian American literature; hence the dearth of calls for revolution.[81]

While critical of the conference's focus on Asian American identity, Wei Min She historicized that focus, allowing that it had been salient "back in the late 1960s," when it had been used to build a collective Asian consciousness. However, the group claimed that by 1975 the issue of identity was moot when isolated from the struggles of the movement. Wei Min She was suggesting not that culture itself should be divorced from social action but rather that the writers conference had wrongfully done so. In contrast, the group vowed to "begin reevaluating our cultural work" in order to "make our culture a sharp weapon in the hands of the people."[82] Thus, Wei Min She, while critical of the conference, remained dedicated to the ideal of culture as a political tool.

Wei Min She itself produced music, lyrics, and skits to dramatize its beliefs and educate workers. Although these cultural productions have proven more ephemeral than those that were published, even in nonmainstream venues, the fact that they were performed at all demonstrates that the distinction between cultural politics and left radicalism is a false dichotomy. At the Chinatown Workers Festival held in San Francisco in 1974, Wei Min She's May 4th Singers performed songs of struggle that called attention to the history of Chinese workers in the United States. The song "We Must Stand Together" noted Chinese immigrants' long and bitter history of exploitation as workers in mines, garment shops, laundries, and restaurants and on railroads, fishing boats, and farms. It decried "discrimination, oppression, and exploitation" along with "immigration laws that keep workers silent and families apart."[83]

Wei Min She's cultural productions built Asian American identity around opposition to exploitation, in keeping with their anticapitalist politics. The song "Join in Struggle" urged listeners to support the struggle to organize the primarily Chinese immigrant workforces of a Chinatown sweatshop, Jung Sai, and an electronics company, Lee Mah. Unlike Frank Chin, Wei Min She did not view immigrants as fundamentally different from American-born Asians, arguing

> I don't understand Chinese
> But I understand the language
> of struggle against the oppressor
> I don't speak Chinese
> But I speak the language
> of resistance to oppression[84]

These lyrics suggested that the language barrier between Chinese-speaking immigrants and English-speaking Chinese Americans mattered little, for pro-strike actions constituted a common "language of struggle" and "resistance." Thus, in this anti-imperialist schema, American-born Asians and Asian immigrants were joined together by struggle and resistance rather than by a shared language and culture or a common Chinese identity. Though both A Grain of Sand and Wei Min She employed culture as a tool for liberation, they were divided by questions of artistry. Miyamoto, Iijima, and Chin were artists in a conscious sense, and they cared deeply about aesthetics; strove to write beautiful melodies, harmonies, and rhythms; and approached lyrics as poetry. In contrast, despite their political importance, the cultural productions of Wei Min She seem primarily strategic and instrumental.

The members of A Grain of Sand were far from alone in producing cultural expressions that sought to liberate Asian Americans. Indeed, their commitments to multiethnic unity, interracial solidarity, and support for the Vietnamese people were shared by many Asian American cultural workers and radicals. Nor were they the only Asian Americans of the period to create a radical musical critique, for the jazz fusion group Hiroshima, which also emerged from the movement in the 1970s, combined western forms with Japanese instrumentation to perform alternative and oppositional Asian American cultural products.[85] The personal and political journeys of Nobuko Miyamoto, Chris Iijima, and Charlie Chin exemplify the dedication of many Asian American artists to the ideals of liberation and their determination to use culture as a means by which to achieve justice and equality for Asian Americans, for other people of color, and for all those who struggled against U.S. domination around the world. As Miyamoto concludes in retrospect, building an Asian American culture was a way of connecting "with something greater than ourselves," creating caring communities that transcended ethnicity and race, and articulating a "desire for change."[86] The members of A Grain of Sand did not slake their thirst for social justice, empowerment, and community building in the 1970s but rather continued to pursue their artistic and political struggles, even as their paths diverged and reconverged in the decades that ensued.

Conclusion

Fighting for the Heart of Asian America

Chris Iijima passed away on 31 December 2005 after a prolonged battle with amyloidosis. Family and friends gathered in Los Angeles on 11 February 2006 to share their grief but also to celebrate a life and legacy of music and activism. At this gathering, the "Come-Unity Celebration for Our Friend and Brother Chris Kwando Iijima," I saw the spirit of the 1960s and 1970s on full display, with tributes, speeches, and remembrances offered by many who had been intimately involved with Asian American causes.[1] Warren Furutani, Victor Shibata, and Eddie Kochiyama warmly recalled Chris's all-out commitment and zest for life and chuckled about his famous combativeness. They proclaimed that the music performed by A Grain of Sand had been "a living soundtrack" of Asian American radicalism and an "integral" component of the national movement by serving as "a bridge between East and West coasts." Kochiyama called Chris "our Stevie [Wonder] and our Gil Scott [-Heron]." Asian American musicians such as June Kuramoto, Derek Nakamoto, and Akira Tana offered tributes in song. Charlie Chin humorously remembered that he had argued with Chris so much that he had dubbed him "Captain Grumpy" but also spoke of his deep admiration for Chris's songwriting ability and verbal acuity. Chin and Nobuko Miyamoto performed a medley of songs by A Grain of Sand. Miyamoto's voice cracked with emotion as she sang, "He was my brother," and finally failed completely as tears streamed down her face.

At the ceremony, Miyamoto recognized two elderly women, Yuri Kochiyama and Aiko Herzig-Yoshinaga, as the "wisdom keepers" who had inspired young radicals of the 1970s. Both women offered moving eulogies, with Herzig-Yoshinaga recounting Chris's early days in New York and Kochiyama leaning heavily on a walker as she approached the podium to speak of his youthful commitment. On that day, the heads of these grandmother radicals were not the only ones flecked with gray, nor were their faces the only ones whose wrinkles betrayed the passage of years, for as Miyamoto noted, "When I first met Chris, I wasn't an elder, but now I am." This was a moment of torch passing from one generation to the next. Amid the tears, embraces, and remembrances of the past, there was also much talk of the present—updates on jobs, family, and current projects. Many former movement participants took their children to the gathering and proudly introduced them to comrades of days gone by. I witnessed a new nexus being built between the generation of activists who had inspired the Asian American movement, the cohort who had served as its leaders and foot soldiers, and those who might comprise its next generation. These young people, who had not even been born when *A Grain of Sand* was recorded in 1973, inhabit a society profoundly changed by the ideals and dedication of Asian American radicals. Hence, this occasion, which was by turns mournful, nostalgic, and joyous, made me ponder what lessons, both cautionary and inspirational, might be learned from recalling Asian American political actions of the 1960s and 1970s.

It seems to me that the Asian American movement left a threefold legacy. First, it created the term "Asian American" to encompass Asians of all ethnicities in the United States. That label originally connoted a political stance whose contention was that what bound all Asians together as Asian Americans were the twin chains of Babylon—racism and imperialism—and the shared struggle to demolish them. However, the political connotations of "Asian American" have been eviscerated in the decades since its construction. The term has taken on a primarily demographic meaning as a descriptor of race, ethnicity, or national descent. Whereas in the 1960s and 1970s Asian American radicals were concerned about the exploitive nature of capitalism, today we see the emergence of "Asian American" business associations, chambers of commerce, and professional associations.[2] Today these organizations function as umbrella groups uniting professionals and business owners across ethnic lines for the express purpose of providing networking opportunities and leadership training in order to enhance individual advancement and maximize profits. By organizing across ethnic lines they follow in the footsteps of the activists who preceded them. But their critiques of inequality are muted, to the extent that they exist at all, and rather than seeing the political construction of Asian America as a means to fundamentally transform American society, they simply seek to ease their existence within it. In this sense, the diminution of the political meaning of "Asian American" is cautionary, for it demonstrates the power of the state and dominant society to co-opt racial definitions and dim radically alternative visions.

Skeptics of the political project originally signified by adopting the moniker Asian American argue that scholars and activists have been over-eager to find resistance in the histories and the cultural productions of Asians in the United States.[3] But reading is itself a political act, and Asian American history is a complex text that bears a multiplicity of interpretations. My intention throughout this book has been to trace a narrative that accounts for the racial triangulation of Asian Americans with and against both blackness and whiteness and to recuperate the resistance to racism and assimilationism performed by activists and cultural workers in the 1960s and 1970s. I have not claimed that these actors were representative of all Asian Americans, and indeed have gone to lengths to show that they were in constant dialogue, if not dispute, with those within their communities who held other political perspectives.

It is far too easy to find current-day examples of Asian Americans who eschew Asian American identity in favor of chasing whiteness. Eric Liu, a highly successful Chinese American who has served as a speechwriter for President Bill Clinton, commentator on MSNBC, and columnist for *Slate* magazine, typifies the mindset of many of the most privileged Asian Americans. He writes in his memoir, *The Accidental Asian*: "Like so many other Asian Americans of the second generation, I find myself now the bearer of a strange new status: white by acclamation. . . . Some are born white, others achieve whiteness, still others have whiteness thrust upon them."[4] Liu is unabashedly allured by whiteness and its promises of acceptance and privilege. At the same time that Liu is enjoying his "model minority" existence, however, many other Asian Americans continue to contend with the challenges confronting racialized people, including poverty, family breakdown, unemployment and underemployment, criminalization and incarceration, and substandard housing, health care, and education. In contrast to Liu, Asian American activists of the 1960s and 1970s refused whiteness by acclamation. They argued that acceding to assimilation was capitulating to white supremacy, for doing so merely stretched the boundaries of whiteness and its privileges to encompass Asians, to the continuing detriment of racial others. Far from being "accidental Asians," these activists intentionally sought to become Asian Americans through their political actions. Chris Iijima may have expressed their sentiments best when he wrote in retrospect:

> [Asian American] identity was only constructed as a means to organize other Asians for political purposes, to highlight aspects of racism, to escape the hegemony of whites in progressive movements, to support other progressive racial formations, to establish alternative forms of looking at society/history, etc. I'm hoping that someday racial identity becomes a political identity again—not an ethnic marker.[5]

Iijima's hopes for Asian American identity highlight a crucial distinction between demographics and commitment. Monisha Das Gupta's particular observation that "a South Asian identity signals a particular politics of social change that cannot be generalized to all immigrants of South Asian origin" may also be applied more generally to Asian American identity and Asian Americans.[6] Although Asian American radicals may not have managed to displace assimilationism, they created new ways to confront it.

The second legacy of the Asian American activism of the 1960s and 1970s is a usable past for Asian Americans who dream of a more just world. Recuperating this history of commitment and struggle not only gives the lie to the myth of Asian American compliance but also provides a template showing how refusal to be a model minority can enable the building of multiethnic, interracial, and transnational sympathies and alliances. Tram Nguyen provides one such example of the bridge between past and present.[7] As a Vietnamese refugee, she was not even present in the United States when the events discussed in this book took place. Nguyen nevertheless locates herself in the tradition of "older Asian American movement radicals," though she has begun to broaden our understanding of activism by unearthing a history of Vietnamese American radicalism from the 1960s to the present.[8] Her book *We Are All Suspects Now* describes the travails of Pakistanis, Somalis, Iraqis, Salvadorans, African Americans, and Latinos in the aftermath of 9/11. It shows how both Muslims and non-Muslims suffer from surveillance, harassment, profiling, detention, and violence in the name of national security and how these extreme measures are becoming normalized in the treatment of immigrants.[9] Nguyen's work emphasizes the contingent nature of the Asian American coalition, demonstrating that it must be constantly revised to embrace new ethnicities and new needs, a position first staked out by activists and cultural workers in the 1960s. Furthermore, it insists on the need to address race in comparative ways and build interracial solidarities between Asian Americans and other racialized people. Finally, Nguyen reminds us that possessing an Asian American political commitment is distinct from being an Asian American in the demographic sense, contrasting her own story with that of fellow Vietnamese refugee Viet Dinh, who became an architect of the USA Patriot Act.[10]

The third and final legacy of Asian American activism has been its rejection, from its very inception, of the arbitrariness of national boundaries, instead viewing the United States as a hegemon in the global arena. This transnational vision vitally informed efforts to understand the racialization of Asian Americans. Pat Sumi's international journeys to Africa and Asia, the adoption of the moniker "Third World" by San Francisco State students, the Red Guard's admiration of Mao and the Black Panthers, the Asian American antiwar movement's embrace of Vietnamese as fellow Asians, A Grain of Sand's support for Puerto Rican independence—all of these evince a transnational consciousness and refusal to rely on the state and citizenship to attain rights.[11] In the current era of globalization and renewed American imperialism, the Asian American movement's commitment to justice regardless of national borders seems prescient and instructive.

Asian Americans who today combat racism, sexism, economic exploitation, and homophobia by demanding immigrant rights and decent housing, wages, education, and health care—who do so through grassroots organizing and refuse to reify distinctions based on immigrant status and citizenship—continue in the tradition set down before them by those who fought to break the chains of Babylon. However, they continually evolve the ideology of Asian American progressivism by paying greater heed to sexuality, embracing new ethnicities, and building new coalitions with groups such as Arab Americans. Thus, although some aspects of Asian American political identity may have waned in the decades since the 1970s, others still shine brightly.

In a conversation about two years after the memorial service for Chris Iijima, Nobuko Miyamoto urged me to balance head and heart in telling this story, which is to say that she advocated for a reading of A Grain of

Sand—and by extension all Asian American radicals and their cultural and political work—that valued intellectual and ideological perspectives while also honoring affective elements: the love, joy, and deep interpersonal connections enabled and indeed created by a politics of empowerment and liberation. To demonstrate the power of the heart, she shared with me the lyrics to "Song for a Child," which Chris had written in 1974. Nobuko began reading the words, but her musicality could not be restrained, and soon she was crooning a beautiful lullaby into my ear over the telephone:

> Child of mine work for those who labor
> Weep for those who cry in pain
> Fight for children weak from hunger
> Fight for those bound up in chains.[12]

I heard the song not as an elegy for a dead past but instead as a charge to a movement that is young, incipient, and perhaps still growing.

Notes

Preface

1. Lowe, *Immigrant Acts,* 22.
2. Habal, "'We Won't Move'"; Habal, *San Francisco's International Hotel;* Toribio, "Dare to Struggle," 31–46.
3. Elbaum, *Revolution in the Air,* 191–206.

Introduction

1. Information on Sumi is drawn from Editorial Board of the UCLA Asian American Studies Center, "An Interview with Pat Sumi"; Yokota, "Interview with Pat Sumi"; and Takemoto, "Pat Sumi."
2. Editorial Board, "An Interview with Pat Sumi," 253.
3. Takemoto, "Pat Sumi," 108.
4. Ibid.
5. Ibid., 108–9.
6. Editorial Board, "An Interview with Pat Sumi," 255; Takemoto, "Pat Sumi," 109.
7. Moser, *New Winter Soldiers,* 98–99.
8. Ibid., 88, 99.
9. U.S. Congress, House of Representatives, Committee on Internal Security, "Investigation of Attempts to Subvert the United States Armed Services, Part 1," 6382, 6539.
10. Moser, *New Winter Soldiers,* 88.
11. U.S. Congress, House of Representatives, Committee on Internal Security, "Investigation of Attempts to Subvert the United States Armed Services, Part 3," 7357–7358.
12. Ibid., 7259–7272; Yokota, "Interview with Pat Sumi," 20–21; Editorial Board, "Interview with Pat Sumi," 256.
13. Committee on Internal Security, "Investigation of Attempts to Subvert the United

States Armed Forces, Part 3," 7295–7296. Sumi's dossier appears as Exhibit 40-A in ibid., 7399–7402.

14. Ibid., 7273, 7269.

15. Ibid., 7265, 7272.

16. Heinl, "The Collapse of the Armed Forces," 331.

17. Committee on Internal Security, "Investigation of Attempts to Subvert the United States Armed Forces, Part 3," 7269; Editorial Board, "Interview with Pat Sumi," 256. The Oceanside Police Department deemed the marine's injury nonserious, while Sumi described him as having been "nearly killed."

18. Moser, *New Winter Soldiers*, 88.

19. Brown, *A Taste of Power*, 220; Yokota, "Interview with Pat Sumi," 25.

20. *Black Panther*, 8 August 1970, 19, quoted in U.S. Congress, House of Representatives, Committee on Internal Security, "The Black Panther Party," 66.

21. Cleaver, "Back to Africa," 232; Brown, *A Taste of Power*, 226.

22. *Black Panther*, 8 August 1970, 19, quoted in Committee on Internal Security, "The Black Panther Party," 66.

23. Clemons and Jones, "Global Solidarity," 33–34.

24. Yokota, "Interview with Pat Sumi," 27–30.

25. Patrell [no first name given], "Glad They're Back," *Gidra*, October 1970, 4; Takemoto, "Pat Sumi," 110; Yokota, "Interview with Pat Sumi," 26.

26. Pat Sumi, "December 7, 1971 . . . Japan Militarism Rising," *Gidra*, December 1970, 7; Pat Sumi, "Activism, 1946 Style," *Gidra*, December 1970, 14; Pat Sumi, "Atrocities against Chinese Amerikans . . . a Partial List," *Gidra*, February 1971, 4; Pat Sumi, "Anti-Asian Legislation . . . a Partial List," *Gidra*, February 1971, 5; Patricia Sumi, "Hiroshima-Nagasaki-Indochina," *Gidra*, August 1971, 15; Pat Sumi, "Laos," *Gidra*, March 1971, 10–14. See also the May 1971, June 1971, July 1971, and August 1971 issues of *Gidra*.

27. Wu, "Journeys for Peace and Liberation."

28. Pat Sumi, "To My Asian American Brothers," *Gidra*, November 1970, 3.

29. Sumi, "Laos," 13.

30. Sumi, "To My Asian American Brothers," 3.

31. Zia, *Asian American Dreams*, 4.

32. Pulido, *Black, Brown, Yellow, and Left*, 23–25.

33. Kim, "The Racial Triangulation of Asian Americans," 40–41.

34. Chang, "America's First Multiethnic 'Riots'"; Min, *Caught in the Middle*; Kim, *Bitter Fruit*; Joyce, *No Fire Next Time*.

35. A/A; *The Afro/Asian Century*.

36. Yu, *Thinking Orientals*; Jung, *Coolies and Cane*; Jung, "Outlawing 'Coolies.'"

37. Lipsitz, *The Possessive Investment in Whiteness*; Allen, "Waiting for Tojo"; Gallicchio, *The African American Encounter with Japan and China*; Kelley and Esch, "Black Like Mao."

38. Pulido, "Race and Revolutionary Politics"; Pulido, *Black, Brown, Yellow, and Left*; Widener, "'Perhaps the Japanese Are to Be Thanked?'"; Kurashige, "Transforming Los Angeles"; Kurashige, *Shifting Grounds of Race*; Prashad, "Kung Fusion." See also Raphael-Hernandez, Steen, and Prashad, *AfroAsian Encounters*.

39. Dudziak, *Cold War Civil Rights*; Borstelman, *The Cold War and the Color Line*.

40. Simpson, *An Absent Presence*; Klein, *Cold War Orientalism*.

41. Lee, *Orientals*.

42. Koshy, "Morphing Race into Ethnicity."

43. Ong, *Buddha Is Hiding*, 86.

44. Lee, *Urban Triage*, 81–83, 92–93; Viet Thanh Nguyen, *Race and Resistance*, 169.

To be fair, Lee argues not that Asian Americans become indistinguishable from whites but rather that their racial positioning above blacks makes their interests complicit with whiteness, and Nguyen differentiates between being white and being structurally aligned with whiteness.

45. Zhou, "Are Asian Americans Becoming 'White'?" 29.

46. Solomon, "'No Evictions'"; Habal, "'We Won't Move'"; Fu, "Keeping Close to the Ground," 109–72.

47. Farber and Bailey, *The Columbia Guide to America in the 1960s*; Gitlin, *The Sixties*; Anderson, *The Movement and the Sixties*, 299; Bloom and Breines, *Takin' It to the Streets*.

48. Fu, "Keeping Close to the Ground," 171.

49. Yip, "Serve the People," 18, 20–21. On the alliances and tensions within and surrounding the I-Hotel, see Fu, "Keeping Close to the Ground," 109–16, 163–72, and Habal, "We Won't Move," 306–9, 336–45.

50. J. K. Dineen, "I Hotel Begins New Life," *San Francisco Examiner*, 30 June 2003; Habal, "We Won't Move," 431–32.

51. On the transitions within the left during the mid-1970s, see Elbaum, *Revolution in the Air*.

52. Burner, *Making Peace with the 60s*, 50, 81; Gitlin, *Twilight of Common Dreams*, 99–100.

53. For a devastating critique of Gitlin's model, see Kelley, "Looking Extremely Backward." In addition to making the charge of racial separatism, Gitlin and others denigrate the post-1968 period for its turn toward Marxist-Leninist-Maoist theory and party building. While Asian American radicals partook in the party building of the 1970s, my point here is that an emphasis on racial identity, far from being separatist, provided points of alliance between nonwhite social movements.

54. Espiritu, *Asian American Panethnicity*.

55. In particular, see Espiritu, *Asian American Panethnicity*, and Vo, *Mobilizing an Asian American Community*.

56. Clearly, the degree to which the state recognizes racially based claims is waning, as successful attacks on affirmative action in places such as Michigan (Michigan Civil Rights Initiative, 2006) and California (Proposition 209, 1996) demonstrate.

57. Lowe, *Immigrant Acts*, 22–26.

58. Pat Sumi, "Third World People: Shoulder to Shoulder," *Gidra*, April 1974, 66–67.

1. Before Asian America

1. Said, *Orientalism*; Okihiro, *Margins and Mainstreams*, 3–30.

2. Bonacich, "Asian Labor in the Development of California and Hawaii."

3. Takaki, *Strangers from a Different Shore*, 31.

4. Saxton, *The Indispensable Enemy*.

5. Peffer, *If They Don't Bring Their Women Here*, xi, 105.

6. Salyer, *Laws Harsh as Tigers*, 17.

7. Hing, *Making and Remaking Asian America*, 23–26; Daniels, *Asian America*, 55–58.

8. Takaki, *Strangers from a Different Shore*, 45, 189–90.

9. Azuma, *Between Two Empires*, 30–31.

10. Hing, *Making and Remaking Asian America*, 28–30; Daniels, *Asian America*, 120–26.

11. Takaki, *Strangers from a Different Shore*, 46–47.

12. Chan, *Asian Americans*, 15, 38–39.

13. Hing, *Making and Remaking Asian America*, 27.

14. Jensen, *Passage from India*, 27.

15. Hing, *Making and Remaking Asian America*, 70.

16. Jensen, *Passage from India*, 15–16.

17. Ibid., 44.

18. Hing, *Making and Remaking Asian America*, 31–32.

19. Takaki, *Strangers from a Different Shore*, 58.

20. Ibid., 316–24.

21. Hing, *Making and Remaking Asian America*, 33–36.

22. Volpp, "'Obnoxious to Their Very Nature,'" 57.

23. Ngai, "The Architecture of Race in American Immigration Law."

24. Ancheta, *Race, Rights, and the Asian American Experience*, 23; Lopez, *White by Law*, 42–44; Peffer, *If They Don't Bring Their Women Here*, 33.

25. Kim, "'Yellow' Skin, 'White' Masks."

26. Lopez, *White by Law*, 49–53, and Appendix A: The Racial Prerequisite Cases, 203–8.

27. Koshy, "Morphing Race into Ethnicity," 168–69; Lopez, *White by Law*, 83–84.

28. Salyer, *Laws Harsh as Tigers*, 18.

29. Ichioka, "The Early Japanese Immigrant Quest for Citizenship," 10–12.

30. *Ozawa v. United States*.

31. Lopez, *White by Law*, 80–86.

32. *United States v. Thind*.

33. Lopez, *White by Law*, 86–92.

34. *Toyota v. United States*; Gordon, "The Racial Barrier to American Citizenship," 243–44; "Status of Filipinos for Purposes of Immigration and Naturalization."

35. Takaki, *Double Victory*, 125; Lopez, *White by Law*, 206.

36. Guglielmo, *White on Arrival*.

37. Pascoe, "Miscegenation Law, Court Cases, and Ideologies of 'Race'"; Koshy, *Sexual Naturalization*.

38. Yu, *Thinking Orientals*; Yu, "Mixing Bodies and Cultures."

39. Osumi, "Asians and California's Anti-Miscegenation Laws," 2, 6.

40. The 1880 legislation amended Section 69 of the Civil Code, which governed the issuance of marriage licenses. However, a concurrent attempt to amend Section 60, another antimiscegenation statute that dealt with the legality of existing marriages, failed and thus, for the next two decades, California's code featured conflicting antimiscegenation statutes, one that barred Mongolians and another that did not. The discrepancy was resolved in 1901, when Section 60 was amended to bar marriage of whites to "Mongolians." Though Section 60 was declared unconstitutional in 1902, it was reenacted in 1905 (Osumi, "Asians," 11, 13).

41. Osumi, "Asians," 18–21.

42. Pascoe, "Miscegenation Law," 49, 61–69.

43. Yen Le Espiritu uses the term "ethnic disidentification" to refer to attempts by various Asians to dissociate from other Asians (*Asian American Panethnicity*, 20).

44. Lee, "The Hidden World of Asian Immigrant Radicalism," 264.

45. Espiritu, *Five Faces of Exile*, 189–92.

46. For examples of Chinese transnationalism during Exclusion, see especially Hsu, *Dreaming of Gold, Dreaming of Home*, and Chen, *Chinese San Francisco, 1850–1943*, 99–108, 217–38.

47. Jensen, *Passage from India*; Puri, *Ghadar Movement*; Mathur, *Indian Revolutionary Movement in the United States of America*, 72–129; Sohi, "Echoes of Mutiny."

48. Choy, *Koreans in America*; Lyu, "Korean Nationalist Activities in Hawaii and the Continental United States, 1900–1945," Parts I and II; Kim, "Inaugurating the American Century," 61–62.

49. Kim, "Inaugurating the American Century," 52–59.

50. McKee, "The Chinese Boycott of 1905–1906 Reconsidered"; Pomerantz, "The Chinese Bourgeoisie and the Anti-Chinese Movement in the United States."

51. Ma, *Monarchists, Revolutionaries, and Chinatowns*; Lai, "China Politics and the U.S. Chinese Communities," 152–59; Lai, "The Kuomintang in Chinese American Communities before World War II," 175, 181–83, 196.

52. Ichioka, *The Issei*, 249–50.

53. Chen, *Chinese San Francisco*, 200.

54. Takaki, *Strangers from a Different Shore*, 271, 281–82.

55. Yung, *Unbound Feet*, 224–248; Chen, *Chinese San Francisco*, 233–35.

56. Ichioka, *Before Internment*, 180–203; Daniels, *Asian America*, 167–69.

57. Espiritu, *Asian American Panethnicity*, 23.

58. Ibid., 26.

59. *Japanese-American Courier* (Seattle), 17 September 1938, 1. For an insider's account of Sakamoto's election as President of the JACL in 1936, see Hosokawa, *JACL*, 95–97.

60. James Sakamoto, "Seattle JACL History," James Y. Sakamoto Papers (hereafter JYSP), Box 1, Folder 1, n.p. This document is a response to a set of questions posed by Bill Hosokawa for his article on Sakamoto, which was subsequently published in the *Pacific Citizen*; Niiya, *Japanese American History*, s.v. "Sakamoto, James Yoshinori (1903–1955)," 300–301; Miyamoto, *Social Solidarity among the Japanese in Seattle*, xix.

61. Sakamoto, "Autobiography," JYSP, Box 15, Folder 1, 15.

62. Ichioka, "A Study in Dualism," 75; Yoo, *Growing Up Nisei*, 72.

63. Hosokawa, *Out of the Frying Pan*, 12.

64. Masaoka, "To: National Board Members, National Council Members, Active and Associated Members, Sponsors, Friends, and Supporters of the National Japanese American Citizens League," 17, 22 April 1944, Japanese American Evaluation and Resettlement Records, BANC MSS 67/14c (JERS), Bancroft Library, University of California–Berkeley, Folder T6.15, Microfilm Reel 84. This document starts on frame 256.

65. Sakamoto, "Autobiography," 2.

66. Azuma, *Between Two Empires*, 131.

67. Sakamoto, "Autobiography," 32–33.

68. Roediger, *The Wages of Whiteness*, 13–20; Jacobson, *Whiteness of a Different Color*, 72–75.

69. Clark Frasier to James Sakamoto, 25 October 1937, JYSP, Box 4, Folder 64.

70. Harry Weingarten to T. T. Yatabe, no date, JYSP, Box 11, Folder 9.

71. Fred M. Fueker to James Sakamoto, 7 February 1938, JYSP, Box 11, Folder 9; Fred M. Fueker to James Sakamoto, 24 December 1937, JYSP, Box 16, Folder 7.

72. Quoted in Salyer, "Baptism by Fire," 847.

73. "California First Biennial Convention of the Federation of Northern District Councils of the Japanese-American Citizens' League," JYSP, Box 13, Folder 13.

74. Tokie Slocum to Sim [Togasaki], 6 June 1937, JYSP, Box 11, Folder 19.

75. *Japanese-American Courier*, 16 September 1933, 3.

76. Mrs. W. C. Dingle to Roy Nishimura, no date, JYSP, Box 11, Folder 11. Although the letter is not dated, it most likely refers to the same flag presentation that the *Japanese American Courier* describes in the 16 September 1933 issue.

77. *Japanese-American Courier*, 13 July 1935, 1.

78. Ibid., 29 September 1928, 1. On his membership in the American Legion, see *Japanese-American Courier*, 6 September 1930. Horr's address to the First Biennial was entitled "Value of Citizenship" ("First Biennial," 2).

79. *Japanese-American Courier*, 23 August 1930, 1.

80. Jacobson, *Whiteness of a Different Color,* 223–26.

81. Friday, "Asian American Labor and Historical Interpretation."

82. Chan, *Asian Americans,* 81–82.

83. Bulosan, *America Is in the Heart;* Evangelista, *Carlos Bulosan and His Poetry.*

84. Takaki, *Strangers from a Different Shore,* 151.

85. Azuma, *Between Two Empires,* 194–205.

86. Takaki, *Strangers from a Different Shore,* 152–154.

87. Espiritu, *Asian American Panethnicity,* 24; Takaki, *Strangers from a Different Shore,* 154.

88. Friday, *Organizing Asian American Labor,* 149–92.

89. Almaguer, "Racial Domination and Class Conflict in Capitalist Agriculture."

90. DeWitt, "The Filipino Labor Union"; Cordova, *Filipinos, Forgotten Asian Americans.*

91. Kwong, *Chinatown, New York,* 116–30.

92. Posadas, "The Hierarchy of Color and Psychological Adjustment in an Industrial Environment."

93. Jung, *Reworking Race.*

94. Ichioka, *The Issei,* 91–145.

95. Yoneda, *Ganbatte.* Unlike AFL unions, CIO unions were racially inclusive.

96. Raineri, *The Red Angel.*

97. Omatsu, "Always a Rebel," 93–94, 96.

98. Ichioka, *The Issei,* 144–45.

99. Yoneda, *Ganbatte,* 67.

100. Omatsu, "Always a Rebel," 93–96.

101. Lai, "A Historical Survey of the Chinese Left in American Society"; Lai, "A Historical Survey of Organization of the Left among the Chinese in America"; Lai, "The Chinese Marxist Left in America to the 1960s."

102. Lai, "Historical Survey of the Chinese Left," 65–69; Yu, *To Save China, To Save Ourselves.*

103. Lai, "China Politics," 153–59.

104. Boggs, *Living for Change,* 45–75, 196–97; Choi, "At the Margin of Asian American Political Experience."

105. Wei, *The Asian American Movement,* 31.

106. As executive director of the Southern Christian Leadership Conference, Baker organized the conference of black student protest leaders that led to the formation of the Student Nonviolent Coordinating Committee, one of the most important civil rights organizations of the early to mid-1960s. See Clayborne Carson, *In Struggle,* 19–21; Ransby, *Ella Baker and the Black Freedom Movement.*

107. Alex Hing, interview with Fred Ho and Steve Yip, in *Legacy to Liberation,* ed. Ho et al., 284–85, 289.

108. Gitlin, *The Sixties,* 110–111.

109. Lai, "Historical Survey of the Chinese Left," 63–80.

2. "Down with Hayakawa!"

1. *San Francisco Examiner,* 22 February 1969; *San Francisco Chronicle,* 22 February 1969. Another report listed the number of attendees as 200 and the number of protesters as 125 (Roger Oyama and Tom Mayehara, "Division in the Community: Hayakawa and the Japanese-American," *Oakland [Calif.] Sun Reporter,* 1 March 1969, 8).

2. Laura Ho, "Pigs, Pickets and a Banana," *Gidra* 1, no. 2 (May 1969): 1.

3. *New York Times*, 28 February 1992, B6: 1; S. I. Hayakawa, "Why I Want America to Win," Unpublished paper, circa 1943, Hoover Institution Archives, S. I. Hayakawa Papers (hereafter, SIH), Box 411, Folder "Writings," Subfolder "Papers, Unpublished," 2–3; Hayakawa, *The English Language Amendment*, 1–4, 13–15.

4. Hayakawa, *Language in Action*. Some academics considered Hayakawa a mere popularizer of the theories of Polish (and later American) scholar Alfred Korzybski. While acknowledging the centrality of Korzybski to his thinking, Hayakawa also cited I. A. Richards, Bronislaw Malinowski (which is particularly interesting given Malinowski's cultural pluralist anthropology), Jean Piaget, and others (iv). Two years before the Harcourt, Brace edition of *Language in Action* appeared, Hayakawa had published a brief 100-page predecessor (Madison, Wisc.: College Typing Co., 1939). The much longer 1941 version (which contained more than 300 pages) was the one that gained widespread distribution and garnered Hayakawa popular acclaim; hence I treat the 1941 edition as the first full-fledged voicing of Hayakawa's theories.

5. Hayakawa, *Language in Action*, 27.

6. Ibid., 42–56.

7. Ibid., 106–9.

8. Hayakawa, "General Semantics," 164–65.

9. Hayakawa, "The Non-Aristotelian Revision of Morality," 167.

10. Charles Hughes, letter to S. I. Hayakawa, 31 December 1941, SIH, Box 415, unmarked folder (brown), Subfolder "Language in Action."

11. Geraldine Rugg, letter to S. I. Hayakawa, 6 January 1942, SIH, Box 415, unmarked folder (brown), Subfolder "Language in Action."

12. H. F. Anderson, letter to S. I. Hayakawa, 10 December 1941, SIH, Box 415, unmarked folder (brown), Subfolder "Language in Action."

13. S. I. Hayakawa, "The Address of Dr. S. I. Hayakawa to Japanese-Americans on Their Problems at the Present Time," SIH, Box 411, Folder "Writings—S.I.H."

14. Hayakawa, "Why I Want America to Win," 8.

15. Hayakawa, "General Semantics," 160.

16. Hayakawa, "Second Thoughts," *Chicago Defender*, 3 July 1943, 15.

17. Myrdal, *An American Dilemma*.

18. Southern, *Gunnar Myrdal and Black-White Relations*; Jackson, *Gunnar Myrdal and America's Conscience*.

19. Hayakawa, "Second Thoughts."

20. Hayakawa, *English Language Amendment*, 2. Because Hayakawa was in Chicago at the outbreak of war, he was not subject to internment or relocation.

21. Hayakawa, "Second Thoughts." For other columns on consumer co-ops, see issues from 1943 dated 20 February, 27 February, 20 March, 27 March, 15 May, 29 May, 10 July, 2 October, and 20 November. In a 29 May piece, commenting on the number of columns devoted to co-ops, he admits to having a "one-track mind" about the topic.

22. Hayakawa, "Second Thoughts."

23. Hayakawa, "Address of Dr. S. I. Hayakawa to Japanese-Americans," 5.

24. Hayakawa, "Second Thoughts."

25. Bob Fuchigami, e-mail to the author, 4 March 2008. Fuchigami and Hayakawa engaged in some disagreements in their correspondence and, strangely enough, Hayakawa sent Fuchigami a copy of Norman Mailer's essay "The White Negro."

26. The Hayakawa letter was quoted by Fuchigami in *Hokubei Mainichi*, 6 December 1955, 1. See also *Rafu Shimpo*, 15 December 1955, 3.

27. Information on CINO and Nisei clubs is drawn from Bob Fuchigami, e-mail to the author, 4 March 2008.

28. Three years after Hayakawa's rebuff, CINO did disband, claiming that increased tolerance of Japanese Americans made the organization unnecessary ("Nisei Unit Notes Tolerance Boost, Will Disband," *Fresno (Calif.) Bee,* 28 December 1958; "Intercollegiate Nisei Group Ends Meeting," *San Francisco Examiner,* 4 January 1959).

29. "Yesterday's TV Ad-Viewing Tots Are Now Integration Advocates: Hayakawa," *Advertising Age,* 19 August 1963, 1, 75; "The Impact of TV on Negroes," *San Francisco Chronicle,* 3 September 1963, 11; "TV Shows Way to Race Equality, Nisei Semanticist Says in Talk," *Nichi Bei Times,* 4 September 1963, 1; "Seeds of Negro Demands Sowed by TV, Says Professor," *Seattle Times,* 2 September 1963; "Dr. Hayakawa Rides Again," *Honolulu Star-Bulletin,* 8 October 1963.

30. "A Semanticist Lays It on the Line," *Variety,* 30 September 1959.

31. Orrick lists the six constituent organizations of the TWLF at its birth as BSU, LASO, MASC, ICSA, PACE, and AAPA (*Shut It Down!* 100), as does Umemoto in "'On Strike!'" (40, n. 72). According to Kuregiy Hekymara, the Native American Student Organization was also a TWLF member (Hekymara, "The Third World Movement and Its History," 127, quoting Third World Liberation Front, "School of Third World Studies," San Francisco, 1968, 4).

32. "Ten Demands of the Black Student Union" and "Five Demands of the Third World Liberation Front," reprinted in Orrick, Jr., *Shut It Down!* 151.

33. Smith, Axen, and Pentony, *By Any Means Necessary,* 96–129; Orrick, *Shut It Down!* 30–33. The speech appears in George Murray, "The Necessity of a Black Revolution," *Black Panther,* 16 November 1968, 13.

34. Despite this fact, many accounts of the strike incorrectly treat the BSU as the primary agitator, with the TWLF acting strictly in a secondary or support role. In fact, the decision-making body of the strike, the twelve-member TWLF Central Committee, was composed of two representatives each from the BSU, LASO, MASC, ICSA, PACE, and AAPA. White students (particularly members of Students for a Democratic Society and Progressive Labor Party members) also participated in the strike but as troops rather than leaders. White students, under the aegis of the Strike Committee, agreed to support the strike without adding further demands to those put forward by the TWLF.

35. Umemoto, "'On Strike!'" 11–15; Wei, *The Asian American Movement,* 17–18.

36. Umemoto, "'On Strike!'" 15–17; Wei, *The Asian American Movement,* 18–19.

37. Umemoto, "'On Strike!'" 17–19; Yuji Ichioka, interview with Yen Le Espiritu, quoted in Espiritu, "Conflict and Cooperation," 51–52.

38. Wei, *Asian American Movement,* 19–20.

39. *San Francisco Chronicle,* 2 January 1969, 26.

40. *San Francisco Chronicle,* 22 February 1969; *San Francisco Examiner,* 22 February 1969.

41. "Public Statement by President S. I. Hayakawa," 30 November 1968, in Strike Collection, Special Collections, J. Paul Leonard Library, San Francisco State University (hereafter SFSU), "Hayakawa Folder #1 (81)."

42. "Declaration of Emergency," 2 December 1968, in SFSU, "Hayakawa Folder #1 (81)."

43. "Hayakawa Rips Off Truck," *Daily Gater,* 3 December 1968, 3; *San Francisco Chronicle,* 3 December 1968, 18; Hayakawa, "From Semantics to the U.S. Senate," 208–10.

44. "Scholar in a Vortex: Samuel Ichiye Hayakawa," *New York Times,* 6 December 1968, 39.

45. Hayakawa, "From Semantics to the U.S. Senate," 210–14.

46. *San Francisco Chronicle,* 15 May 1969, 21.

47. *San Francisco Chronicle*, 14 May 1969.

48. "Minutes of the Thirty-eighth Annual Meeting of the Pacific Coast Coffee Association," 27, in SFSU, "Hayakawa Folder #3 (83)" (emphasis mine).

49. *San Francisco Chronicle*, 27 November 1968, 7.

50. *Time*, 6 December 1968, 83.

51. Brown and Paris, *Quotations from Chairman S. I. Hayakawa*, n.p.

52. Hayakawa and Hayakawa, "From Semantics to the U.S. Senate," 148, 371.

53. "Hayakawa's True Colors," *Strike Daily*, 10 December 1968, 2.

54. Quoted in Bill Barlow and Peter Shapiro, "The Emperor Has New Clothes," *Open Process*, 4 December 1968, 4–5.

55. "Another Bloody Day," *Daily Gater*, 4 December 1968, 1 (emphasis mine).

56. Glazer and Moynihan, *Beyond the Melting Pot*.

57. *San Francisco Examiner*, 22 February 1969.

58. Hayakawa, "Education in Ferment," 207.

59. Tom Wieder, "A Little Segregation Might Help the Negro, Says Dr. S. I. Hayakawa," *Monterey (Calif.) Peninsula Herald*, 4 December 1965.

60. "Dr. S. I. Hayakawa . . . Progress of Negroes Held Back by Inferiority Complex Induced by Whites, Declares Noted Nisei Semanticist," *Nichi Bei Times*, 24 August 1965; "Negro Progress Held Back By Built-in Inferiority Complex, Hayakawa Says," *Hokubei Mainichi*, 25 August 1965.

61. Hayakawa, "Education in Ferment," 207.

62. *San Francisco Examiner*, 22 February 1969.

63. Wieder, "A Little Segregation Might Help the Negro."

64. S. I. Hayakawa, "Why the English Language Amendment? An Autobiographical Statement," in Hoover Institution Archives, Lillian Baker Papers (hereafter LB), Box 8, Folder "Hayakawa, S. I. 1986–," 2.

65. *San Francisco Chronicle*, 11 April 1968.

66. Smith, Axen, and Pentony, *By Any Means Necessary*, 205–6. This insiders' account—Smith served as president and Pentony as deputy president of San Francisco State—exhibits all of the biases and partialities one might expect. It consistently represents the liberal administration as virtuous, longsuffering, and rational in contrast to its opponents on both the left and the right. Caught between conservative politicians and the trustees of the California State Colleges on the one hand and radical faculty and students on the other, the administration is portrayed as well-intentioned yet impotent. Furthermore, this narrative focuses on institutional politics between faculty, administrators, and trustees while treating student activism much less richly. Finally, it adopts an antiradical perspective, calling "tragic" and "unfortunate" events that others might find instigated valuable changes in the college itself and in academe at large.

67. Litwak and Wilner, *College Days in Earthquake Country*, 126.

68. President Smith, in explaining his own resignation, strongly implied that Hayakawa orchestrated a coup d'état and positioned himself as the next president (Smith, Axen, and Pentony, *By Any Means Necessary*, 193–94, 206–7); Hayakawa recalls writing a memorandum to the trustees of the California State College system on the steps that needed to be taken to restore order on campus during Smith's presidency and prior to his ascension (Hayakawa, "From Semantics to the U.S. Senate," 206). On Hayakawa as a member of the Faculty Renaissance, see Orrick, *Shut It Down!* 56. Hayakawa, "Education in Ferment," 199.

69. Hayakawa, "From Semantics to the U.S. Senate," 203–4, 217. That Hayakawa accepted without protest the joking quid pro quo of Pearl Harbor for San Francisco State suggests how unconcerned he was with prior racism, which had conflated Japanese Americans

with the imperial Japanese militarists and justified their mass incarceration during World War II.

70. *San Francisco Chronicle*, 10 December 1968, 25.

71. *Seminar: A Quarterly Review for Newspapermen* 12 (June 1969): 7, reprinted from the *Denver Post*, 29 November 1968, 20.

72. *Strike Daily*, 10 December 1968, in Hoover Institution Archives, New Left Collection (hereafter NLC), Box 21, Folder "Strike Daily."

73. Richard Gumbiner, "Doctor Hayakawa's Next Duty as Samurai (a tanka: to be chanted)," *Open Process*, 8 and 9 January 1969, 10, in NLC, Box 20, Folder "Open Process."

74. *San Francisco Express Times*, 4 December 1968.

75. Reginald Major, "SF State Still in Trouble: Uncle Sam Hayakawa," *Oakland (Calif.) Sun Reporter*, 14 December 1968, 2.

76. Oyama and Mayehara, "Division in the Community," 8.

77. McEvoy and Miller, "On Strike . . . Shut It Down," 29. McEvoy and Miller's account, while generally antistrike, is also critical of the administration. Although at various times they acknowledge the participation of nonblack students of color, McEvoy and Miller tend to cast the strike in black-and-white terms.

78. Poster, San Francisco Historical Center, San Francisco Public Library (hereafter SFPL), Folder "SFSU Strike. Flyers."

79. "Seven Arrests: Hayakawa Foes Nailed on Poster," *San Francisco Chronicle*, 11 December 1968.

80. *Open Process*, 4 December 1968; *Open Process*, 8 January 1969.

81. San Francisco Strike Committee, "On Strike: Shut It Down," n.p., quoted in Orrick, *Shut It Down!* 60. This staff report is not to be confused with the actual report of the San Francisco State College Study Team. The Strike Committee was composed of white students who supported the TWLF demands. Although a number of SDS members were also members of the Strike Committee, it remained independent of SDS.

82. Ho, "Pigs, Pickets and a Banana," 1.

83. Editorial Board of the UCLA Asian American Studies Center, "An Interview with Pat Sumi," 260.

84. *Hokubei Mainichi*, 1 January 1969.

85. Oyama and Mayehara, "Division in the Community," 8.

86. Takahashi, *Nisei/Sansei*.

87. *Nichi Bei Times*, 8 February 1969; *Hokubei Mainichi*, 8 February 1969.

88. *Nichi Bei Times*, 14 February 1969.

89. *San Francisco Chronicle*, 6 December 1968, 21. The *Chronicle* story does not name the organization behind the pro-Hayakawa petition, but in view of the information in the other sources specified later, my interpretation of the evidence seems plausible. In her essay "The San Francisco State College Story" (1 January 1969), Kai-yu Hsu described a scroll emblazoned "Banzai Sam!" presented to Hayakawa by the Nisei Junior Chamber of Commerce (SFSU, Kai-Yu Hsu folder [87]). The *San Francisco Examiner* mentions this same scroll and reports that it bore two hundred signatures but does not specify what organization bestowed it upon Hayakawa (7 December 1968, 4).

90. *San Francisco Chronicle*, 5 December 1968.

91. Yoneda, "100 Years of Japanese Labor History in the USA," 158.

92. James Hirabayashi, interview with the author, 13 October 2006.

93. *Hokubei Mainichi*, 3 February 1969, 1.

94. *Nichi Bei Times*, 25 February 1969; *Hokubei Mainichi*, 25 February 1969.

95. *Hokubei Mainichi*, 18 February 1969.

96. Jeff Matsui, "Sounding Board," *Pacific Citizen*, 10 January 1969, 5.

97. *San Francisco Chronicle,* 11 January 1969, 1.

98. SFSU, "AAPA Folder."

99. SFSU, "AAPA Folder." See also the *San Francisco Examiner* and *San Francisco Chronicle,* 4 December 1968, for reporting on the letter.

100. "Nisei and Sansei Students!" SFSU, "AAPA Folder" (emphasis in original).

101. "Japanese Community Meets on Hayakawa," *Oakland (Calif.) Sun Reporter,* 14 December 1968, 2.

102. *Pacific Citizen,* 18 April 1969.

103. Jeff Matsui, "Sounding Board," *Pacific Citizen,* 10 January 1969, 5. Matsui mistakenly cites the date of Hayakawa's naturalization as 1953 and that of the CINO incident as 1957. Barlow and Shapiro claim that a similar incident occurred in 1946 (see *An End to Silence,* 250). For 1954 as the date of his naturalization, see Hayakawa, "Why the English Language Amendment?" 2.

104. Mrs. Katherine Reyes, Letter to the Editor, *Nichi Bei Times,* 21 February 1969.

105. *Time,* 31 January 1969; *Hokubei Mainichi,* 3 February 1969, 1.

106. *Hokubei Mainichi,* 3 February 1969, 1.

107. Ibid., 1.

108. Hayakawa, "Education in Ferment," 202.

109. AAPA, "To Asian-American Students and Faculty," in SFSU, "Asian-American Political Alliance Folder (14)."

110. Ibid.

111. James Hirabayashi, interview with the author, 13 October 2006.

112. Umemoto, "On Strike!" 36.

113. Omatsu, "The 'Four Prisons' and the Movements of Liberation," 59–60.

114. Elbaum, "What Legacy from the Radical Internationalism of 1968?" 49.

115. Chang, "Expansion and Its Discontents," 181–206.

116. Iwamoto, "Once, There Was a Professor of English," 4.

117. S. I. Hayakawa, "Racism by Any Other Name," Exclusive to Weeklies, Semi-Weeklies, and the Ethnic Press in California, Column 20, November 1977, in LB, Box 8, Folder "Hayakawa, Dr. S. I."

118. For differing accounts of the multiple campaigns for redress and reparations, see Hohri, *Repairing America;* Hatamiya, *Righting a Wrong;* and Shimabukuro, *Born in Seattle.* The definitive work is Maki, Kitano, and Berthold, *Achieving the Impossible Dream.*

119. S. I. Hayakawa, letter to Senator Larry Pressler, 17 May 1988, in LB, Box 8, Folder "Hayakawa, S. I. 1986–." At the end of the letter, Hayakawa invites Pressler to place it in the Congressional Record. He did so, and it is included in Congressional Record—Senate, 9 August 1988, 100th Congress, 2nd Session, 1988, 134:118:11257.

120. Hayakawa, "'Giri,' to One's Name: Notes on the Wartime Relocation and the Japanese Character," 15 December 1975, in LB, Box 8, Folder "Hayakawa, Fr. S. I.," 8. A version of this essay appeared as a response to the NBC airing of "Farewell to Manzanar," as "Farewell to Manzanar: An Unorthodox View of the World War II Internment of Japanese-Americans," *TV Guide,* 6 March 1976, 13, 14, 16.

121. Lillian Baker, letter to Hayakawa aide Pat Agnew, 8 August 1979, in LB, Box 8, Folder "Hayakawa, S. I.—Ltrs."; *Kashu Mainichi,* 11 May 1976, in idem.

122. S. I. Hayakawa, letter to Lillian Baker, 7 January 1976, in LB, Box 8, Folder "Hayakawa, Dr. S. I." The list of materials sent to Hayakawa appears in Lillian Baker, letter to S. I. Hayakawa, 21 August 1981, in LB, Box 8, Folder "Hayakawa, S. I.—Ltrs."

123. Hayakawa, *English Language Amendment,* 12–18.

124. Patrick Andersen, "Hayakawa Claims Asians Support English as the Official Language," *AsianWeek,* 17 January 1986, 1.

125. Clifford I. Uyeda, "'U.S. English' Is a Threat," *AsianWeek,* 13 June 1986, 7.

126. Laird Harrison, "Governor Joins Prop. 63 Foes," *AsianWeek,* 5 September 1986, 1.

127. This comprised the "five precincts at the core of Chinatown." Laird Harrison, "Prop. 63 Rejected 3–1 By S.F. Asian Neighborhoods: Proponents May Sue to Stop the City's Bilingual Ballots," *AsianWeek,* 7 November 1986, 3.

128. Laird Harrison, "Exclusive: U.S. English," *AsianWeek,* 15 August 1986, 1; Laird Harrison, "'Hidden Agenda' Denied by U.S. English Leaders: Immigrant Groups Charge Language Movement Is Racist," *AsianWeek,* 22 August 1986, 1. To his credit, Hayakawa attempted to distance himself from Tanton after these remarks. See Hayakawa, "From Semantics to the U.S. Senate," 263–65, 348–52; S. I. Hayakawa to Stanley Diamond, 10 October 1990, reprinted in Hayakawa, "From Semantics to the U.S. Senate," 353a.

129. Southern Poverty Law Center, "The Puppeteer," www.splcenter.org/intel/intel report/article.jsp?pid=180 (accessed 21 July 2004).

3. Black Panthers, Red Guards, and Chinamen

1. *AAPA Newspaper* 1, no. 4, (March 1969): 1; Lyman, "Red Guard on Grant Avenue."

2. Terkel, *Race,* 310.

3. Wei, *The Asian American Movement,* 207–17.

4. Chin, *The Chickencoop Chinaman and Year of the Dragon,* xiv.

5. Shimakawa, *National Abjection,* 61–62; Chin et al., eds., *Aiiieeeee!*

6. Chin, "Come All Ye Asian American Writers." On the Chin-Kingston feud, see, among others, Cheung, "The Woman Warrior versus the Chinaman Pacific," and Li, *Imagining the Nation,* 49–55.

7. Kim, "'Such Opposite Creatures,'" 75–79.

8. Espiritu, *Asian American Panethnicity,* 20–24.

9. Espiritu labels this solidarity "Asian American panethnicity." I propose instead the admittedly somewhat unwieldy term "multiethnic Asian American racial identity" because it underlines the process of racialization that binds Asian ethnic groups together.

10. See, among others, Roediger, *The Wages of Whiteness.*

11. Burner, *Making Peace with the 60s,* 50, 81; Gitlin, *Twilight of Common Dreams,* 99–100.

12. Terkel, *Race,* 311.

13. Chin et al., "An Introduction to Chinese- and Japanese-American Literature," xxi–xlviii.

14. Documentary collections include Louie and Omatsu, eds., *Asian Americans;* Ho et al., eds., *Legacy to Liberation; Amerasia Journal* 13 (1989); and Tachiki, Wong, and Odo, eds., *Roots.* Literary studies that emphasize Asian American cultural nationalism include Eng, *Racial Castration,* 8, 20–21; Palumbo-Liu, *Asian/American,* 303–8, 317; Wong, "Denationalization Reconsidered"; Dirlik, "Asians on the Rim," 5; and Lowe, *Immigrant Acts,* 22–26. Wong, Dirlik, and Lowe allow for complexities in the origins of Asian American identity but tend to argue that American nationalism formed its basis.

15. *AAPA Newspaper* 1, no. 4 (March 1969): 4.

16. Daniels, *The Politics of Prejudice,* 65–78; Lee, *Orientals,* 106–44; Okihiro, *Margins and Mainstreams,* 129–38.

17. Simpson, *An Absent Presence,* 171–85.

18. William Petersen, "Success Story, Japanese-American Style," *New York Times Magazine,* 9 January 1966, 21, 33, 36, 38, 40, 41, 43.

19. "Success Story of One Minority Group in the U.S.," *U.S. News and World Report,* 26 December 1966; Okihiro, *Margins and Mainstreams,* 139–40.

20. Van Deburg, *New Day in Babylon,* 112–91.

21. Carmichael and Hamilton, *Black Power,* 37, 11, 29–31.

22. Alex Hing, quoted in Lyman, "Red Guard," 185.

23. Chin, *Chickencoop,* 59.

24. Ibid., 3.

25. Ibid., 32, 37–38.

26. Terkel, *Race,* 313.

27. Ernest Allen Jr., "Waiting for Tojo"; Lipsitz, *The Possessive Investment in Whiteness,* 184–98; Deutsch, "'The Asiatic Black Man,'" 194–98.

28. Tyson, "Robert F. Williams, 'Black Power,' and the Roots of the African American Freedom Struggle," 568–69; Clemons and Jones, "Global Solidarity," 30; Elbaum, *Revolution in the Air,* 67; Kelley and Esch, "Black Like Mao."

29. Marqusee, *Redemption Song,* 162–80; Remnick, *King of the World,* 287; Deutsch, "'The Asiatic Black Man,'" 193–94.

30. Hilliard and Cole, *This Side of Glory,* 247.

31. Omi and Winant, *Racial Formation in the United States,* 88–91 (emphasis in original).

32. Prashad, *Everybody Was Kung Fu Fighting,* 136.

33. On Los Angeles as the "Afro-Asian City," see Widener, "'Perhaps the Japanese Are to Be Thanked?'"

34. Seattle's black population nearly tripled between 1940 and 1945 (Taylor, *The Forging of a Black Community,* 173–74). San Francisco's black population increased by 798 percent in the 1940s, Oakland's by 462 percent, and Los Angeles's by 167 percent (Taylor, *In Search of the Racial Frontier,* 254).

35. Maya Angelou, quoted in Taylor, *Racial Frontier,* 273.

36. Terkel, *Race,* 310.

37. Okihiro, *Margins and Mainstreams,* 60.

38. Steve Louie, interview with the author, 20 July 1997.

39. Boggs, *Living for Change,* xi, 45–74, 118; Choi, "At the Margin of Asian American Political Experience."

40. Simpson, *Absent Presence,* 147–48; Fujino, "Revolution's from the Heart," 169; Fujino, "To Serve the Movement"; Kochiyama, *Passing It On;* Fujino, *Heartbeat of Struggle.*

41. Wong, "Panther Brotherhood," 76–77. The term *jackanape* refers to individuals who, while espousing a radical line, engaged mostly in thug activities that were not politically motivated.

42. Wong, "Yellow Panther," 66–69.

43. Seale, *Seize the Time,* 72–73. Seale later (79) identifies the "Japanese radical" as Richard Aoki (whom he renders as "Iokey"). See also Pearson, *Shadow of the Panther,* 112, and Ogbar, *Black Power,* 168.

44. Seale, *Seize the Time,* 79; Pearson, *Shadow of the Panther,* 113; Wong, "Berkeley and Beyond," 70–71; Aoki, "Interview by Dolly Veale," 324, 327. Aoki claims an even closer collaboration: he remembers co-writing the Panthers' famous 10-Point Program with Newton and Seale over a "bottle of scotch" but allows for "different interpretations" of that event (326).

45. Louie interview. Karenga, also known as Maulana Karenga, was the leader of the U.S. organization, an Afrocentric black nationalist group. See Brown, *Fighting for US.*

46. Pearson, *Shadow of the Panther,* 167; "Why I'm Marching to Free Huey," and "'Free Huey, Free Huey'—An Awesome Outburst," *San Francisco Chronicle,* 16 July 1968.

47. Young Lords Party, *Palante;* Melendez, *We Took the Streets;* Chavez, *Mi Raza Primero!* Smith and Warrior, *Like a Hurricane,* 129.

48. Wolfe, *Radical Chic and Mau-Mauing the Flak-Catcher.*

49. Louie interview.

50. Lyman, "Red Guard," 31.

51. "A History of the Red Guard Party," *IWK Journal* 2 (May 1975), 81–83, reprinted from *Getting Together* 4, nos. 3–5.

52. Hing, "Former Minister of Information for the Red Guard Party and Founding Member of I Wor Kuen," 284.

53. Ibid., 285.

54. Ibid., 296.

55. "History of the Red Guard Party," 81; Wong, "Red Star in America," 80; Lyman, "Red Guard," 32; *Red Guard Community Newspaper,* 25 June 1969, 1. For examples of slogans and terminology, see *Red Guard Community Newspaper,* 9 April 1999, 2; 25 June 1969, 1; and many others issues.

56. *Red Guard Community Newspaper,* 12 March 1969, 1.

57. Hing, "Former Minister," 288.

58. *Red Guard Community Newspaper,* 25 June 1969, 3.

59. "Our Political Program," "Rules of the Red Guard," "8 Points of Attention," and "3 Main Rules of Discipline," *Red Guard Community Newspaper,* 12 March 1969, 6–9, and subsequent issues. See also "Black Panther Party Platform and Program: What We Want, What We Believe," "Rules of the Black Panther Party," "8 Points of Attention," and "3 Main Rules of Discipline," reprinted in *The Black Panthers Speak,* 2nd edition, ed. Foner, 2–6.

60. Prashad, *Kung Fu Fighting,* 139–140.

61. Hing, "Former Minister," 286–87.

62. *Red Guard Community Newspaper,* 8 September 1969, 2.

63. Hing, "Former Minister," 292.

64. Ibid., 287.

65. *Red Guard Community Newspaper,* 12 March 1969, 7.

66. "History of the Red Guard Party," 84.

67. Lai, "The Kuomintang in Chinese American Communities before World War II," 175, 181–83, 196.

68. Nee and Nee, "The Kuomintang in Chinatown," 146–51; Yu, *To Save China, To Save Ourselves;* Amy Chen, director, *The Chinatown Files,* DVD (New York: Third World Newsreel, 2001).

69. Hing, "Former Minster," 286–87.

70. Ibid., 289; Dong, "Transforming Student Elites," 202.

71. Aoki, "Interview," 323.

72. Hing, "Former Minister," 282–84.

73. Roediger, *Wages of Whiteness,* 100–120.

74. Morrison, *Playing in the Dark.*

75. Terkel, *Race,* 310. In contrast to Chin's assertion, groups like Yellow Brotherhood and Asian American Hardcore in Los Angeles organized Asian American gangsters and worked to prevent drug abuse. See Tasaki, "Wherever There Is Oppression," and Nagatani, "'Action Talks and Bullshit Walks.'"

76. Chin, *Chickencoop,* 13.

77. Ibid., 3, 20, 21, 9 (ellipses in original).

78. Ibid., 40.

79. Ibid., 19.

80. Terkel, *Race,* 310.

81. Roediger, *Wages of Whiteness;* Rogin, *Blackface, White Noise,* 13.

82. Lott, *Love and Theft,* 50–52.

83. Bhabha, *The Location of Culture,* 86.

84. Matthews, "'No One Ever Asks, What a Man's Place in the Revolution Is,'" 278–80.

85. Eldridge Cleaver, "Message to Sister Erica Huggins of the Black Panther Party," *Black Panther,* 5 July 1969, reprinted in *The Black Panthers Speak,* ed. Foner, 98–99.

86. Matthews, "No One Ever Asks," 285–92.

87. Wei, *Asian American Movement,* 212–14; "History of the Red Guard Party," 86–87. I Wor Kuen (IWK, Righteous Harmonious Fists) was named in honor of the Chinese anti-imperialist fighters of the Boxer Rebellion.

88. Kuen, "12 Point Platform and Program," 406.

89. Wei, *Asian American Movement,* 215, 226.

90. "Political Summation of the Jung Sai Strike," *IWK Journal* 2 (May 1975): 49–55.

91. "History of the Red Guard Party," 81, 86–87; League of Revolutionary Struggle, Statements on the Founding of the League of Revolutionary Struggle, 42.

92. Lee, *Performing Asian America,* 61–88; Shimakawa, *National Abjection,* 91–97.

93. Chin, *Chickencoop,* 20.

94. Chin relates a nearly identical incident that occurred while he was traveling through New Orleans in 1960 (*Bulletproof Buddhists and Other Essays,* 13–15).

95. Chin, *Chickencoop,* 25.

96. Ibid., 14.

97. Ibid., 48.

98. Ibid., 48–49.

99. Ibid., 63.

100. Ibid., 20.

101. Ibid., 51–52.

102. Ibid., 53.

103. Chin, *Chinaman Pacific and Frisco R.R. Co.;* Chin, *Donald Duk.*

104. Chin, *Chickencoop,* 64.

105. Wei, *Asian American Movement,* 75–76; "Asian Women as Leaders," *Rodan* 1, no. 9 (April 1971), reprinted in *Roots,* 297–98.

106. Wei, *Asian American Movement,* 76–77; Tomi Tanaka, "from a lotus blossom cunt," *Gidra* (July 1971), reprinted in *Roots,* ed. Tachiki, Wong, and Odo, 109.

107. Ling, "The Mountain Movers."

108. Kim Geron and Pam Tau Lee, interview with the author, 31 January 2003.

109. Yokota, "Interview with Pat Sumi," 24–26.

110. "Political Summation of the Jung Sai Strike," *IWK Journal* 2 (May 1975): 49–72; "Who Dares to Make Waves?" *Wei Min Newspaper* 4, no. 1 (October–November 1974): 5; Wei, *Asian American Movement,* 210–11.

4. "Are We Not Also Asians?"

1. "May 12th Demo," *Getting Together* 3, no. 8 (May 27–June 9, 1972): 1.

2. Kim, *A History of Asian American Theatre,* 62.

3. Tom Wells provides a comprehensive overview of the mainstream antiwar movement in *The War Within.*

4. Stokely Carmichael, quoted in Wells, *The War Within,* 124.

5. Huey P. Newton, "Message on the Peace Movement," *Black Panther,* 27 September 1969, reprinted in Foner, *The Black Panthers Speak,* 70

6. Oropeza, *¡Raza Sí! ¡Guerra No!* 99–100.

7. Chavez, *Mi Raza Primero!* 68.

8. *La Causa,* quoted in Oropeza, *¡Raza Sí! ¡Guerra No!* 154.

9. Mike Watanabe, interview with Yen Le Espiritu, 19 July 1989, quoted in Espiritu, "Conflict and Cooperation," 65.

10. Kim Geron and Pam Tau Lee, interview with the author, 31 January 2003, Berkeley, Calif.

11. Loo et al., "Race-Related Stress among Asian American Veterans," 77.

12. Kiang, "About Face," 24. The figure of 250 killed is a significant undercount, for it ignores Filipinos with Hispanic surnames and Asians and Pacific Islanders with family names of ambiguous ethnicity, such as Lee and Young.

13. "Scott Shimabukuro," in John Kerry and Vietnam Veterans Against the War, *The New Soldier,* 42. The transcript of the Winter Soldier Investigation in Detroit was read into the *Congressional Record* by Senator Mark Hatfield of Oregon. Kiang asserts that Mike Nakayama and Nick Nakatani testified before a tribunal in California ("About Face," 37–38 n. 15), but because they participated in California rather than Michigan, their testimony does not appear in the *Congressional Record.* Furthermore, it is likely that Mike Nakayama and Mike Nakayamo are the same individual.

14. Christopher, *The Viet Nam War,* 2.

15. Asian Americans are absent from the most comprehensive synthesis of the antiwar movement, Tom Wells's *The War Within,* as well as Staughton Lynd and Michael Ferber's *The Resistance* and Charles DeBenedetti and Charles Chatfield's *An American Ordeal.* Richard Stacewicz's *Winter Soldiers* entirely omits Asian Americans, as does Richard R. Moser's *The New Winter Soldier.* None of the veterans interviewed by Stacewicz and Moser had Asian surnames. (Clearly, this methodology of determining ethnicity is heuristic at best.)

16. Moser, *The New Winter Soldier,* 46–47, 53, 57, 59–67, 70–71, 76–77, 84–85.

17. Terry, *Bloods;* Trujillo, *Soldados.* For further work on black soldiers, see Gill, "Black Soldiers' Perspectives on the War"; Gill, "From Maternal Pacifism to Revolutionary Solidarity"; and Goff, Sanders, and Smith, *Brothers.* On Latinos, see Mariscal, *Aztlán and Viet Nam;* Oropeza, *¡Raza Sí! ¡Guerra No!;* Ybarra, "Perceptions of Race and Class among Chicano Vietnam Veterans"; and Escobar, "The Dialectics of Repression."

18. Nelson Nagai, interview with the author, 1 February 2003, Stockton, Calif.

19. *BAACAW Newsletter,* reprinted in "Asians Against the War," *Getting Together* 3, no. 8 (May 27–June 9, 1972): 2.

20. Genny Lim, "'Honey Bucket,' a Play on a War-Scarred Asian GI," *East/West,* 3 November 1976, 7.

21. Frank Abe, interview with the author, 26 August 2001, Seattle.

22. Frank Abe, actor's note, 25 October 1976, Folder "October 2, 1971–March 13, 1978. Actor," Frank Abe Personal Files (hereafter ABE), copy in the author's possession.

23. *Honey Bucket* AATW Program, 12, in the Asian American Theater Company Papers, California Ethnic and Multicultural Archives, University of California, Santa Barbara (hereafter AATC), Box 19, Folder 12.

24. Ibid., 5, 11, 12; Press Release sent to City College, 16 September 1976, in AATC Box 19, Folder 12; Press Release, 26 September 1976, in AATC Box 19, Folder 12; *Honey Bucket* AATW Program and Swords to Ploughshares–Veterans Fair Program, 2, in AATC Box 19, Folder 12; Escueta, letter applying for a position on the AATW Board of Directors, in AATC Box 12, Folder 12. In addition, see Ben Tong, "Asian American Theater Workshop—Alive and Well in San Francisco!" *Bridge: An Asian American Perspective,* Summer 1977, 7–10.

25. Press Release sent to City College, 16 September 1976, in AATC Box 19, Folder 12; Press Release, 26 September 1976, in AATC Box 19, Folder 12; *Honey Bucket* AATW Program, 12.

26. "Honey Bucket Ticket Revenue," 2, in AATC Box 19, Folder 12; "Honey Bucket Budget Report," 5, in AATC Box 19, Folder 12 (depending on the version of the report, the budget was $1,725.02 or $1,701.13).

27. I want to make it clear that by "imaginary" I mean not false but rather constructed, in the sense of Benedict Anderson's imagined communities.

28. The text of the investigation was read into the *Congressional Record* by Senator Mark Hatfield of Oregon. *Congressional Record,* 92nd Congress, 1st session, 6 April 1971, 9974.

29. *Congressional Record,* 92nd Congress, 1st Session, Vol. 117, Part 8, 10010–11.

30. Lorenzo "Larry" Silvestre, interview with Jose Velasquez, 27 January 1999, Federal Way, Wash., in Asian Pacific American Veterans Project collection, Wing Luke Asian Museum, Seattle (hereafter APAV).

31. Maehara, "Think on These Things," 124.

32. Welchel, *From Pearl Harbor to Saigon,* 104. Welchel assigned pseudonyms to all of his informants to protect their privacy.

33. Welchel, *Pearl Harbor to Saigon,* 19.

34. Ron Chinn, interview with Ken Mochizuki, 9 November 1998, Seattle, in APAV.

35. *Congressional Record,* 92nd Congress, 1st Session, Vol. 117, Part 8, 10010–11.

36. Mike Muromoto, interview with Ken Mochizuki, date unknown, Everett, WA, in APAV.

37. Silvestre interview.

38. Jose Velasquez, interview with Ken Mochizuki, 1986 or 1987, location unknown, in APAV.

39. Matsuoka et al., "Asian-Pacific American Vietnam Veterans," 107.

40. Ken Mochizuki, "Don Woo, 1st Force Reconnaissance Company, United States Marine Corps," *International Examiner,* 5 November 1986, 8.

41. Velasquez interview.

42. Matsuoka et al., "Asian-Pacific American Vietnam Veterans," 107.

43. Melvyn Escueta, *Honey Bucket,* 1. The script of *Honey Bucket,* dated 9 October 1976, is available in AATC, Box 32, Folder 3. The videotape of the AATW-staged production appears in AATC, Box 19, Folder 12.

44. Escueta, *Honey Bucket,* 31.

45. Ibid., 36.

46. Ken Mochizuki, "Larry Wong, United States Marine Corps, Phu Bai," *International Examiner,* 5 November 1986, 12.

47. Escueta, *Honey Bucket,* 46.

48. Ibid., 36, 46.

49. Ibid., 30.

50. Ken Mochizuki, "Mike Higashi, 172nd Preventive Medicine, United States Army," and "Gary Ikeda, Headquarters Company I Force, United States Army," *International Examiner,* 5 November 1986, 14.

51. Mike Higashi, interview with Pei Pei Sung, 5 February 1999, Seattle, in APAV.

52. "Bay Area Asian Coalition Against the War," *New Dawn* 1, no. 10 (July 1972): 9.

53. "August 6, Hiroshima-Nagasaki Day," *New Dawn* 2, no. 1 (August 1972): 7.

54. "Asian Veterans Hold Meeting in Nihonmachi," *New Dawn* 2, no. 5 (December 1972): 9

55. "J-Town Community Night against the War," *New Dawn* 2, no. 7 (February 1973): 6–7.

56. "J-Town Regional Plans Anti-War Calendar Sale," *New Dawn* 2, no. 5 (December 1972): 5; "BAACAW, AMMO and N.Y. Asian Coalition Begin Medical Drive," *New Dawn* 2, no. 6 (January 1973): 5.

57. Gotanda, *Fish Head Soup and Other Plays.*

58. Ibid., 24.

59. Ibid., 37.

60. Ibid., 49–50 (ellipses in original). Two other times Victor flashes back to the VC soldier with his gun pointed at Victor's face, about to shoot (32, 34).

61. Nagai interview.

62. Gotanda, *Fish Head Soup,* xii.

63. Escueta, *Honey Bucket,* 43.

64. Ibid., 54.

65. Loo et al., "Race-Related Stress," 75–90.

66. Matsuoka et al., "Asian-Pacific American Vietnam Veterans," 107.

67. Chinn interview.

68. Loo et al., "Race-Related Stress," 80–83.

69. *Bridge* 1, no. 2 (September–October 1971): 30.

70. *Getting Together* 1, no. 2 (April 1970): 12–13, reprinted in *Gidra* 2, no. 5 (May 1970): 10.

71. Nakamura, "The Nature of G.I. Racism."

72. Marshall, *In the Combat Zone,* 221–22.

73. Ibid., 18–19.

74. Lim, "'Honey Bucket,'" 7.

75. Christopher Chow to AATW, 24 October 1976, in AATC, Box 19, Folder 12.

76. Escueta, *Honey Bucket,* 48.

77. Frank Abe journal, 21 October 1976, Folder "October 2, 1971–March 13, 1978. Actor," ABE.

78. Escueta, *Honey Bucket,* 35.

79. Ibid., 32, 33 (ellipses in original). This scene was omitted from the AATW production.

80. Escueta, *Honey Bucket,* 14, 41.

81. Yoshimura, "G.I.s and Asian Women."

82. "Notes on Women's Liberation," *AAPA Newspaper* 1, no. 5 (Summer 1969): 4–5.

83. For example, see the cover of *Gidra* 2, no. 3 (March 1970), "Why an Asian War?" flyer (circa 1970), reprinted in Louie and Omatsu, *Asian Americans,* 98, and "Join the Asian Contingent" flyer (circa 1971), reprinted in Louie and Omatsu, *Asian Americans,* 103).

84. Geron and Lee interview.

85. Yokota, "Interview with Pat Sumi," 24–26.

86. Nagai interview.

87. "Anti-War Benefit," *Getting Together* 3, no. 12 (July 22–August 5, 1972): 2; "Anti-War Basketball," *New Dawn* 2, no. 1 (August 1972): 7.

88. Oropeza, *¡Raza Sí! ¡Guerra No!* 111–12.

89. Escueta, *Honey Bucket,* 22.

90. Ibid., 9.

91. Ibid., 31 (ellipsis in original).

92. Christopher, *The Viet Nam War,* 122; Welchel, *From Pearl Harbor,* 18.

93. Miller, *Benevolent Assimilation,* 33.

94. Toribio, "Dare to Struggle," 31.

95. Ed Diokno, "'Honey Bucket': Triumph of Vietnam War," *Philippine News,* 16–22 October 1976.

96. Lim, "'Honey Bucket,'" 7.

97. Escueta, *Honey Bucket,* 51.

98. Ibid., 43 (ellipses in original).

99. Tagatac, "The New Anak."

100. Ibid., 159–63.

101. Ibid., 152, 166.

102. Ibid., 160.

103. Christopher, *The Viet Nam War,* 148.

104. Ibid., 165–66.

105. "Bay Area Asian Coalition Against the War," *New Dawn* 1, no. 10 (July 1972): 12.

106. *BAACAW Newsletter,* reprinted in "Asians Against the War," *Getting Together* 3, no. 8 (May 27–June 9, 1972): 2.

107. *AAPA Newspaper* 1, no. 6 (October 1969): 1.

108. *AAPA Newspaper* 1, no. 5 (September 5–20, 1969): 7.

109. "Asians Against the War," *Getting Together* 3, no. 8 (May 27–June 9, 1972): 2.

110. "Bay Area Asian Coalition Against the War," *New Dawn* 1, no. 10 (July 1972): 8.

111. "BAACAW Picnic," *New Dawn* 2, no. 1 (August 1972): 14.

112. Wells, *The War Within,* 497–98. Another seed was a letter from Glenn Omatsu and others from Yale University calling for the creation of an Asian American antiwar movement.

113. Editorial Board of the UCLA Asian American Studies Center, "An Interview with Pat Sumi," 254–59.

114. "Demonstrate Inaugural Day," *New Dawn* 2, no. 6 (January 1973): 1.

115. The discussion of the 1973 inaugural day festivities in this paragraph relies on Merilynne Hamano, "A Cold Resistance, Anti-War Demonstration: A Report of Asian Americans in New York Marching in Washington D.C.," *Gidra* 5, no. 3 (March 1973): 4, 5.

116. Wells cites a crowd size of eighty thousand (*The War Within,* 563–64).

117. Hamano, "Cold Resistance," 5.

118. Paul Wong, "The Emergence of the Asian-American Movement," *Bridge* 2, no. 1 (September–October 1972): 35–36 (emphasis in original).

119. Information on this incident is drawn from the Geron and Lee interview and from Nelson Nagai, interview with the author, 1 February 2003, Stockton, Calif.

120. "Moratorium," *Rodan* 1, no. 10 (May 1971): 10. In another example of Asian American invisibility, in their discussion of this moratorium Zaroulis and Sullivan note that "militant Hispanic and Indian (native American) groups forcibly took control of the microphone on the speaker's platform" but do not mention Asian Americans (Zaroulis and Sullivan, *Who Spoke Up?* 360).

121. Geron and Lee interview. The NLF was the National Front for the Liberation of South Vietnam.

122. Wong, "Emergence of the Asian-American Movement," 35–36.

123. Asians Against Fascism, "Hypocrites," *Gidra* 2, no. 5 (May 1970): 11.

124. Steve Louie, interview with the author, 20 July 1997, San Francisco.

125. Carol Mochizuki and Vivian Matsushige, "Peace Rally," *Gidra* 2, no. 5 (May 1970): 5.

126. Asian Coalition, "On the White Antiwar Movement," *Gidra* 5, no. 3 (March 1973): 20.

127. On the PCPJ and NPAC rivalry, see Wells, *The War Within,* 472–73, 479–80, 528; Garfinkle, *Telltale Hearts,* 193; and Hunt, *The Turning,* 83.

128. "Moratorium," 10.

5. Performing Radical Culture

1. "Nobuko Miyamoto," 325.

2. Nobuko Miyamoto, e-mail to the author, 15 January 2008.

3. Genny Lim, "Kearny Street Workshop—A Story of Survival," *Bridge* 3, no. 5 (May 1975): 28–30; Wei, *The Asian American Movement*, 185–90; Frank Chin et al., *Aiiieeeee!*

4. Van Deburg, *New Day in Babylon*, 9–10.

5. Arif Dirlik finds that the Asian American movement's vision of identity was "informed by a radical historicism" that sought to uncover Asian Americans' deeply American "roots" ("Asians on the Rim," 5). Similarly, Sau-ling Wong emphasizes the extent to which the Asian American movement adopted a stance of "claiming America" ("Denationalization Reconsidered"). In fairness, Dirklik and Wong also note that Asian American identity recognized linkages between Asian Americans and other people of color in the United States and between Asians in the United States and Asians abroad, but the thrust of their arguments hinges upon the idea that American nationalism underpinned the origins of Asian American identity.

6. For example, Wei's characterization of the founders of New York's Basement Workshop as "cultural nationalists" simply cannot do justice to the varied and complicated politics they espoused (Wei, *Asian American Movement*, 184).

7. Wei, *Asian American Movement*, 44–71.

8. Odo, "Preface," x–xi.

9. Dividing Asian American artists into camps undoubtedly leads to overstating differences while understating areas of congruence. However, I do so as a heuristic device so that different strands of thought within the movement can be seen more clearly.

10. Nobuko Miyamoto, telephone conversation with the author, 15 January 2008.

11. Unless otherwise noted, personal information on Nobuko Miyamoto is drawn from Nobuko Miyamoto, interview with the author, 13 February 2006, Los Angeles. See also "Nobuko Miyamoto," 324–26. In general, I refer to Miyamoto by the first name (JoAnne or Nobuko) she used contemporarily.

12. On the Boyle Heights in the postwar period, see Sánchez, "'What's Good for Boyle Heights Is Good for the Jews.'"

13. Loring was a world-class dancer and choreographer who choreographed the ballet *Billy the Kid*.

14. At the time, Nobuko did not recognize the racial politics of the musical, which is discussed by Christina Klein in *Cold War Orientalism*, 191–221.

15. Klein, *Cold War Orientalism*, 236.

16. Hamamoto, *Monitored Peril*, 8–9.

17. "Nobuko Miyamoto," 325.

18. The film was released in Italy in 1973 as *Afferra il Tempo* (Seize the time).

19. On the Young Lords church takeover, see Melendez, *We Took the Streets*, 112–29.

20. Miyamoto interview.

21. Hing, "Former Minister of Information for the Red Guard Party . . . Interviewed by Fred Ho and Steve Yip," 284–85, 289.

22. Omatsu, "Always a Rebel," 93–94, 96.

23. Takahashi, *Nisei/Sansei*, 66–72.

24. Yoneda, *Ganbatte*, 67.

25. Omatsu, "Always a Rebel," 96.

26. Fujino, *Heartbeat of Struggle*, 360 n. 7.

27. Omatsu, "Always a Rebel," 96; Raineri, *The Red Angel*, 182, 303–4.

28. Fujita-Rony, "'Destructive Force,'" 41; Wei, *Asian American Movement*, 25–26.

29. Fujino, *Heartbeat*, 236–44.

30. "Come-Unity Celebration for Our Friend and Brother, Chris Kwando Iijima," field notes, 11 February 2006, Los Angeles, in the author's possession.

31. "Chris Iijima"; for a discussion of Basement Workshop and I Wor Kuen, see Wei, *Asian American Movement*, 185–90 and 212–17, respectively.

32. On Hampton's murder, see Churchill and Vander Wall, *Agents of Repression*, 63–77.

33. Miyamoto interview.

34. Ibid.

35. "Chris Iijima," 319–21; "Nobuko Miyamoto," 325.

36. "Girl Is Slain in Chicago Hotel Room; Roommate Is Seriously Slashed," *New York Times*, 18 July 1970, 20.

37. Prior to coming to Chicago, in New York they had met with a delegation of Californians including Victor Shibata and Warren Furutani. Both the East and West Coasters were astounded by the parallels between Asian American organizing in the different locales.

38. Unless otherwise noted, the information on Chin is from Charlie Chin, interview with the author, 10 April 2006, San Francisco.

39. Chin and Miyamoto both recounted this first performance in their respective interviews with the author.

40. Chin interview; "William David 'Charlie' Chin."

41. Chin interview.

42. Wang, "Between the Notes," 451.

43. "Chris and JoAnn" from New York City are labeled "revolutionary minstrels" in "Calendar of Events," *Gidra* 3, no. 1 (January 1971): 19.

44. Miyamoto interview.

45. Chin interview.

46. Miyamoto interview.

47. Ling, "Introduction," 6.

48. Chris Iijima, e-mail to the author, 14 October 1999.

49. Miyamoto interview.

50. Iijima, "Pontifications on the Distinction between Grains of Sand and Yellow Pearls," 4.

51. Chin interview.

52. Iijima, "Pontifications," 5.

53. JoAnne Miyamoto and Chris Iijima, "Yellow Pearl," song on *A Grain of Sand*, a sound recording by Miyamoto, Ijima, and Chin. The song's lyrics are also printed in *Bridge* 1, no. 2 (September–October 1971): 21.

54. Charlie Chin, "Wandering Chinaman," song on *A Grain of Sand*.

55. JoAnne Miyamoto and Chris Iijima, "We Are the Children," song on *A Grain of Sand*.

56. JoAnne Miyamoto and Chris Iijima, "Something about Me Today," song on *A Grain of Sand* (ellipses in original).

57. *Gidra* 1, no. 7 (October 1969): 5.

58. Mirikitani et al., *Time to Greez!*

59. Janice Mirikitani, "Firepot," poem in *Time to Greez!* 3.

60. In writing "We have been fractured," Mirikitani proposes an original state of Asian solidarity prior to the imposition of these false distinctions. Indeed, much of the movement literature laments a declension from this idealized state of Asian unity—which of course never existed in reality—and narrates the emergence of Asian American identity as a return to this state of grace.

61. Mirikitani, "Firepot."

62. JoAnne Miyamoto and Chris Iijima, "Jonathan Jackson," song on *A Grain of Sand*.

63. Fujino, *Heartbeat*, 177–79, 215–16; Miyamoto interview.

64. JoAnne Miyamoto and Chris Iijima, "Warriors of the Rainbow," song on *A Grain of Sand*.

65. Miyamoto and Iijima, "We Are the Children."

66. Marlene Tanioka and Aileen Yamaguchi, "Asians Make Waves to Alcatraz . . . ," *Gidra*, March 1970, 6–7. On the takeovers of Alcatraz, see Johnson, *The Occupation of Alcatraz Island*, and Johnson, Nagel, and Champaign, *American Indian Activism*.

67. Merilynne Hamano, "From Manzanar to Wounded Knee," *Gidra*, May 1973, 8–9; "Asians Go to Wounded Knee," *Insight* newsletter, reprinted in *Asian Americans*, ed. Louie and Omatsu, 178. On the Wounded Knee occupation, see Burnette and Koster, *The Road to Wounded Knee*, and Crow Dog, *Lakota Woman*, 128–69.

68. "In Support of the Knee," *Gidra* 5, no. 6 (June 1973): 8–9.

69. JoAnne Miyamoto and Chris Iijima, "Somos Asiáticos," song on *A Grain of Sand*.

70. Miyamoto interview.

71. "Nobuko Miyamoto," 326.

72. Chin interview.

73. JoAnne Miyamoto and Chris Iijima, "Divide and Conquer," song on *A Grain of Sand*.

74. JoAnne Miyamoto and Chris Iijima, "War of the Flea," song on *A Grain of Sand*.

75. Janice Mirikitani, "Jungle Rot & Open Arms," poem in *Time to Greez!* 13–14.

76. Wing Tek Lum, "Chinese New Year," poem in *Time to Greez!* 61.

77. Brenda Paik Sunoo, "I can understand . . . ," poem in *Time to Greez!* 19.

78. George Leong, "Bach Mai," poem in *Time to Greez!* 17.

79. Stacewicz, *Winter Soldiers*, 347, 359.

80. *Wei Min Newspaper* 4, no. 3 (April–May 1975): 10.

81. Dale Yu Nee, "'See, Culture Is Made, Not Born . . .' Asian American Writers Conference," *Bridge* 3, no. 6 (August 1975): 42–48.

82. *Wei Min Newspaper* 4, no. 3 (April–May 1975): 10.

83. *Wei Min Newspaper* 3 (September 1974): 7.

84. Ibid., 8.

85. Wang, "Between the Notes," 453–54.

86. Miyamoto e-mail.

Conclusion

1. All observations and quotations from the "Come-Unity Celebration" are drawn from the author's field notes, West Los Angeles College, 11 February 2006. For coverage of a memorial service for Chris Iijima held in New York City, see Phil Tajitsu Nash, "A Man and a Movement," *AsianWeek* 27, no. 32 (March 31–April 6, 2006): 6.

2. Vo, *Mobilizing an Asian American Community*, 92–128.

3. Nguyen, *Race and Resistance*.

4. Liu, *The Accidental Asian*, 34–35.

5. Chris Iijima, e-mail to the author, 14 October 1999.

6. Das Gupta, *Unruly Immigrants*, 256.

7. I am greatly indebted to an anonymous reader for the University of Minnesota Press for suggesting Nguyen's story as emblematic of the types of solidarities enabled by Asian American racial politics.

8. Nguyen, "Caring for the Soul of Our Community," 285–89.

9. Nguyen, *We Are All Suspects Now*.

10. Ibid., 137.

11. On the failures of the state and inadequacies of citizenship, see especially Lowe, *Immigrant Acts*, and Das Gupta, *Unruly Immigrants*.

12. Chris Iijima, "Song for a Child," unpublished, 1974. Lyrics in author's possession; special thanks to Nobuko Miyamoto for sharing them.

Bibliography

Books and Articles

A/A: African American–Asian American Cross-Identifications. Special issue, *Journal of Asian American Studies* 5, no. 1 (February 2002).

The Afro/Asian Century. Special issue, *positions: east asia cultures critique* 11, no. 1 (April 2003).

Allen, Ernest Jr.. "Waiting for Tojo: The Pro-Japan Vigil of Black Missourians, 1932–1943." *Gateway Heritage* 16, no. 2 (1995): 38–55.

Almaguer, Tomás. "Racial Domination and Class Conflict in Capitalist Agriculture: The Oxnard Sugar Beet Workers' Strike of 1903." *Labor History* 25 (1984): 325–50.

Ancheta, Angelo N. *Race, Rights, and the Asian American Experience.* New Brunswick, N.J.: Rutgers University Press, 1998.

Anderson, Terry H. *The Movement and the Sixties.* New York: Oxford University Press, 1996.

Aoki, Richard. "Interview by Dolly Veale." In *Legacy to Liberation: Politics and Culture of Revolutionary Asian Pacific America,* ed. Fred Ho et al., 319–34. San Francisco: AK Press, 2000.

Azuma, Eiichiro. *Between Two Empires: Race, History, and Transnationalism in Japanese America.* New York: Oxford University Press, 2005.

Barlow, William, and Peter Shapiro. *An End to Silence.* New York: Bobbs-Merrill, 1971.

Bhabha, Homi K. *The Location of Culture.* New York: Routledge, 1994.

Bloom, Alexander, and Wini Breines, eds. *Takin' It to the Streets: A Sixties Reader.* New York: Oxford University Press, 1995.

Boggs, Grace Lee. *Living for Change.* Minneapolis: University of Minnesota Press, 1998.

Bonacich, Edna. "Asian Labor in the Development of California and Hawaii." In *Labor Immigration under Capitalism: Asian Workers in the United States before World War II,* ed. Lucie Cheng and Edna Bonacich, 130–82. Berkeley: University of California Press, 1984.

Borstelman, Thomas. *The Cold War and the Color Line: American Race Relations in the Global Arena.* Cambridge: Harvard University Press, 2001.

Brown, Elaine. *A Taste of Power: A Black Woman's Story.* New York: Doubleday, 1992.

Brown, Janet, and Richard Paris, eds. *Quotations from Chairman S. I. Hayakawa.* San Francisco: Fred and Gobi, 1969.

Brown, Scot. *Fighting for US: Maulan Karenga, the US Organization, and Black Cultural Nationalism.* New York: NYU Press, 2003.

Bulosan, Carlos. *America Is in the Heart.* Seattle: University of Washington Press, 1973.

Burner, David. *Making Peace with the 60s.* Princeton, N.J.: Princeton University Press, 1996.

Burnette, Robert, and John Koster. *The Road to Wounded Knee.* New York: Bantam, 1974.

Carmichael, Stokely, and Charles V. Hamilton. *Black Power: The Politics of Liberation in America.* New York: Vintage Books, 1967.

Carson, Clayborne. *In Struggle: SNCC and the Black Awakening of the 1960s.* Cambridge: Harvard University Press, 1981.

Chang, Edward T. "America's First Multiethnic 'Riots.'" In *The State of Asian America: Activism and Resistance in the 1990s,* ed. Karin Aguilar–San Juan, 110–17. Boston: South End Press, 1994.

Chang, Mitchell J. "Expansion and Its Discontents: The Formation of Asian American Studies Programs in the 1990s." *Journal of Asian American Studies* 2, no. 2 (June 1999): 181–206.

Chan, Sucheng. *Asian Americans: An Interpretive History.* Boston: Twayne, 1991.

Chavez, Ernesto. *Mi Raza Primero! Nationalism, Identity, and Insurgency in the Chicano Movement in Los Angeles, 1966–1978.* Berkeley: University of California Press, 2002.

Chen, Yong. *Chinese San Francisco, 1850–1943: A Trans-Pacific Community.* Palo Alto, Calif.: Stanford University Press, 2000.

Cheung, King-kok. "The Woman Warrior versus the Chinaman Pacific: Must a Chinese American Critic Choose between Feminism and Heroism?" In *Conflicts in Feminism,* ed. Marianne Hirsch and Evelyn Fox Keller, 234–51. New York: Routledge, 1990.

Chin, Frank. *Bulletproof Buddhists and Other Essays.* Honolulu: University of Hawaii Press, 1998.

———. *The Chickencoop Chinaman and Year of the Dragon: Two Plays by Frank Chin.* Seattle: University of Washington Press, 1981.

———. *Chinaman Pacific and Frisco R.R. Co.* Minneapolis: Coffee House Press, 1988.

———. "Come All Ye Asian American Writers of the Real and the Fake." In *The Big AIIIEEEEE! An Anthology of Chinese American and Japanese American Literature,* ed. Jeffery Paul Chan et al., 1–92. New York: Meridian, 1991.

———. *Donald Duk: A Novel.* Minneapolis: Coffee House Press, 1991.

Chin, Frank, et al. "An Introduction to Chinese- and Japanese-American Literature," in *Aiiieeeee! An Anthology of Asian-American Writers,* ed. Frank Chin et al., xxi–xlviii. Washington, D.C.: Howard University Press, 1974.

———, eds. *Aiiieeeee! An Anthology of Asian-American Writers.* Washington, D.C.: Howard University Press, 1974.

Choi, Jennifer Jung Hee. "At the Margin of Asian American Political Experience: The Life of Grace Lee Boggs." *Amerasia Journal* 25, no. 2 (1999): 18–40.

Choy, Bong-Youn. *Koreans in America.* Chicago: Nelson-Hall, 1979.

"Chris Iijima: Lawyer, Singer, and Songwriter." In *Yellow Light: The Flowering of Asian American Arts,* ed. Amy Ling, , 319–21. Philadelphia: Temple University Press, 1999.

Christopher, Renny. *The Viet Nam War/The American War: Images and Representations in Euro-American and Vietnamese Exile Narratives.* Amherst, Mass.: University of Massachusetts Press, 1995.

Churchill, Ward, and Jim Vander Wall. *Agents of Repression: The FBI's Secret Wars against the Black Panther Party and the American Indian Movement.* Boston: South End Press, 2002.

Cleaver, Kathleen. "Back to Africa: The Evolution of the International Section of the Black Panther Party (1969–1972)." In *The Black Panther Party Reconsidered,* ed. George E. Jones, 211–54. Baltimore: Black Classic Press, 1998.

Clemons, Michael L., and Charles E. Jones. "Global Solidarity: The Black Panther Party in the International Arena." In *Liberation, Imagination, and the Black Panther Party: A New Look at the Panthers and Their Legacy,* ed. Kathleen Cleaver and George Katsiaficas, 20–39. New York: Routledge, 2001.

Cordova, Fred. *Filipinos, Forgotten Asian Americans: A Pictorial Essay, 1763–circa 1963.* Dubuque, Iowa: Kendall/Hunt, 1983.

Crow Dog, Mary. *Lakota Woman.* New York: Perennial, 1994.

Daniels, Roger. *Asian America: Chinese and Japanese in the United States since 1850.* Seattle: University of Washington Press, 1988.

———. *The Politics of Prejudice: The Anti-Japanese Movement in California and the Struggle for Japanese Exclusion.* Berkeley: University of California Press, 1962.

Das Gupta, Monisha. *Unruly Immigrants: Rights, Activism, and Transnational South Asian Politics in the United States.* Durham, N.C.: Duke University Press, 2006.

DeBenedetti, Charles, and Charles Chatfield. *An American Ordeal: The Antiwar Movement of the Vietnam Era.* Syracuse, N.Y.: Syracuse University Press, 1990.

Deutsch, Nathaniel. "'The Asiatic Black Man': An African American Orientalism?" *Journal of Asian American Studies* 4, no. 3 (October 2001): 193–208.

DeWitt, Howard A. "The Filipino Labor Union: The Salinas Lettuce Strike of 1934." *Amerasia Journal* 5, no. 2 (1978): 1–22.

Dirlik, Arif. "Asians on the Rim: Transnational Capital and Local Community in the Making of Contemporary Asian America." *Amerasia Journal* 22, no. 3 (1996): 1–24.

Dong, Harvey. "Transforming Student Elites into Community Activists: A Legacy of Asian American Activism." In *Asian Americans: The Movement and the Moments,* ed. Steve Louie and Glenn Omatsu, 186–204. Los Angeles: UCLA Asian American Studies Center Press, 2001.

Dudziak, Mary L. *Cold War Civil Rights: Race and the Image of American Democracy.* Princeton, N.J.: Princeton University Press, 2000.

Editorial Board of the UCLA Asian American Studies Center. "An Interview with Pat Sumi." In *Roots: An Asian American Reader,* ed. Amy Tachiki et al., 253–64. Los Angeles: UCLA Asian American Studies Center Press, 1971.

Elbaum, Max. *Revolution in the Air: Sixties Radicals Turn to Lenin, Mao and Che.* London: Verso, 2002.

———. "What Legacy from the Radical Internationalism of 1968?" *Radical History Review* 82 (Winter 2002): 37–64.

Eng, David. *Racial Castration: Managing Masculinity in Asian America.* Durham, N.C.: Duke University Press, 2001.

Escobar, Edward J. "The Dialectics of Repression: The Los Angeles Police Department and the Chicano Movement, 1968–71." *Journal of American History* 79, no. 4 (March 1993): 1483–1514.

Espiritu, Augusto Fauni. *Five Faces of Exile: The Nation and Filipino American Intellectuals.* Palo Alto, Calif.: Stanford University Press, 2005.

Espiritu, Yen Le. *Asian American Panethnicity: Bridging Institutions and Identities.* Philadelphia: Temple University Press, 1992.

————. "Conflict and Cooperation: Panethnicity among Asian Americans." Ph.D. diss., University of California, Los Angeles, 1990.

Evangelista, Susan. *Carlos Bulosan and His Poetry: A Biography and Anthology.* Seattle: University of Washington Press, 1985.

Farber, David, and Beth Bailey. *The Columbia Guide to America in the 1960s.* New York: Columbia University Press, 2001.

Foner, Philip S., ed. *The Black Panthers Speak,* 2nd edition. New York: Da Capo Press, 1995.

Friday, Chris. "Asian American Labor and Historical Interpretation." *Labor History* 35, no. 4 (Fall 1994): 524–46.

————. *Organizing Asian American Labor: The Pacific Coast Canned Salmon Industry, 1870–1942.* Philadelphia: Temple University Press, 1994.

Fu, May Chuan. "Keeping Close to the Ground: Politics and Coalition in Asian American Community Organizing, 1969–1977." Ph.D. diss., University of California–San Diego, 2005.

Fujino, Diane C. *Heartbeat of Struggle: The Revolutionary Life of Yuri Kochiyama.* Minneapolis: University of Minnesota Press, 2005.

————. "Revolution's from the Heart: The Making of an Asian American Woman Activist, Yuri Kochiyama." In *Dragon Ladies: Asian American Feminists Breathe Fire,* ed. Sonia Shah, 169–81. Boston: South End Press, 1997.

————. "To Serve the Movement: The Revolutionary Practice of Yuri Kochiyama." In *Legacy to Liberation: Politics and Culture of Revolutionary Asian Pacific America,* ed. Fred Ho et al., 257–66. San Francisco: AK Press, 2000.

Fujita-Rony, Thomas Y. "'Destructive Force': Aiko Herzig-Yoshinaga's Gendered Labor in the Japanese American Redress Movement." *Frontiers: A Journal of Women Studies* 24, no. 1 (2003): 38–60.

Gallicchio, Marc. *The African American Encounter with Japan and China: Black Internationalism in Asia, 1895–1945.* Chapel Hill: University of North Carolina Press, 2003.

Garfinkle, Adam. *Telltale Hearts: The Origins and Impact of the Vietnam Antiwar Movement.* New York: MacMillan, 1997.

Gee, Emma, ed. *Counterpoint: Perspectives on Asian America.* Los Angeles: Asian American Studies Center Press, 1976.

Gill, Gerald. "Black Soldiers' Perspectives on the War." In *The Vietnam Reader,* ed. Walter Capps. New York: Routledge, 1991.

————. "From Maternal Pacifism to Revolutionary Solidarity: African American Women's Opposition to the Vietnam War." In *Sights on the Sixties,* ed. Barbara L. Tischler, 177–95. New Brunswick, N.J.: Rutgers University Press, 1992.

Gitlin, Todd. *The Sixties: Years of Hope, Days of Rage.* New York: Bantam, 1993.

————. *Twilight of Common Dreams: Why America Is Wracked by Culture Wars.* New York: Metropolitan Books, 1995.

Glazer, Nathan, and Daniel Patrick Moynihan. *Beyond the Melting Pot: The Negroes, Puerto Ricans, Jews, Italians, and Irish of New York City.* Cambridge, Mass: MIT Press, 1963.

Goff, Stanley, Robert Sanders, and Clark Smith, eds. *Brothers: Black Soldiers in Nam.* Novato, Calif.: Presidio Press, 1982.

Gordon, Charles. "The Racial Barrier to American Citizenship." *University of Pennsylvania Law Review* 93, no. 3 (March 1945): 237–58. Reprinted in *Asian Indians, Filipinos, Other Asian Communities and the Law,* ed. Charles McClain, 287–308. New York: Garland, 1994.

Gotanda, Philip Kan. *Fish Head Soup and Other Plays.* Seattle: University of Washington Press, 1995.

Guglielmo, Thomas A. *White on Arrival: Italians, Race, Color, and Power in Chicago, 1890–1945.* New York: Oxford University Press, 2003.

Habal, Estella. *San Francisco's International Hotel: Mobilizing the Filipino American Community in the Anti-Eviction Movement.* Philadelphia: Temple University Press, 2007.

———. "'We Won't Move': The International Hotel Anti-Eviction Movement, 1968–1979, and the Filipino Community." Ph.D. diss., University of California–Davis, 2003.

Hamamoto, Darrell. *Monitored Peril: Asian Americans and the Politics of TV Representation.* Minneapolis: University of Minnesota Press, 1994.

Hatamiya, Leslie. *Righting a Wrong: Japanese Americans and the Passage of the Civil Liberties Act of 1988.* Palo Alto, Calif.: Stanford University Press, 1993.

Hayakawa, S. I. "Education in Ferment." In *Black Power and Student Rebellion,* ed. James McEvoy and Abraham Miller. Belmont, Calif.: Wadsworth, 1969.

———. *The English Language Amendment: One Nation . . . Indivisible?* Washington, D.C.: Washington Institute for Values in Public Policy, 1985.

———. "General Semantics: An Introductory Lecture." *ETC.: A Review of General Semantics* 2, no. 3 (Spring 1945): 164–65.

———. *Language in Action: A Guide to Accurate Reading and Writing.* New York: Harcourt, Brace and Co., 1941.

———. "The Non-Aristotelian Revision of Morality." *ETC.: A Review of General Semantics* 3, no. 3 (Spring 1946): 167.

Hayakawa, S. I., and Margedant Peters Hayakawa. "From Semantics to the U.S. Senate, Etc., Etc." Oral history conducted in 1989 by Julie Gordon Shearer. Regional Oral History Office, Bancroft Library, University of California, Berkeley, 1994.

Heinl, Robert D. "The Collapse of the Armed Forces." In *Vietnam and America: A Documented History,* ed. Marvin E. Gettlemen et al., 326–41. New York: Grove, 1995.

Hekymara, Kuregiy. "The Third World Movement and Its History in the San Francisco State College Strike of 1968–1969." Ph.D. diss., University of California, Berkeley, 1972.

Hilliard, David, and Lewis Cole. *This Side of Glory.* Boston: Little, Brown, 1993.

Hing, Alex. "Former Minister of Information for the Red Guard Party and Founding Member of I Wor Kuen, Interviewed by Fred Ho and Steve Yip." In *Legacy to Liberation: Politics and Culture of Revolutionary Asian Pacific America,* ed. Fred Ho et al., 279–96. San Francisco: AK Press, 2000.

Hing, Bill Ong. *Making and Remaking Asian America through Immigration Policy, 1850–1990.* Palo Alto, Calif.: Stanford University Press, 1993.

Ho, Fred, et al., eds. *Legacy to Liberation: Politics and Culture of Revolutionary Asian/Pacific America.* San Francisco: AK Press, 2000.

Hohri, William. *Repairing America: An Account of the Movement for Japanese American Redress.* Pullman: Washington State University Press, 1988.

Hosokawa, Bill. *JACL: In Quest of Justice.* New York: William Morrow, 1982.

———. *Out of the Frying Pan: Reflections of a Japanese American.* Niwot: University Press of Colorado, 1998.

Hsu, Madeline Y. *Dreaming of Gold, Dreaming of Home: Transnationalism and Migration between the United States and South China, 1882–1943.* Palo Alto, Calif.: Stanford University Press, 2000.

Hunt, Andrew. *The Turning: A History of Vietnam Veterans Against the War.* New York: New York University Press, 1999.

Ichioka, Yuji. *Before Internment: Essays in Prewar Japanese American History.* Ed. Gordon H. Chang and Eiichiro Azuma. Palo Alto, Calif.: Stanford University Press, 2006.

———. "The Early Japanese Immigrant Quest for Citizenship: The Background of the 1922 Case." *Amerasia Journal* 4, no. 2 (1977): 1–22.

———. *The Issei: The World of the First Generation Japanese Immigrants, 1885–1924.* New York: Free Press, 1988.

———. "A Study in Dualism: James Yoshinori Sakamoto and the *Japanese American Courier*, 1928–1942." *Amerasia Journal* 13, no. 2 (1986–87): 49–81.

Iijima, Chris. "Pontifications on the Distinction between Grains of Sand and Yellow Pearls." In *Asian Americans: The Movement and the Moment*, ed. Steve Louie and Glenn Omatsu, 3–14. Los Angeles: UCLA Asian American Studies Center Press, 2001.

Jackson, Walter. *Gunnar Myrdal and America's Conscience: Social Engineering and Racial Liberalism, 1938–1987.* Chapel Hill: University of North Carolina Press, 1990.

Jacobson, Matthew Frye. *Whiteness of a Different Color: European Immigrants and the Alchemy of Race.* Cambridge, Mass.: Harvard University Press, 1998.

Jensen, Joan. *Passage from India: Asian Indian Immigrants in North America.* New Haven, Conn.: Yale University Press, 1988.

Johnson, Troy R. *The Occupation of Alcatraz Island: Indian Self-Determination and the Rise of Indian Activism.* Urbana: University of Illinois Press, 1996.

Johnson, Troy, Joane Nagel, and Duane Champaign, eds. *American Indian Activism: Alcatraz to the Longest Walk.* Urbana: University of Illinois Press, 1997.

Joyce, Patrick D. *No Fire Next Time: Black Korean Conflicts and the Future of America's Cities.* Ithaca, N.Y.: Cornell University Press, 2003.

Jung, Moon-Ho. *Coolies and Cane: Race, Labor, and Sugar in the Age of Emancipation.* Baltimore, Md.: Johns Hopkins University Press, 2006.

———. "Outlawing 'Coolies': Race, Nation, and Empire in the Age of Emancipation." *American Quarterly* 57, no. 3 (2005): 677–701.

Jung, Moon-Kie. *Reworking Race: The Making of Hawaii's Interracial Labor Movement.* New York: Columbia University Press, 2006.

Kelley, Robin D. G. "Looking Extremely Backward: Why the Enlightenment Will Only Lead Us into the Dark." In *Yo' Mama's Disfunktional! Fighting the Culture Wars in Urban America*, 103–24. Boston: Beacon, 1997.

Kelley, Robin D. G., and Betsy Esch. "Black Like Mao: Red China and Black Revolution." *Souls* 1, no. 4 (Fall 1999): 6–41.

Kerry, John, and Vietnam Veterans Against the War. *The New Soldier.* New York: Collier, 1971.

Kiang, Peter Nien-Chu. "About Face: Recognizing Asian and Pacific American Vietnam Veterans in Asian American Studies." *Amerasia Journal* 17, no. 3 (1991): 22–40.

Kim, Claire Jean. *Bitter Fruit: The Politics of Black–Korean Conflict in New York City.* New Haven, Conn.: Yale University Press, 2000.

———. "The Racial Triangulation of Asian Americans." In *Asian Americans and Politics: Perspectives, Experiences, Prospects*, ed. Gordon H. Chang, 39–78. Washington, D.C.: Woodrow Wilson Center Press, 2001.

Kim, Elaine. "'Such Opposite Creatures': Men and Women in Asian American Literature." *Michigan Quarterly Review* 39, no. 1 (Winter 1990): 68–93.

Kim, Esther. *A History of Asian American Theatre.* Cambridge: Cambridge University Press, 2006.

Kim, Richard S. "Inaugurating the American Century: The 1919 Philadelphia Korean Congress, Korean Diasporic Nationalism, and American Protestant Missionaries." *Journal of American Ethnic History* 26, no. 1 (Fall 2006): 50–76.

Kim, Suzanne A. "'Yellow' Skin, 'White' Masks: Asian American 'Impersonations' of Whiteness and the Feminist Critique of Liberal Equality." *Asian Law Journal* 8, no. 1: 89–109.

Klein, Christina. *Cold War Orientalism: Asia in the Middlebrow Imagination, 1945–1961.* Berkeley: University of California Press, 2003.

Kochiyama, Yuri. *Passing It On: A Memoir.* Los Angeles: UCLA Asian American Studies Center Press, 2004.

Koshy, Susan. "Morphing Race into Ethnicity: Asian Americans and Critical Transformations of Whiteness." *boundary 2* 28, no. 1 (2001): 153–94.

———. *Sexual Naturalization: Asian Americans and Miscegenation.* Palo Alto, Calif.: Stanford University Press, 2004.

Kuen, I Wor. "12 Point Platform and Program." In *Legacy to Liberation: Politics and Culture of Revolutionary Asian Pacific America,* ed. Fred Ho et al., 405–6. San Francisco: AK Press, 2000.

Kurashige, Scott. *The Shifting Grounds of Race: Black and Japanese Americans in the Making of Multiethnic Los Angeles.* Princeton, N.J.: Princeton University Press, 2007.

———. "Transforming Los Angeles: Black and Japanese American Struggles for Racial Equality in the 20th Century." Ph.D. diss., UCLA, Los Angeles, 2000.

Kwong, Peter. *Chinatown, New York: Labor and Politics, 1930–1950.* New York: Monthly Review Press, 1979.

Lai, Him Mark. "China Politics and the U.S. Chinese Communities." In *Counterpoint: Perspectives on Asian America,* ed. Emma Gee et al., 152–59. Los Angeles: Asian American Studies Center Press, 1976.

———. "The Chinese Marxist Left in America to the 1960s." *Chinese America: History and Perspectives* 1992: 3–82.

———. "A Historical Survey of Organization of the Left among the Chinese in America." *Bulletin of Concerned Asian Scholars* 4, no. 3 (Fall 1972): 10–21.

———. "A Historical Survey of the Chinese Left in American Society." In *Counterpoint: Perspectives on Asian America,* ed. Emma Gee et al., 63–80. Los Angeles: Asian American Studies Center Press, 1976.

———. "The Kuomintang in Chinese American Communities before World War II." In *Entry Denied: Exclusion and the Chinese Community in America, 1882–1943,* ed. Sucheng Chan, 170–212. Philadelphia: Temple University Press, 1991.

League of Revolutionary Struggle. *Statements on the Founding of the League of Revolutionary Struggle (Marxist-Leninist).* New York: Getting Together Publications, 1978.

Lee, James Kyung-Jin. *Urban Triage: Race and the Fictions of Multiculturalism.* Minneapolis: University of Minnesota Press, 2004.

Lee, Josephine. *Performing Asian America: Race and Ethnicity on the Contemporary Stage.* Philadelphia: Temple University Press, 1997.

Lee, Robert G. "The Hidden World of Asian Immigrant Radicalism." In *The Immigrant Left in the United States,* ed. Paul Buhle and Dan Georgakas, 256–88. Albany: State University of New York Press, 1996.

———. *Orientals: Asian Americans in Popular Culture.* Philadelphia: Temple University Press, 1999.

Li, David Leiwei. *Imagining the Nation: Asian American Literature and Cultural Consent.* Palo Alto, Calif.: Stanford University Press, 1998.

Ling, Amy. "Introduction." In *Yellow Light: The Flowering of Asian American Arts,* ed. Amy Ling, 1–8. Philadelphia: Temple University Press, 1999.

———, ed. *Yellow Light: The Flowering of Asian American Arts.* Philadelphia: Temple University Press, 1999.

Ling, Susie. "The Mountain Movers: Asian American Women's Movement in Los Angeles." *Amerasia Journal* 15, no. 1 (1989): 51–67.

Lipsitz, George. *The Possessive Investment in Whiteness: How White People Profit from Identity Politics.* Philadelphia: Temple University Press, 1998.

Litwak, Leo, and Herbert Wilner. *College Days in Earthquake Country*. New York: Random House, 1970.

Liu, Eric. *The Accidental Asian: Notes of a Native Speaker*. New York: Random House, 1998.

Loo, Chalso M., et al. "Race-Related Stress among Asian American Veterans: A Model to Enhance Diagnosis and Treatment." *Cultural Diversity and Mental Health* 4, no. 2 (1998): 75–90.

Lopez, Ian F. Haney. *White by Law: The Legal Construction of Race*. New York: New York University Press, 1996.

Lott, Eric. *Love and Theft: Blackface Minstrelsy and the American Working Class*. New York: Oxford University Press, 1993.

Louie, Steve, and Glenn Omatsu, eds. *Asian Americans: The Movement and the Moment*. Los Angeles: UCLA Asian American Studies Center Press, 2001.

Lowe, Lisa. *Immigrant Acts: On Asian American Cultural Politics*. Durham: University of North Carolina Press, 1996.

Lyman, Stanford M. "Red Guard on Grant Avenue." In *Culture and Civility in San Francisco*, ed. Howard S. Becker, 20–52. Chicago: Transaction Books, 1971.

Lynd, Staughton, and Michael Ferber. *The Resistance*. Boston: Beacon, 1970.

Lyu, Kingsley. "Korean Nationalist Activities in Hawaii and the Continental United States, 1900–1945," Part I (1910–1919). *Amerasia Journal* 4, no. 1 (1977): 23–90.

———. "Korean Nationalist Activities in Hawaii and the Continental United States, 1900–1945," Part II (1920–1945). *Amerasia Journal* 4, no. 2 (1977): 53–100.

Ma, Eve Armentrout. *Monarchists, Revolutionaries, and Chinatowns: Chinese Politics in the Americas and the 1911 Revolution*. Honolulu: University of Hawaii Press, 1990.

Maehara, G. Akito. "Think on These Things: A Perspective from a Vietnam Era Veteran." *Amerasia Journal* 17, no. 1 (1991): 123–27.

Maki, Mitchell T., Harry H. L. Kitano, and S. Megan Berthold. *Achieving the Impossible Dream: How Japanese Americans Obtained Redress*. Urbana: University of Illinois Press, 1999.

Mariscal, George. *Aztlán and Viet Nam: Chicano and Chicana Experiences of the War*. Berkeley: University of California Press, 1999.

Marqusee, Mike. *Redemption Song: Muhammad Ali and the Spirit of the Sixties*. London: Verso, 2000.

Marshall, Kathryn. *In the Combat Zone: An Oral History of American Women in Vietnam, 1966–1975*. Boston: Little, Brown, 1987.

Mathur, L. P. *Indian Revolutionary Movement in the United States of America*. Delhi, India: S. Chand and Company, 1970.

Matsuoka, Jon, et al. "Asian-Pacific American Vietnam Veterans: An Exploratory Study of Wartime Experiences and Post-war Adjustment." *Journal of Multicultural Social Work* 2 (1992): 102–11.

Matthews, Tracye. "'No One Ever Asks, What a Man's Place in the Revolution Is': Gender and the Politics of the Black Panther Party, 1966–1971." In *The Black Panther Party Reconsidered*, ed. Charles E. Jones, 267–304. Baltimore: Black Classics Press, 1998.

McEvoy, James, and Abraham Miller. "On Strike . . . Shut It Down." In *Black Power and Student Rebellion*, eds. James McEvoy and Abraham Miller. Belmont, Calif.: Wadsworth, 1969.

McKee, Delber L. "The Chinese Boycott of 1905–1906 Reconsidered: The Role of Chinese Americans." *Pacific Historical Review* 55 (1986): 165–91.

Melendez, Mickey. *We Took the Streets: Fighting for Latino Rights with the Young Lords*. New York: St. Martin's, 2003.

Miller, Stuart Creighton. *Benevolent Assimilation: The American Conquest of the Philippines, 1899–1903.* New Haven, Conn.: Yale University Press, 1982.

Min, Pyong Gap. *Caught in the Middle: Korean Merchants in America's Multiethnic Cities.* Berkeley: University of California Press, 1996.

Mirikitani, Janice, et al., eds. *Time to Greez! Incantations from the Third World.* San Francisco: Glide Publications, 1975.

Miyamoto, JoAnne, Chris Iijima, and Charlie Chin. *A Grain of Sand.* Sound recording. New York: Paredon Records, 1973.

Miyamoto, S. Frank. *Social Solidarity among the Japanese in Seattle.* Reprint, Seattle: University of Washington Press, 1984.

Morrison, Toni. *Playing in the Dark: Whiteness and the Literary Imagination.* Cambridge, Mass.: Harvard University Press, 1992.

Moser, Richard R. *The New Winter Soldiers: GI and Veteran Dissent during the Vietnam Era.* New Brunswick, N.J.: Rutgers University Press, 1996.

Myrdal, Gunnar. *An American Dilemma: The Negro Problem and Modern Democracy.* New York: Harper, 1944.

Nagatani, Nick. "'Action Talks and Bullshit Walks': From the Founders of Yellow Brotherhood to the Present." In *Asian Americans: The Movement and the Moment,* ed. Steve Louie and Glenn Omatsu, 148–55. Los Angeles: UCLA Asian American Studies Press, 2001.

Nakamura, Norman. "The Nature of G.I. Racism." In *Roots: An Asian American Reader,* ed. Amy Tachiki et al., 24–26. Los Angeles: UCLA Asian American Studies Center Press, 1971. Reprinted from *Gidra,* June–July 1970.

Nee, Brett de Bary, and Victor Nee. "The Kuomintang in Chinatown." In *Counterpoint: Perspectives on Asian America,* ed. Emma Gee et al., 146–51. Los Angeles: Asian American Studies Center Press, 1976.

Ngai, Mae M. "The Architecture of Race in American Immigration Law: A Reexamination of the Immigration Act of 1924." *Journal of American History* 86, no. 1 (June 1999): 67–92.

Nguyen, Tram Quang. "Caring for the Soul of Our Community: Vietnamese Youth Activism in the 1960s and Today." In *Asian Americans: The Movement and the Moment,* ed. Steve Louie and Glenn Omatsu, 285–89. Los Angeles: UCLA Asian American Studies Center Press, 2001.

———. *We Are All Suspects Now: Untold Stories from Immigrant Communities after 9/11.* Boston: Beacon, 2005.

Nguyen, Viet Thanh. *Race and Resistance: Literature and Politics of in Asian America.* New York: Oxford University Press, 2002.

Niiya, Brian, ed. *Japanese American History: An A-to-Z Reference from 1868 to the Present.* New York: Facts on File, 1993.

"Nobuko Miyamoto: Dancer, Singer, and Songwriter." In *Yellow Light: The Flowering of Asian American Arts,* ed. Amy Ling, 325. Philadelphia: Temple University Press, 1999.

Odo, Franklin. "Preface." In *Roots: An Asian American Reader,* ed. Amy Tachiki et al. Los Angeles: UCLA Asian American Studies Center, 1971.

Ogbar, Jeffrey O. G. *Black Power: Radical Politics and African American Identity.* Baltimore: Johns Hopkins University Press, 2004.

Okihiro, Gary Y. *Margins and Mainstreams: Asians in American History and Culture.* Seattle: University of Washington Press, 1994.

Omatsu, Glenn. "Always a Rebel: An Interview with Kazu Iijima." *Amerasia Journal* 13, no. 2 (1986–87): 83–98.

———. "The 'Four Prisons' and the Movements of Liberation: Asian American Activism from the 1960s to the 1990s." In *Contemporary Asian America: A Multidisciplinary Reader*, 2nd ed., ed. Min Zhou and J. V. Gatewood, 56–88. New York: New York University Press, 2007.

Omi, Michael, and Howard Winant. *Racial Formation in the United States: From the 1960s to the 1990s*. New York: Routledge, 1994.

Ong, Aihwa. *Buddha Is Hiding: Refugees, Citizenship, the New America*. Berkeley: University of California Press, 2003.

Oropeza, Lorena. *¡Raza Sí! ¡Guerra No! Chicano Protest and Patriotism during the Viet Nam War Era*. Berkeley: University of California Press, 2005.

Orrick, William H. Jr. *Shut It Down! A College in Crisis: San Francisco State College, October 1968–April 1969; A Report to the National Commission on the Causes and Prevention of Violence*. Washington, D.C.: U.S. Government Printing Office, 1969.

Osumi, Megumi Dick. "Asians and California's Anti-Miscegenation Laws." In *Asian and Pacific American Experiences: Women's Perspectives*, ed. Nobuya Tsuchida, 1–37. Minneapolis: Asian/Pacific American Learning Resource Center, University of Minnesota, 1982.

Palumbo-Liu, David. *Asian/American: Historical Crossings of a Racial Frontier*. Palo Alto, Calif.: Stanford University Press, 1999.

Pascoe, Peggy. "Miscegenation Law, Court Cases, and Ideologies of 'Race' in Twentieth Century America." *Journal of American History* 83, no. 1 (June 1996): 44–69.

Pearson, Hugh. *Shadow of the Panther: Huey Newton and the Price of Black Power in America*. Reading, Mass.: Addison-Wesley, 1994.

Peffer, George Anthony. *If They Don't Bring Their Women Here: Chinese Female Immigration before Exclusion*. Urbana: University of Illinois Press, 1999.

Pomerantz, Linda. "The Chinese Bourgeoisie and the Anti-Chinese Movement in the United States, 1850–1905." *Amerasia Journal* 11, no. 1 (1984): 1–33.

Posadas, Barbara. "The Hierarchy of Color and Psychological Adjustment in an Industrial Environment: Filipinos, The Pullman Company, and the Brotherhood of Sleeping Car Porters." *Labor History* 23 (1982): 349–73.

Prashad, Vijay. *Everybody Was Kung Fu Fighting: Afro-Asian Connections and the Myth of Cultural Purity*. Boston: Beacon, 2002.

———. "Kung Fusion: Organize the 'Hood' Under I-Ching Banners." In *Everybody Was Kung Fu Fighting: Afro-Asian Connections and the Myth of Cultural Purity*, 126–49. Boston: Beacon, 2002.

Pulido, Laura. *Black, Brown, Yellow, and Left: Radical Activism in Los Angeles*. Berkeley: University of California Press, 2006.

———. "Race and Revolutionary Politics: Black, Chicana/o, and Asian American Leftists in Southern California." *Antipode* 34, no. 4 (2002): 762–88.

Puri, Harish K. *Ghadar Movement: Ideology, Organization, and Strategy*. Amritsar, India: Guru Nanak Dev University Press, 1983.

Raineri, Vivian McGuckin. *The Red Angel: The Life and Times of Elaine Yoneda Black, 1906–1988*. New York: International Publishers, 1991.

Ransby, Barbara. *Ella Baker and the Black Freedom Movement: A Radical Democratic Vision*. Chapel Hill: University of North Carolina Press, 2003.

Raphael-Hernandez, Heike, Shannon Steen, and Vijay Prashad, eds. *AfroAsian Encounters: Culture, History, Politics*. New York: New York University Press, 2006.

Remnick, David. *King of the World: Muhammad Ali and the Rise of an American Hero*. New York: Random House, 1998.

Roediger, David R. *The Wages of Whiteness: Race and the Making of the American Working Class*. New York: Verso, 1991.

Rogin, Machael. *Blackface, White Noise: Jewish Immigrants in the Hollywood Melting Pot.* Berkeley: University of California Press, 1993.

Said, Edward. *Orientalism.* New York: Vintage Books, 1979.

Salyer, Lucy E. "Baptism by Fire: Race, Military Service, and U.S. Citizenship Policy, 1918–1935." *Journal of American History* 91, no. 3 (December 2004): 847–76.

———. *Laws Harsh as Tigers: Chinese Immigrants and the Shaping of Modern Immigration Law.* Chapel Hill: University of North Carolina Press, 1995.

Sánchez, George J. "'What's Good for Boyle Heights Is Good for the Jews': Creating Multiracialism on the Eastside during the 1950s." *American Quarterly* 56, no. 3 (September 2004): 633–61.

Saxton, Alexander. *The Indispensable Enemy: Labor and the Anti-Chinese Movement in California.* Berkeley: University of California Press, 1971.

Seale, Bobby. *Seize the Time: The Story of the Black Panther Party and Huey P. Newton.* 1970. Baltimore: Black Classics Press, 1991.

Shimabukuro, Robert Sadamu. *Born in Seattle: The Campaign for Japanese American Redress.* Seattle: University of Washington Press, 2001.

Shimakawa, Karen. *National Abjection: The Asian American Body Onstage.* Durham, N.C.: Duke University Press, 2002.

Simpson, Caroline Chung. *An Absent Presence: Japanese Americans in Postwar American Culture, 1945–1960.* Durham, N.C.: Duke University Press, 2001.

Smith, Paul Chaat, and Robert Allen Warrior. *Like a Hurricane: The Indian Movement from Alcatraz to Wounded Knee.* New York: W. W. Norton, 1996.

Smith, Robert, Richard Axen, and DeVere Pentony. *By Any Means Necessary: The Revolutionary Struggle at San Francisco State.* San Francisco: Josey-Bass, 1970.

Sohi, Seema. "Echoes of Mutiny: Race, Empire, and Indian Anticolonialism in North America." Ph.D. diss., University of Washington, Seattle, 2008.

Solomon, Larry R. "'No Evictions: We Won't Move!' The Struggle to Save the I-Hotel." In *Roots of Justice: Stories of Organizing in Communities of Color,* 93–104. Berkeley, Calif.: Chardon, 1998.

———. *Roots of Justice: Stories of Organizing in Communities of Color.* Berkeley, Calif.: Chardon, 1998.

Southern, David. *Gunnar Myrdal and Black-White Relations: The Use and Abuse of an American Dilemma, 1944–1969.* Baton Rouge: Louisiana State University Press, 1987.

Stacewicz, Richard. *Winter Soldiers: An Oral History of the Vietnam Veterans Against the War.* New York: Twayne Publishers, 1997.

"Status of Filipinos for Purposes of Immigration and Naturalization." *Harvard Law Review* 42, no. 6 (April 1929): 809–12. Reprinted in *Asian Indians, Filipinos, Other Asian Communities and the Law,* ed. Charles McClain, 69–72 (New York: Garland, 1994).

Tachiki, Amy, Eddie Wong, and Franklin Odo, eds. *Roots: An Asian American Reader.* Los Angeles: UCLA Asian American Studies Center Press, 1971.

Tagatac, Sam. "The New Anak." In *AIIIEEEEE!* ed. Frank Chin et al., 151–68. Washington, D.C.: Howard University Press, 1974.

Takahashi, Jere. *Nisei/Sansei: Shifting Japanese American Identities and Politics.* Philadelphia: Temple University Press, 1997.

Takaki, Ronald. *Double Victory: A Multicultural History of America in World War II.* Boston: Back Bay Books, 2001.

———. *Strangers from a Different Shore: A History of Asian Americans.* New York: Penguin, 1989.

Takemoto, Cindy. "Pat Sumi: Off the Pedestal." In Asian Women's Journal, *Asian Women,* 107–11 (Los Angeles: UCLA Asian American Studies Center Press, 1975).

Tasaki, Ray. "Wherever There Is Oppression." In *Asian Americans: The Movement and the Moment,* ed. Steve Louie and Glenn Omatsu, 81–86. Los Angeles: UCLA Asian American Studies Center Press, 2001.

Taylor, Quintard. *The Forging of a Black Community: Seattle's Central District from 1870 through the Civil Rights Era.* Seattle: University of Washington Press, 1994.

———. *In Search of the Racial Frontier: African Americans in the American West.* New York: W. W. Norton, 1998.

Terkel, Studs. *Race: How Blacks and Whites Think and Feel about the American Obsession.* New York: New Press, 1992.

Terry, Wallace. *Bloods: An Oral History of Vietnam.* New York: Random House, 1984.

Toribio, Helen C. "Dare to Struggle: The KDP and Filipino American Politics." In *Legacy to Liberation: Politics and Culture of Revolutionary Asian Pacific America,* ed. Fred Ho et al., 31–46. San Francisco: AK Press, 2000.

Trujillo, Charley. *Soldados: Chicanos in Viet Nam.* San Jose, Calif.: Chusma House, 1990.

Tyson, Timothy. "Robert F. Williams, 'Black Power,' and the Roots of the African American Freedom Struggle." *Journal of American History* 85, no. 2 (September 1998): 540–70.

Umemoto, Karen. "'On Strike!' San Francisco State College Strike, 1968–69: The Role of Asian American Students." *Amerasia Journal* 15, no. 1 (1989): 3–41.

Van Deburg, William. *New Day in Babylon: The Black Power Movement and American Culture, 1965–1975.* Chicago: University of Chicago Press, 1992.

Vo, Linda Trinh. *Mobilizing an Asian American Community.* Philadelphia: Temple University Press, 2004.

Volpp, Leti. "'Obnoxious to Their Very Nature': Asian Americans and Cultural Citizenship." *Citizenship Studies* 5, no. 1 (2001): 57–71.

Wang, Oliver. "Between the Notes: Finding Asian America in Popular Music," *American Music* 19, no. 4 (Winter 2001): 439–65.

Wei, William. *The Asian American Movement.* Philadelphia: Temple University Press, 1993.

Welchel, Toshio. *From Pearl Harbor to Saigon: Japanese American Soldiers and the Vietnam War.* London: Verso, 1999.

Wells, Tom. *The War Within: America's Battle over Vietnam.* Berkeley: University of California Press, 1994.

Widener, Daniel. "'Perhaps the Japanese Are to Be Thanked?' Asia, Asian Americans, and the Construction of Black California." *positions: east asia cultures critique* 11, no. 1 (April 2003): 135–81.

"William David 'Charlie' Chin: Musician, Composer, and Writer." In *Yellow Light: The Flowering of Asian American Arts,* ed. Amy Ling, 310–12. Philadelphia: Temple University Press, 1999.

Wolfe, Tom. *Radical Chic and Mau-Mauing the Flak-Catcher.* New York: Farrar, Straus, and Giroux, 1970.

Wong, Martin. "Berkeley and Beyond." *Giant Robot* 10 (Spring 1998): 70–71.

———. "Panther Brotherhood." *Giant Robot* 10 (Spring 1998): 76–77.

———. "Red Star in America." *Giant Robot* 10 (Spring 1998): 80.

———. "Yellow Panther." *Giant Robot* 10 (Spring 1998): 66–69.

Wong, Sau-ling C. "Denationalization Reconsidered: Asian American Cultural Criticism at a Theoretical Crossroads." *Amerasia Journal* 21 nos. 1 and 2 (1995): 1–27.

Wu, Judy Tzu-Chun. "Journeys for Peace and Liberation: Third World Internationalism and Radical Orientalism during the U.S. War in Vietnam." *Pacific Historical Review* 76, no. 4 (November 2007): 575–84.

Ybarra, Lea. "Perceptions of Race and Class among Chicano Vietnam Veterans." *Vietnam Generation* 1, no. 2 (Spring 1989): 69–93.

Yip, Steve. "Serve the People—Yesterday and Today: The Legacy of Wei Min She." In *Legacy to Liberation: Politics and Culture of Revolutionary Asian Pacific America*, ed. Fred Ho et al., 15–30. San Francisco: AK Press, 2000.

Yokota, Ryan Masaaki. "Interview with Pat Sumi." In *Asian Americans: The Movement and the Moment*, ed. Steve Louie and Glenn Omatsu, 16–31. Los Angeles: UCLA Asian American Studies Center Press, 2001.

Yoneda, Karl. "100 Years of Japanese Labor History in the USA." In *Roots: An Asian American Reader*, ed. Amy Tachiki et al., 150–58. Los Angeles: UCLA Asian American Studies Center Press, 1971.

———. *Ganbatte: Sixty-Year Struggle of a Kibei Worker*. Los Angeles: Asian American Studies Center Press, 1983.

Yoo, David K. *Growing Up Nisei: Race, Generation and Culture among Japanese Americans of California, 1924–49*. Urbana: University of Illinois Press, 2000.

Yoshimura, Evelyn. "G.I.s and Asian Women." In *Roots: An Asian American Reader*, ed. Amy Tachiki et al., 27–29. Los Angeles: UCLA Asian American Studies Program, 1971. Reprinted from *Gidra*, January 1971.

Young Lords Party. *Palante: Young Lords Party*. New York: McGraw-Hill, 1971.

Yu, Henry. "Mixing Bodies and Cultures: The Meaning of America's Fascination with Sex between 'Orientals' and 'Whites.'" In *Sex, Love, Race: Crossing Boundaries in North American History*, ed. Martha Hodes, 448–51. New York: New York University Press, 1999.

———. *Thinking Orientals: Migration, Contact, and Exoticism in Modern America*. New York: Oxford University Press, 2002.

Yu, Renqiu. *To Save China, to Save Ourselves: The Chinese Hand Laundry Alliance of New York*. Philadelphia: Temple University Press, 1994.

Yung, Judy. *Unbound Feet: A Social History of Chinese Women in San Francisco*. Berkeley: University of California Press, 1995.

Zaroulis, Nancy, and Gerald Sullivan. *Who Spoke Up? American Protest against the War in Vietnam, 1963–1975*. Garden City, N.Y.: Doubleday, 1984.

Zhou, Min. "Are Asian Americans Becoming 'White'?" *Contexts* 3, no. 1 (Winter 2004): 29–37.

Zia, Helen. *Asian American Dreams: The Emergence of an American People*. New York: Farrar, Strauss, and Giroux, 2000.

Government Documents

U.S. Congress. House. Committee on Internal Security. "The Black Panther Party: Its Origins and Development as Reflected in Its Official Weekly Newspaper, *The Black Panther Community News Service*." 91st Cong., 2nd sess. *Staff Study by the Committee on Internal Security, House of Representatives*. Washington, D.C.: U.S. Government Printing Office, 1970.

U.S. Congress. House. Committee on Internal Security. "Investigation of Attempts to Subvert the United States Armed Services, Part 1." 92nd Cong., 1st sess. *Hearings before the Committee on Internal Security*. Washington, D.C.: U.S. Government Printing Office, 1972.

U.S. Congress. House. Committee on Internal Security. "Investigation of Attempts to Subvert the United States Armed Services, Part 3." 92nd Cong., 2nd sess. *Hearings before the Committee on Internal Security*. Washington, D.C.: U.S. Government Printing Office, 1972.

Ozawa v. United States, 260 U.S. 178 (1922).

Toyota v. United States, 268 U.S. 402 (1925).

United States v. Thind, 261 U.S. 204 (1923).

Newspapers and Periodicals

AAPA Newspaper (Berkeley, Calif.)
Advertising Age
AsianWeek (San Francisco)
Black Panther (Oakland, Calif.)
Bridge (New York)
Chicago Defender
Daily Gater (San Francisco)
Denver Post
East/West (San Francisco)
San Francisco *Express Times*
Fresno (Calif.) Bee
Getting Together (New York)
Gidra (Los Angeles)
Hokubei Mainichi (San Francisco)
Honolulu Star-Bulletin
International Examiner (Seattle)
IWK Journal
Japanese-American Courier (Seattle)
La Causa (Los Angeles)
Monterey (Calif.) Peninsula Herald
New Dawn (San Francisco)
New York Times
Nichi Bei Times (San Francisco)
Open Process (San Francisco)
Pacific Citizen (Los Angeles)
Philippine News (San Francisco)
Rafu Shimpo (Los Angeles)
Red Guard Community Newspaper (San Francisco)
Rodan (San Francisco)
San Francisco Chronicle
San Francisco Examiner
Seattle Times
Seminar: A Quarterly Review for Newspapermen
Strike Daily (San Francisco)
Oakland (Calif.) Sun Reporter
Time
Variety (Los Angeles)
Wei Min Newspaper (San Francisco)

Manuscript Collections

Asian American Theater Company Papers, California Ethnic and Multicultural Archives, University of California, Santa Barbara
Asian Pacific American Veterans Project collection, Wing Luke Asian Museum, Seattle
Frank Abe Personal Files, copy in the author's possession
James Y. Sakamoto Papers, Manuscripts, Special Collections, and University Archives, University of Washington Libraries, University of Washington, Seattle

Japanese American Evacuation and Resettlement Records, 1930–74 (Bulk 1942–64), Bancroft Library, University of California, Berkeley

Japanese American Research Project Collection of Material about Japanese in the United States, 1893–1985, Manuscripts Division, Charles E. Young Research Library, UCLA, Los Angeles

Lillian Baker Papers, Hoover Institution Archives, Stanford University, Stanford, Calif.

New Left Collection, Hoover Institution Archives, Stanford University, Stanford, Calif.

San Francisco Historical Center, San Francisco Public Library, San Francisco

San Francisco State University Strike Collection, San Francisco Historical Center, San Francisco Public Library, San Francisco

S. I. Hayakawa Papers, Hoover Institution Archives, Stanford University, Stanford, Calif.

Social Protest Collection, Bancroft Library, University of California, Berkeley

Special Collections, Labadie Collection, Harlan Hatcher Graduate Library, University of Michigan, Ann Arbor

Strike Collection, Special Collections, J. Paul Leonard Library, San Francisco State University, San Francisco

Index

Abe, Frank, 102, 112
African Americans: and Asian Americans, 3, 67, 79–82; identification with Asians, 79–80
Alcatraz Island occupation, 146
Ali, Muhammad, 80
Allen, Ernest, 11
American Cannery Workers Union, 35
American Communist Party (CPUSA), 36
American Federation of Labor (AFL), 35, 37
American Federation of Teachers (AFT), 41
American Indian Movement (AIM), 17, 83, 146
American Indians, 17, 136, 145–46
American Legion, 30–34
Anderson, Terry, 14
antiassimilation. *See* blackness; fellow Asians line against the Viet Nam war; interracial solidarity; Third World solidarity
anti-imperialism, 4, 6, 8, 99; in antiwar movement, 116–22; in culture, 129
anti-Marcos movement, 122
antimiscegenation legislation and court rulings, 26–27

antiwar movement: Asian American differences from the mainstream movement, 122–25; multiethnic solidarity within, 115, 120–22; people of color within, 98–99
Aoki, Richard, 82, 88
Asian American identity, 75–77
Asian American Political Alliance (AAPA), 52, 76, 82–84, 100, 120–21; at San Francisco State College, 50, 52, 64–65, 68
Asian Americans for Action (AAA), 77, 100, 134–35, 150
Asian American Theater Workshop (AATW), 102
Asian American veterans, 100, 104–7; race-based stress and, 109–10; women's experiences, 111–13
Asian American Writers Conference, 150–51
Asian Community Center, 14, 101
Asian contingents, 100, 121–23
Asian Exclusion League, 22
Asian nationalism, 27; Chinese, 28–29; Indian, 28; Korean, 28
Asian Political Alliance, 38
assimilation, 2–3, 12, 77–78; and Americanism (liberal assimilationism), 30–34. *See also* Hayakawa, Samuel

Ichiyé (S. I.): as assimilationist; whiteness
Azuma, Eiichiro, 35

BAACAW (Bay Area Asian Coalition Against War), 7, 97–98, 101–2, 107–8, 120–25
Basement Workshop, 128, 135, 139, 150
Bellecourt, Clyde, 17
Bhabha, Homi, 90–92
blackness: as antiassimilation, 78; Asian American performances of, 89–95; Asian Americans and, 5, 12, 56–57, 80–81, 84. *See Chickencoop Chinaman, The:* masculinity in; Red Guard Party: and blackness
Black Panther Party, 51–52, 145: and antiwar movement, 4–5, 17; Asian Americans and, 81, 84, 133, 135–36, 135. *See* Red Guard Party: Black Panther Party and
Black Power, 5, 78
Black Student Union, 50–52
Boggs, Grace Lee, 38, 81
Bonifacio, Andres, 117
Brown, Elaine, 6
Brown Berets, 83, 99, 123, 125
Bulosan, Carlos, 34, 38
Burner, David, 15, 76

California Intercollegiate Nisei Organization (CINO), 49, 67, 72
Cannery Workers and Farm Laborers Union (CWFLU), 35
Carmichael, Stokely (Kwame Toure), 78, 81, 98
Castro, Fidel, 85
Chan, Patsy, 123
Chicago Defender, 46–49
Chicanos: and antiwar movement, 4, 98–99, 123, 125; and Asian American workers, 35–36
Chickencoop Chinaman, The (Chin), 73–74; assimilationism in, 79; masculinity in, 93–95
Chin, Charlie, 127, 129, 137, 154
Chin, Frank, 5, 73–74, 102–3, 151. *See also Chickencoop Chinaman, The*
China, People's Republic of: as symbol of radicalism, 86–88

China Daily News, 37–38
Chinese Consolidated Benevolent Association (CCBA), 38, 88
Chinese Exclusion Act, 21
Chinese Hand Laundry Alliance (CHLA), 37–38
Chinese Progressive Association, 14
Chinese Workers Mutual Aid Association (CWMAA), 37
citizenship. *See* naturalization
Cleaver, Eldridge, 6, 85, 92, 133
Cold War, 12
Comité, El, 147
common racialization of Asian Americans and Vietnamese, 104–5, 110
Community Interest Committee of Nihonmachi (CICN), 62–64
Congress of Industrial Organizations (CIO), 36–37
cultural nationalism, 75–7, 128–29

Das Gupta, Monisha, 157
Daughters of the American Revolution (DAR), 30–34, 47
Davis, Angela, 4, 17
diasporism, 129
Dong, Harvey, 88

Elbaum, Max, xi
English language movement, 71–72
Esch, Betsy, 11
Escueta, Melvyn, 7, 97–98, 102–3. *See also Honey Bucket*
Espiritu, Augusto, 27
Espiritu, Yen Le, 16, 35
ethnic studies, 50–51, 68–69
exclusion. *See* immigration

Fanon, Frantz, 81, 85
Federation for Immigration Reform (FAIR), 72
fellow Asians line against the Viet Nam War, 99, 103–7, 110, 116–18. *See also* common racialization of Asian Americans and Vietnamese
Fish Head Soup (Gotanda), 108–9
Fonda, Jane, 4
Fu, May, 14
Fuchigami, Bob, 49

Gallicchio, Marc, 11
Gentlemen's Agreement, 21–22
Ghadar Party, 28
Gidra, 7, 9, 41, 61, 110, 124
Gitlin, Todd, 13–14, 60, 76
Gotanda, Philip Kan, 108–9
Grain of Sand, A (album), 141–43, 144–49
Grain of Sand, A (band), 9, 127, 139–41
Guevara, Che, 85
Guglielmo, Thomas, 25

Habal, Estella, x
Hampton, Fred, 136–37
Hayakawa, Samuel Ichiyé (S. I.), 2, 40–42; as assimilationist, 44–45, 48–50, 56–57, 67–68, 70–71; belief that racism stems from ignorance and irrationality, 42–43, 46, 49; conservative political career after San Francisco State College, 70–72; on general semantics as theory of and solution to racism, 42–43, 45–46; Japanese American debate over, 61–68, 136; as President of San Francisco State, 52–55, 58; racialization of, 55–61
Hayden, Tom, 4
Herzig-Yoshinaga, Aiko, 135, 155
Hilliard, David, 77, 80
Hing, Alex, 79, 84, 88, 114
Hirabayashi, James, 62–63
Hokubei Mainichi (San Francisco), 61–63
Honey Bucket (Escueta), 7, 102, 105–7, 116–18
Hosokawa, Bill, 31

Ichioka, Yuji, 36, 52
Iijima, Chris, 127, 129, 134–37, 157, 159; memorial service for, 154–55
Iijima, Kazu, 38, 134–35
immigration, 20–23
Intercollegiate Chinese for Social Action (ICSA), 50–51
International Hotel (I-Hotel), 13, 102, 119
International Labor Defense (ILD), 36–37
interracial solidarity, 15, 17, 52, 118, 129, 145–48. *See also* Third World solidarity
I Wor Kuen (IWK), 14, 92, 96, 100–101, 122, 135, 150

Jackson, George, 145
Jackson, Jonathan, 145
Jacobson, Matthew Frye, 34
Japanese American Citizens League (JACL), 30–34, 62, 64, 71–72, 136–37
Japanese-American Courier, 29–31
Japanese and Korean Exclusion League. *See* Asian Exclusion League
Japanese-Mexican Labor Association (JMLA), 35, 38
J-Town Collective, 102, 122
Jung, Moon-Ho, 11
Jung, Moon-Kie, 36

Kalayaan, 14, 122
Katayama, Sen, 36–38
KDP (Katipunan Ng Ma Demokratikong, Union of Democratic Pilipinos), x, 14
Kearny Street Workshop, 14, 127
Kelley, Robin D. G., 11
Kim, Claire Jean, 10
Kim, Richard S., 28
Klein, Christina, 131
Kochiyama, Yuri, 81, 133–34, 145, 154–55
Koshy, Susan, 11, 26
Kuomintang Party (KMT), 28–29, 88
Kurashige, Scott, 11

Lai, Him Mark, 37, 39
Language in Action (Hayakawa), 42–43
Latin American Student Organization, 50
Lee, James Kyung-Jin, 13
Lee, Robert G., 27
Leong, George, 149
Leway (Legitimate Ways), 51, 84
Lipsitz, George, 11
Liu, Eric, 156
Lopez, Ian Haney, 24
Los Siete de la Raza, 4
Lott, Eric, 90
Louie, Steve, 81–82, 84, 124
Lowe, Lisa, ix
Lum, Wing Tek, 149

Malcolm X, 79–80, 133
Mao Zedong, 77, 85, 87–88
Martínez, Elizabeth "Betita," 98
Masaoka, Mike, 81

masculinity: Asian American performances of, 89, 92–95
Matsuda, Minn, 135
Mexican American Student Coalition (MASC), 50
Mirikitani, Janice, 52, 128, 143–45, 149
Miyamoto, Nobuko "JoAnne," 127, 129–37, 154–55, 158–59
model minority, 12, 41, 59, 67–68, 77, 156–57
Moser, Richard, 101
Movement for a Democratic Military (MDM)/Green Machine, 3–6
multiethnic solidarity, 52, 83–84, 86, 99, 142–45; in contrast to panethnicity, 16; lack of, 29, 35. *See also* antiwar movement: multiethnic solidarity within
Muniz, Ramsey, 17
Murray, George Mason, 51
Myrdal, Gunnar, 47

Nagai, Nelson, 101, 115
Nakatsu, Penny, 64, 66
Nakayamo, Mike, 100, 104
Native Americans. *See* American Indians
National Maritime Union (NMU), 36
National Peace Action Coalition (NPAC), 125
naturalization: Chinese, 23–24; Filipinos, 25; Indian (Thind), 24–25; Japanese, 24, 32–33; Koreans, 24–25
Newton, Huey, 81, 83–84, 98
Ngai, Mae, 23
Nguyen, Tram, 157–58
Nguyen, Viet, 13
1917 Immigration Act, 22
1924 Immigration Act, 22
North Korea, 6
North Viet Nam. *See* Viet Nam, North

Odo, Franklin, 128
Okamura, Raymond, 62, 66
Omatsu, Glenn, 69
Ong, Aihwa, 13
Orientalism, 20

Pace College, 138–39
Page Law, 21
Pascoe, Peggy, 26

Peace and Freedom Party, 52
Peffer, George Anthony, 21
People's Coalition for Peace and Justice (PCPJ), 125
Peterson, William, 78
Pilipino American Collegiate Endeavor (PACE), 50
Prashad, Vijay, 11, 80
Pratt, Geronimo, 133
Pre-sixties Asian American politics. *See* Asian nationalism; assimilation; radicalism: pre-sixties
Provisional Revolutionary Government (of the Republic of South Viet Nam) (PRG), 97, 102
Puerto Ricans, 146–48
Pulido, Laura, 10–11

Quidachay, Ron, 52

racial triangulation, 10–11
radicalism: pre-1960s, 34–39
Ramparts, 4
Red Guard Party, 5, 73, 76; and blackness, 86; Black Panther Party and, 77, 84–86; formation of, 84–86; ideology of, 78, 86; programs of, 78–79, 85, 87
redress and reparations, 70–71
Republic of New Africa (RNA), 145
Rodan, 101, 123, 125
Roediger, David, 89

Said, Edward, 20
Sakamoto, James Y., 29, 134
Salavar, Pat, 52
San Francisco State College, 40–41, 50–70
Saxton, Alexander, 21
Seale, Bobby, 81, 85
Seamen's International Union (SIU), 36
1790 Naturalization Act, 23
Shimabukuro, Scott, 100, 104
sixties historiography, 14–15
Slocum, Tokutaro "Tokie," 32–33
snake dance, 123–24
Students for a Democratic Society (SDS), 59, 61
Sumi, Pat, 1–9, 17, 61, 95, 114, 122
Sunoo, Brenda Paik, 149
Sun Reporter (Oakland), 60

Tagatac, Sam, 118–19
Takahashi, Jere, 62
Takaki, Ronald, 22, 34
Terry, Wallace, 101
Third World Liberation Front (TWLF),
 40–41, 50, 68–70
Third World Liberation Front strike at
 San Francisco State College. *See* San
 Francisco State College
Third World solidarity, 17, 40–41, 68–69,
 118, 148
transnational sympathy, 148–50, 158. *See
 also* common racialization of Asian
 Americans and Vietnamese; fellow
 Asians line against the Viet Nam War
Triple-A. *See* Asian Americans for Action
 (AAA)
Trujillo, Charley, 101
Tydings-McDuffie Act, 23

Umemoto, Karen, 69
Uno, Edison, 62,
U.S. People's Anti-Imperialist Delegation,
 6

Van Deburg, William, 128
Veterans of Foreign Wars (VFW), 30–34
Viet Nam, North, 6; as antiwar symbol,
 4, 80
Vietnam Veterans Against the War
 (VVAW), 100

Viet Nam War: as anti-Asian, 6–7, 104–11
Volpp, Leti, 23

Wada, Yori, 62, 67
Wake, Lloyd, 62, 66
Wang, Oliver, 139
Wei, William, 15
Wei Min She (WMS), 14, 76, 93, 96,
 100–102, 122; cultural productions of,
 150–52
whiteness, 2–3, 12–13, 79, 156–57
Widener, Daniel, 11
Williams, Robert, 80
women: hypersexualization in Viet Nam,
 111–13; liberation in the Asian Ameri-
 can movement, 3, 93, 95–96, 113–15,
 137
Wong, Mason, 51
Woo, George, 51
Wounded Knee occupation, 146

Yellow Peril, 12
Yip, Steve, 38
Yoneda, Karl, 36, 38, 63, 134
Yoshimura, Evelyn, 95, 113–14
Young Lords, 83, 133, 136
Yu, Henry, 11, 26
Yu, Renqiu, 37

Zhou, Min, 13
Zia, Helen, 10

DARYL J. MAEDA is assistant professor of ethnic studies at the University of Colorado–Boulder, where he teaches Asian American studies and comparative ethnic studies.